Indian and Scout

F. S. Brereton

[ZHINGOORA BOOKS]

Contents

Chap.

I.	Tusker Joe	
II.	Jack Kingsley's Dilemma	
III.	A Rude Awakening	
IV.	The Road to California	
V.	On the Railway	
VI.	A Hold-up	
VII.	Friends and Hunters	
VIII.	Out on the Prairie	
IX.	Only a Youngster	
X.	A Buffalo Hunt	
XI.	Surrounded by Indians	
XII.	A Tight Corner	
XIII.	Dodging the Enemy	
XIV.	An Attack in Force	
XV.	Giving 'em Pepper	
XVI.	The Bashful Jacob	
XVII.	Black Bill to the Rescue	
XVIII.	The Gold Rush	
XIX.	Tom makes a Find	
XX.	An Ambuscade	
XXI.	The Outwitting of Tusker	
XXII.	A Double Recognition	
XXIII.	Steve Leads the Way	
XXIV.	A Great Acquittal	

CHAPTER I

Tusker Joe

"Ef there was a man here as was a man, guess it'd be some use waitin' and talkin'. But as thar ain't sich a thing handy, why, I'll git. Once and fer all, aer thar a one here as don't think I did it fair? Eh?"

The man who spoke swept his eyes round the narrow, ugly room, and pulled the brim of his wideawake hat down over his eyes just a trifle lower; whether to hide the scowl in them, or the fear which lurked in his dilated pupils, it would be difficult to say. Tusker Joe was not anxious that his companions in the room, which went by the name of saloon, should guess that he was anything but self-composed and full of courage. But to give the bare truth, Tusker Joe was by no means easy in his mind. Even the smoking revolver in his hand, in which four unused cartridges yet remained, failed to reassure him. It was not only fear for his own wretched life that haunted him. Tusker Joe had a conscience at this day, and it smote him just then harder than all else. Even as he swept his eyes round the room he was struggling hard to drown that ready conscience, to still the voice which whispered persistently in his ear: "Murderer, murderer!"

"Yer don't speak," he went on, after a minute's awkward silence, raising his voice till he almost shouted the words, as if the sounds helped to encourage him and drown that still, small whisper. "Then I takes it that ye're all in agreement. It was fair done. Me alone against them two, and they quarrelsome. I'd stop and face the sheriff hisself with that. But what's the use? A man has ter work nowadays, and a sheriff wastes time. Yer can jest give him the facts for yerselves; but, at the same time, yer can jest mind. Tusker Joe ain't a playsome girl. He ain't a weaklin', likely ter take sauce from no one. And lies he don't have at no price, not at all. Ef there's a man here as feels at this second as he don't agree that it war all fair and square, jest let him speak up. That's what I say. Let him open his mouth, here and now, before what's left of us."

The man's voice was truculent now. His words deafened those within the saloon, and there was no excuse for not hearing them. But no answer came. Not one of the three men seated at a table at one end ventured to open his lips. Instead, all, as if by common arrangement, kept their eyes fixed on the wall opposite them, as if intent on counting the planks which helped to make it, while their open palms lay exposed on the table.

TUSKER JOE'S CHALLENGE

Right opposite Tusker Joe a solitary individual sat awkwardly on a rough bench. He was a man of some thirty years of age, with red hair and beard, and a weak expression. The long, pointed chin, the narrow eyes switching restlessly from side to side, even the diminutive proportions of this fellow, spoke of indecision, of one accustomed to follow and not to lead, of one inclined at all times to shirk difficulties. Red Sam, for that was the name he went by in this mining camp, was not even his own master. He was a hired labourer, who had come to the mining camps not to test his own luck, and to risk all he had in the hope that hard work and a strenuous fight with Dame Fortune would bring him the riches which many a man had won. Sam had not the courage for such a venture. He preferred good wages, and a certainty, to any risk. He was not quarrelsome, nor over-talkative, and he did not frequent the drinking saloon at Salem Falls more often than others. He was just an average miner, content with his lot so far, and indistinguishable from the others who worked at the camp save in respect to his beard. He wore the same gaudy shirt and neckerchief, high boots, a wide-brimmed hat, and a belt big enough to circle a horse, in the holster of which was a revolver. Tusker's eyes, which during the last few moments had been searching the cracked mirror opposite him, at the back of the bar on which he leaned, suddenly lit upon Sam—Red Sam, the weakling—whom all in that camp knew to be harmless and the reverse of dangerous. And as they did so, that still, small voice whispered with even greater persistence in Tusker's ear: "Murderer, murderer!" till the man became savage. He swung round again, his eyes flashing, his pistol pointed.

"What's that?" he demanded menacingly. "Yer didn't speak, I know, but yer looked what yer thought. Draw!"

Sam was utterly disconcerted. Had he been able, he would have straightway sunk beneath the rough boards which formed the floor of the saloon. To retreat, to get away from such a terrible man and such an ugly encounter, was all that he desired. But that pointed pistol held him rooted to the spot.

"Me?" he stuttered, gripping the bench with both hands. "Me think anything! Why——"

He stared at Tusker with wide-open mouth, and eyes which were dilated with terror.

"Yer looked it," retorted Tusker, his face scowling horribly. "Ef I thought for one moment as yer'd forget, I'd put daylight clean through yer now. Clean through yer, Sam."

The very idea of such a terrible happening almost caused Red Sam to faint. He positively shivered, and when his shifting eyes happened to pass to the far end of the saloon, where were the men whom Tusker had already fired upon, the shiver became a tremble. His fingers twitched as he endeavoured to clutch the bench, his hair stood erect beneath the wide-brimmed hat, which gave this modest fellow such a desperate appearance at ordinary times, while the end of his beard shook.

"Clean through yer," repeated Tusker grimly: the sight of this harmless and trembling individual seeming to appease the bully for the moment. "Through yer and any others as dares ter think—think, mind yer—that all warn't fair and square. For the last time, aer thar a man here as has got a word ter say agin it."

Tall and broad, his face and neck and arms burned to a brick red by exposure to the sun, Tusker Joe would have at ordinary times been pronounced a handsome fellow. His long, curling, black moustache set off features which, though never pleasant, were regular and distinctly prepossessing. His red mining shirt, corduroy breeches, and high boots made up, with the brilliant handkerchief round his throat and the draggled and untidy hat upon his head, an appearance which was picturesque, if nothing more; while the breadth of his shoulders, and the size of his limbs, told of a man used to labour, of a strong fellow, able to look well to himself. Unfortunately, however, there was something about the face which detracted from the general air of picturesqueness. Tusker Joe's features were marked by heavy lines, some across a somewhat narrow forehead, and others about the corners of the eyes and the mouth. Even at rest the features wore an air the reverse of frank and straightforward. The eyes were shifty, even more so than those of the weak Red Sam. And now, when his passions were stirred, the face which looked out from beneath the pulled-down brim of his hat was seamed with other lines—lines which told of hate, of avarice, of fear, of a thousand passions flitting through the man's mind. Bluff and brag at his best, Tusker Joe was in those days too young a man to carry off such a situation with absolute tranquillity. True, he had been in saloon brawls before, and had shot men; but he had never murdered. In those rough days, down at the diggings, when men spent a goodly part of their gains in the saloons, quarrels were of frequent occurrence, and revolvers came readily to the hand. Bullies arose, too, and for a while terrorized even these lawless, gambling men. But sheer murder was hardly attempted, for then even the miners arose in anger, and when that was the case lynch law was the order—a short shrift was given to the guilty party, and either he was riddled with bullets or, if a rope happened to be handy, he was strung to the nearest tree. Often enough there was no suitable tree, and then the bullets of the miners finished the matter.

Tusker Joe had turned from Red Sam by now, and for one brief moment cast his eyes to that far end where lay the men at whom he had fired. Even he shuddered ever so little, and from contemplating them turned to the rough bar again and leaned one arm upon it. Then his eyes sought the cracked mirror which was nailed to the boarded wall behind the bar, reflecting from its golden-circled frame the whole of the saloon. In the glass he could see the three men seated at the table, their palms still prominently exposed. Not one had moved so much as a finger. They sat riveted to their chairs, their eyes fixed on the plank wall as before, knowing that Tusker Joe's eyes were upon them, and that to carry a hand to a pocket meant a shot from his revolver in an instant.

"Cowed! Jest don't dare ter move a finger, the skunks," growled the murderer beneath his breath. "And thar ain't one of 'em as don't know Tusker well enough ter guess what'll follow if they get ter blabbin'. Blabbin'! What's that I said? Thar ain't no need ter fear that. It was fair and square. Lord Tom had no need fer ter call me a liar and a thief. He knew that a man don't take sich words hereabouts, and that bullets git flyin' when names are called. He asked fer trouble, and, by thunder, he's had it! As fer Jim, he'd a hand at his shooter, and ef he's gone under, reckon it's his own fault. Yer don't catch me waitin' fer a man ter shoot."

For some two minutes he stood at the bar, his unseeing eyes fixed upon the reflecting mirror, while his busy brain invented excuse after excuse for the act of which he had just been guilty. But, strive as he might to gloss over this shooting affray, and to paint his own side of the squabble in rosy colours, that still, small voice returned with persistence. "Murderer! murderer!" It echoed even louder in his ears, till the man was distracted and desperate.

"Here! fill it up, will yer?" he shouted, thrusting forward an empty glass, and menacing the frightened negro behind the bar with his revolver. "To the brim, and slippy with it! Hur! Now, again! Hur! Thar's the price fer it. Keep the change."

Gulping down two glasses of spirit within a few seconds, he threw the glass to the floor, where it smashed into a hundred pieces, and then tossed a dollar on to the bar. By now a haunted look had come into the man's face. The fingers which pulled the expended cartridges from his weapon and replenished the chambers trembled obviously. The man was become desperate. His conscience was driving him hard. But with it all he was cunning. He kept his eyes on the men at the table, and then swung round to confront Red Sam, causing that miserable individual to shiver more than ever. Then, with never a glance to the far end of the room, he backed to the door of the saloon, pulled it open with his foot, and backed out. The door slammed to, and Tusker was gone. Those who crossed to the window to watch him saw the miner running down the street for his life, and, conscious now that they were safe themselves, they shook their fists at his retreating figure, and swore beneath their breath.

"I knew as it would come from him," exclaimed one of them, proceeding to fill a pipe. "Tusker Joe is bound ter break out somewhares, and become camp bully and murderer. Up to date he ain't dared attempt anything over much, but ter-day he's done it. He won't never look back. Mark my words, mate, he'll get wusser and wusser. He's the sort that goes on from one thing ter another, and don't stop till the sheriff's got him, or his mates has took the law up themselves, and has strung him six foot up. It war all a plant."

"It war," agreed a second. "Tusker had made up his mind fer a ruction, and Lord Tom war a fool to help him. Ef he hadn't been green, as green as grass, he'd have known what'd happen when he got ter callin' names. He war too free with 'em, and had got no use fer his own shooter. But I'm surprised at Jim. He's been out this way nigh most of his life, and he must have known. Seems he was took by surprise; fer he could shoot, he could."

They nodded their heads at one another, and slowly filled and lit their pipes, while they held their eyes to the window, fearful that Tusker Joe might yet return. Not that he would have terrorized them altogether. When a man finds another holding a revolver levelled at his head, and knows that the slightest movement or protest will bring a bullet in his direction, he by force of circumstances keeps very still. Even if he happens to be a courageous man— and many of these miners were undoubtedly that—common sense teaches him not so much as to lift a finger. He swallows his chagrin, and registers the vow to live for another day, when matters may be more equal. Tusker Joe had got the drop on his comrades in the saloon, to use a mining expression. He had drawn his revolver at the very beginning of the quarrel, and all knew that he was a dead shot. But now he could have no advantage, and had he appeared again, he would undoubtedly have met with strenuous opposition.

"He's cleared, yer bet," said the third man after a while. "Tusker knows as thar won't be no livin' fer him here after this, and he's bound ter git. Suppose it's a case fer the sheriff?"

"Yep; thar ain't nothin' more ter do. Guess the verdict'll be murder. Thar's bound to be a howl in Salem Falls, and men'll get ter swear that they'll shoot Tusker on sight. Then it'll blow over. Tusker won't be fool enough ter show up this side of the grave, and things'll be forgotten. Suppose we git a move on."

The three stepped towards the door, Red Sam rising at the same time and joining them, evidently with the idea of obtaining some sort of protection from their company. He lifted the latch, and was about to emerge, when a sound came from the far end of the room, bringing the four facing round in that direction. And this is what they saw.

Close to the far wall was a second table—a long affair composed of rough boards, with a bench perched just behind it, between the table and the wall. On this bench a man was seated, with his hands sprawled out on the table top, and his head resting on his hands. He might have been asleep for all one could tell, as his posture was the most natural one possible. Certainly one would never have imagined that he was the victim of a shooting affray. But Lord Tom was dead, without any doubt. Closer inspection of his body showed a hole in his forehead, now reclining on his hands, while an ugly dark pool was spreading out between his fingers. At his feet lay a man as dead apparently as he. His feet were pointed towards the centre of the saloon, while his head and shoulders lay beneath the bench, almost directly under his dead comrade. It seemed that he had been holding a paper when the affray started, for he had dragged that to the ground with him, and it now covered his face and chest, while one arm peeped from beneath it, exposing the hand to view, with a revolver gripped in the latter. A moment before Jim had lain an inert mass. Now, at the sound of departure of the others, he stirred and called gently to them. Then the hand which gripped the revolver loosed its hold, and gently drew the paper from his face.

"Jest pull me out from under this here consarn," he asked in the coolest possible voice. "Now set me up on the table. Gently, boys! That ere chap's broken my arm. Now, Peter, something wet ter drink, quick as yer can."

They lifted him on to the table very gently; for these miners, when all was said and done, were exceedingly good and kind to one another when in distress. And there they supported him, while the negro behind the bar mixed some spirit and water and brought it.

"Huh! that'll make me wake up," said Jim, still cool and collected. "So Lord Tom's dead? I guessed it'd come ter that when he got ter flingin' names about. And Tusker's gone. Wall, there ain't nothin' more ter do now but ter git well and started in again at the diggin'. Guess he's took all. A fine pardner he's been, to be sure! He's seen me and Tom slavin' every day and guess he's jest chuckled. He's bided his time, and got clean off with all the stuff. Boys, we'd cleaned up the claim only yesterday, and thar was enough to take every mother's son of us back to New York, with something in hand ter start up business with. And Tusker's got it all, and has rubbed poor Tom out."

He looked round at the miners, and each in turn nodded his agreement.

"Rubbed him clean out, yer bet," said one. "It don't take twice lookin' ter tell that. Tom's dead, and we'd a notion yer was the same. Yer lay that still."

"And yer didn't move over sprightly," came from the wounded man dryly. "I saw every little bit of the theatricals, and thar wasn't a man as dared ter show fight, small blame to yer. For me, he'd got the drop before I'd a hand on my shooter, and jest sent his lead through my arm. I wasn't askin' fer more. I knew a move meant death, sure. And so I did same as you. Lay still as a mouse, with the paper over my face, and jest a small tear in it through which I could watch what was happening. Mates, I'll tell yer somethin'. I've been diggin' and minin' this five years. I've met bad men and good, rough and honest, and downright ruffians. But Tusker's jest a murderer. I gives him notice, here and now, that I shoot on sight at the next meetin'. If only for Lord Tom's sake, I shoot on sight. Tusker's a thief and a murderer."

When the whole matter came to be discussed, it was the decision of the inmates of the camp at Salem Falls that Tusker Joe was indeed a thief and a murderer. It cropped up in the evidence offered to the sheriff, who duly made an enquiry, that this man, some thirty years of age only, had twice before entered into partnership with other miners, and, having waited till the claims panned out well, and earnings were collected, disappeared with all that he could lay his hands on. And on this occasion it was his intention to do the same. But Lord Tom, a man of a different stamp to the miners, had detected his intention, and in an unwary moment had taxed him with the crime, and had not hesitated to call him a thief. Then it was that Tusker had deliberately shot his partner down, and done the same for Jim. It was a clear case of murder. A warrant was issued for the arrest of the man, and in a little while the event was forgotten. But Jim did not forget, while in course of time the news of Lord Tom's death filtered through to New York State, where his widow was living. Mary Kingsley did not forget. She mourned her husband for many a long day, and then, like the sensible woman she was, set herself to think of her son. And that son, Jack Kingsley, is the lad who is the hero of this story.

CHAPTER II

Jack Kingsley's Dilemma

Mary Kingsley may be described as an eminently unfortunate woman. Married at an early age, it was not long before her husband fell out of employment, and found himself hard put to it to make a living. That was in or about the year 1848; and presently, when a fever for gold digging in California spread over the United States of America, Tom Kingsley became badly bitten with the desire to try his own fortune. A town-bred man, he fared but ill at first; but in a little while his fortunes mended, so that he was able to send money to his wife. Then had come a partnership, bringing great profit at first, and later on the disaster with which the reader is acquainted.

Five years after the death of Tom Kingsley, Mary married again—a man of uncertain temper, who quickly began to look upon his stepson Jack as an encumbrance. There were quarrels between himself and his wife with regard to the boy, and very soon Jack himself came in for ill-feeling and frequent chastisement.

"I don't think I shall put up with it much longer, Mother," said Jack one day when there had been an unusually stormy scene. "I learned last year that when I was away from home, on a visit up the Hudson, you and Father got on well together; but immediately I returned there were quarrels, of which I was the cause. I think he's jealous of your care for me."

"It seems so," admitted Mary with tears in her eyes. "I've noticed the same, Jack. Phineas is a good and kind husband when things do not disturb him, but when he's upset, matters are—well, unpleasant for all. If he had had a son of his own perhaps things would have been different; but he hasn't, and so one has to look facts in the face. You know, boy, that your mother would not have you leave. But——"

"Just so, Mother," interrupted Jack. "There is always a but in these affairs. I've talked it over with Uncle up the Hudson, and he thinks I should cut from home and strike out for myself. I'm old enough. I'm seventeen and a half."

"And big enough, bless you!" cried Mary. "Ah, if only the question had never arisen! But I'm not a fool anyway, Jack, and I'm looking facts in the face. I see clearly that it would be better for you, better for me, and happier altogether. Though I shall miss you, boy. How I shall you do not know. What'll you do?"

Jack thought for a moment; and while he stands there, his hands sunk deep in his pockets, let us take a good look at him. Jack Kingsley was of that peculiarly fair complexion which is generally, and too often wrongly, associated with a hasty and hot temper. His hair was distinctly red, not the lank red hair one often meets with, but crisp red curls that clung closely to his head. Indeed the colour suited his general complexion remarkably well, and Jack was by no means a bad-looking fellow. For the rest, he was a typical American; well grown for his age, in fact quite tall, though a little lanky, for he was too young to have filled out yet. Still Jack was well covered with muscle, light and active on his feet, with his head well set back on a pair of stout shoulders. There was a deep white scar on his cheek, which seemed to set off the good lines of his face as a patch sets off that of a lady. That scar was the result of a determined struggle with an old school enemy, whom Jack had fought three times in succession, suffering defeat on the first two occasions. Eyes which looked at you frankly and steadily, a firm chin and expressive lips, hiding a set of excellent teeth, made up an appearance which was as decidedly attractive and confidence—inspiring as Tusker Joe's had been the opposite.

"Yes, I'm old enough and big enough," said Jack, with that easy assurance so common to young Americans. "And I ain't afraid of work."

"A good thing too," echoed his mother. "Because you will have to look to yourself. Your father hasn't enough to be making you allowances, and you've nothing else to look to. I'm not sorry either. A young man should look at the world for himself. The fact that he has to make his way should give him greater determination. If Tom had lived it might have been different. But that rogue who murdered him stole all he possessed, including his papers. But there—I'll not bother you with the tale. What will you do?"

"I've talked it over twenty times, Mother, and Uncle has advised me to go west, down to the camps."

"To dig! Gold prospecting!" exclaimed Mary Kingsley with horror in her voice; for she thought of her first husband.

"Perhaps. But only if other things fail. I'm told that a smith is always wanted down there. There are spades and picks to mend, ironwork to prepare, and, in fact, lots of jobs for a handy man."

"But you don't——"

Mary threw her hands up in consternation. She knew that Jack had but recently left school, and had as yet no knowledge of any trade. He had done a great deal of amateur joinery at home; but then that was not smith's work.

"I've tried it," said Jack sturdily. "Uncle sent me to the forge near his house, and last holidays I did a month on end. I can use a hammer now, and in a few months shall be able to do ordinary jobs, as well as shoeing horses. The older I get the stronger I shall become, no doubt; and strength is what is wanted, once one has the training and knowledge."

"But for the moment you are useless to all intents and purposes," exclaimed Mary.

"I can earn my bread and butter and a trifle for spending in leisure times," said George. "I stopped at Hopeville as I came through from up the Hudson, and James Orring, the smith, will take me at a dollar a week, with board and lodging thrown in. If you're willing I'll go at once."

It may be imagined that Mary was thrown into a condition of unhappiness at her son's news. True, she had begun to realize more and more that the best thing for the boy was to leave home and strike out a career for himself. But she had put the evil day as far from her as possible, satisfied in her unselfishness to put up with her husband's tempers if her son could be near her. And now to hear that he was prepared to go at once, that the day was actually at hand for him to cut adrift from the nest which had held him all these years, was a bitter blow. She shed tears, and then, like the sensible woman she was, encouraged Jack to carry out his determination.

She busied herself for the next two days with his clothes, and then bade farewell to him bravely. So, in due course, our hero reached Hopeville, and took up his residence with James Orring.

"You'll have to fetch and carry besides smithing," said James, a blunt, kind-hearted fellow. "Labour's hard to get hereabouts. Mighty hard, I tell you, and a chap who wants wages has to earn them. But I'll not be stingy. Show us that you're a willing fellow, and the money'll be good and plenty."

For a month Jack laboured steadily in the forge, his sleeves rolled to the elbow, and his leathern apron round his waist. And, little by little, James allowed him to undertake work at the anvil.

"He's shapin' well," he told his wife, "and since that's the case I'm giving him jobs. It'll help to make him know his powers, besides giving a body time for a smoke in his own parlour. He ain't no trouble, that lad."

Three months later Jack had become so good at the work that James was able to enjoy even more leisure. He began to take a holiday every now and again, and left the little township with his wife in order to visit friends. He felt he was justified in doing so, for his apprentice was wonderfully steady, and easily earned the four dollars a week he was now receiving.

"We're off for the day and night," he said when he came to the forge in the early morning, his white cuffs and collar showing that he did not intend to work. "You can manage any ordinary job that comes in. But if it's something big, and you don't fancy tackling it, why, it'll wait till to-morrow. Me and the missus is off to see her sisters, way back of the forest, and we'll be here again by noon to-morrow."

Jack nodded, and stopped hammering for a moment. "There are plenty of small jobs to keep me going to-day," he said. "I'll look to things. Go and enjoy yourself."

Some two hours later he was disturbed at his work by the arrival of a buggy. It was driven up to the door of the forge, and a man whose clothing showed that he came from a town descended briskly.

"Mornin'," he said. "Busy?"

"Moderate," answered Jack, for he was not anxious to lose a job.

"Got time ter do a little bit for me?"

"Depends what it is," said Jack. "If it ain't big, reckon I'll tackle it. But not now. I've a heap to get on with."

"Special money fer special work," exclaimed the stranger. "See here, I've broke the key of my front door, and blest if I know how I'm ter git in again. I could break a window, fer sure, but then that's more expensive than getting another key. The puzzle is that the business end is broken off in the lock, and I ain't got it."

He held up the shank of a big key, one which might have belonged to the lock of a large front door, and handed it to Jack. The stem was broken and twisted halfway up, and the most important item was missing. Jack shook his head.

"I could forge an end to it easy," he said. "But then, what'd be the use? It wouldn't open the lock unless you knew all about the wards. It would be waste of money."

"So it would, so it would, siree," agreed the stranger, a man of some thirty-five years of age, to whom, somehow or other, Jack took an instant dislike. "But I ain't sich a fool as I look. I can give yer a plan."

"Exact?" asked Jack.

"To a T; a wax impression. Thar's care for you! I'm fond of a bit of modelling in wax, and sometimes try my hand at amateur sculpture. Guess it was one of the first things I did ter take a wax impression of that 'ere key. And it's comin' in useful. I'd forgot it almost, and then remembered it was in the drawer."

He stopped suddenly and looked keenly at Jack; for this individual had overstepped himself. If he had broken the key of his own front door, and so locked himself out, how had he been able to get the impression from the drawer? Jack was no duffer, to be sure, but he had at the same time no cause for suspecting anyone who came to offer work. Moreover, he was pondering with all his youthful keenness how to set about the task.

"It's a longish job," he said, scratching his head.

"How much?" demanded the man quickly.

"I don't know for sure. Depends on how long it takes. Besides, I've other work, which can't be left."

"Ten dollars if it's ready in two hours," came from the stranger, making Jack open his eyes.

"Right!" he said promptly. "I'll do it. Leave the shank and the impression. I'll get at the job at once."

As a matter of fact it took our hero rather less than two hours to complete the task, for he was a quick workman, and this was a straightforward matter. In a very little while he had welded a piece of iron on to the broken shank, and had shaped it roughly to form the wards of the key. Then he placed it in the vice, and used a hack saw and file till all was completed.

"And I wonder why he's in such a hurry, and ready to pay such a figure for it," he wondered, as he put the finishing strokes. "Ten dollars would pay for more than window and key, and—jimminy!"

He gave vent to a shrill whistle, and stood looking out of the smoke-grimed window, his hand supported on a file. He was thinking of the stranger, and for the first time felt suspicious. What his suspicions were he could not say for the life of him. They were entirely intangible. But why did the man need that key? Was it actually for his front door, and, if so, how did he obtain the wax impression? Jack picked up the piece of wax and examined it.

"Certainly not old," he said emphatically. "This was moulded perhaps yesterday, or the day before. I wonder if——"

"Got it ready, youngster?" came a voice from the door, and looking there Jack saw the stranger. He had not come in his buggy on this occasion, but afoot; and as he spoke was gingerly stepping round the puddle and soft mud which existed near the door.

"Ready, sure," exclaimed Jack, reddening. "And I hope it'll do. You said it was for the front door?"

"Yes. Ye're right in one guess. It's the front door. That's a good job, lad. Let's see if it'll stand the pressure."

Placing the wards in the vice, the stranger tested the strength of the key by twisting with all his might.

"A strong job too," he exclaimed. "Here's the ten dollars. Four in notes, and the rest cash. Good day!"

He was gone almost before Jack had finished counting the money, and, having stepped again gingerly across the mud, disappeared along the road which led through the town. He left our hero staring after him, and unconsciously examining the wax impression which he still held in his hand.

"It's queer," he said. "Wish James was back home to discuss the matter. Now, if I was older, or had more experience, I suppose I should get to thinking that that fellow wanted the key for some other purpose. That it was not his own front door he wished to open with it. He told me a fib, I'm sure. He made a mistake when he talked about the impression being in his drawer. Well, there's the money, and James will be glad."

At six o'clock our hero shut the forge, took his tea in the house closely adjacent, and, having washed himself and put on a suit of respectable clothes, he went down into the town and out to the other side. He was fond of a sharp walk after being cooped up in the forge all day long, and often went off into the country. It was dark when he had covered six miles, and by then he was almost in the wilderness. The road had almost ceased to exist, while there was forest land on every side. On the left, however, as he faced home again, the country was divided by the Hudson River, beside which the road wound, but elevated from its surface. Indeed, it stood three hundred feet above the water.

"A fine place for a house," thought our hero, as his eyes were attracted by lights ahead and to the left. "The man who selected that site had an eye to beauty. They say he started without a dollar, and made all he has by hard work. I wonder if I shall ever be able to do anything like that. It doesn't seem possible, and yet I dare say he thought the same. It would be grand to have a big house overlooking the Hudson, and give mother a home there."

Jack was not above the building of castles in the air, and as he trudged along, his busy brain conjured up a future for himself, a future in which hard work and care would bring him riches and a rise in the world. For America was the home of numbers and numbers of men who had made wealth from nothing, aided by a strong arm, a firm purpose, and continuous application. Why should he, Jack Kingsley, not be able to follow in their footsteps? What if he were to own a big forge one of these days, and, leaving it to a manager, opened others elsewhere. That would be doing business. That would be rising in the world, and, if the thing were managed properly, money would be gained and would accumulate.

Jack was so entirely lost in the brilliant scenes he was conjuring up that he was barely conscious of his surroundings. He had strayed from the road now, and was traversing a strip of moorland which ran between it and the river. Then of a sudden something attracted his attention. It was a dusky outline right ahead, which presently took on the shape of a buggy. Jack halted when he was within ten paces of the cart and listened. He was no sneak at any time, but a familiar note caught his ear. Someone was speaking, and, since he could not settle the doubt in his mind at that distance, he stepped even closer, making not a sound as his feet trod the soft green carpet beneath them.

"Jest ten o'clock," he heard the voice say, while someone on the far side of the buggy struck a match, shielded it with his hand, and evidently examined his watch with the aid of the flame.

"Jest ten, and Jem Bowen's away down in New York city. That's good."

"Fer us. Guess it ain't fer him," responded someone else. "'Cos, seeing as he ain't here, and don't have need fer certain things, we'll make free with 'em. Did yer get the key?"

"Yer bet," and Jack instantly recognized that this was undoubtedly the voice of the man who had accosted him at the forge. "I ain't lived a while fer nothing. I've been down here for two weeks past lordin' it in Hopeville, and getting ter know the ropes. Thar's a young chap down at James Orring's forge as is a good workman, and soft."

Jack flushed in the darkness at this allusion to himself, and stood undecided how to act. His idea of common fairness bade him decamp at once, and no doubt he would have done so had not the words he had already heard, and others which followed immediately, persuaded him that he ought to stay.

"Soft?" queried the other man with a giggle which roused Jack's indignation. "Perhaps he's made a mistake."

"No fear of that. He's more simple than soft. That's jest what I meant. He's jest mighty keen on his work, and don't give a thought to other matters. I guessed he was the man fer us, so I cleared old man James out with a call from his wife's sisters. Then I went down ter the forge, and the young chap asked no questions. I jest stuffed him with a yarn, and he swallowed it. At any rate, thar's the key. A fine job."

"And it's like the impression?"

An oath escaped the first man. He remembered now for the first time that he had left the wax model behind him.

"'Tain't no matter after all," he said after a while. "The model ain't no use to him, and ten to one he's tossed it into the fire. At any rate I compared the thing he made with the model, and I guess it was exact. Thar ain't a doubt but what it'll fit."

"Then thar's no use in waitin'. The lights yonder has been out fer the last three hours, save in the servants' quarters, and we know the old man who's in charge is as deaf as any adder. The sooner we break the place the better chance of getting clear. How's that?"

"Sense! Nothing more and nothing less. Let's git right now. Thar ain't no need ter exert ourselves. We'll drive pretty close, and walk right in."

The two figures appeared from the far side of the buggy, while Jack slid to the ground and crouched behind a bush. He caught the whiff of someone's pipe, and saw the red end of the barrel. Then the men sprang to their places, the whip cracked, and in a moment the buggy was moving away.

"Ought he to follow? Should he cling to the back of the buggy and give the alarm when they reached the house? Should he leave the matter? It was no affair of his."

The questions raced through Jack's mind, and for a few seconds he was undecided. Care for his own safety prompted him to pursue the easier course, to let matters drift, and not interfere himself. Then his duty—the common duty we owe one another—pulled him in the other direction. He would go and give the alarm. But those few seconds of indecision had altered the complexion of affairs. The buggy was already some yards away, and, though Jack ran, it rapidly increased its distance from him. Then the house to be burgled by these rascals was a good mile and a half away, and before he could arrive their purpose might be carried out.

"Not if I can stop them," said Jack stubbornly. "It's clearly for me to do something. I'll put a spoke in their wheel."

He took to his heels at once and cut straight across towards the house, at that moment hidden from him by a rise in the land. However, he soon sighted the light which had been referred to, and within a little while was at the gates which shut in the surroundings of the park attached to the mansion. They were open, and the buggy stood just within, the reins being secured to the ironwork. Jack stepped boldly through into the park, and ran along on the grass border. In a little while he reached the drive, and, skirting that—for to have stepped into it would have been to make a noise—he presently came to the large front door. It was open.

"And the thieves have gone in. I'll follow, and then kick up a rumpus," he said. "They shall not get away with any booty if I can avoid it."

He stepped across the threshold, and was within the mansion immediately. Listening for a moment, he heard sounds in the distance, and set off in that direction.

"Better catch them red-handed than not," he thought. "Guess this'll be a surprise for 'em."

CHAPTER III

A Rude Awakening

"Guess this'll be a surprise for 'em."

His heart throbbing a little faster than it was wont to do, and his pulses beating tumultuously, Jack crept along a passage, and presently came to a large door which stood ajar. There was someone within the room without a doubt; for he heard whispering voices, while, though the place was not lighted, every now and again a ray swept past the door, and penetrated through the chink beneath it, as if one of the burglars had a lamp and were flashing it to and fro. Then he heard the chink of metal.

"Silver!" he heard someone exclaim.

"H—h—ush! You'll wake the house, booby! Silver it is, and plenty of it. Easier ter take Jem Bowen's glint than dig for gold in Californy. Put 'em in the sack. Never mind bending the things. They'll all come out the same in the melting-pot. Here, leave the job ter me and get to the other cabinet."

The dulled sound of footsteps came to Jack's ear, and every now and again a metallic sound, as the silver articles were dropped into the sack. As for himself, he had made no sound as he came along the passage, for it was luxuriously carpeted. He stood at the door, hesitating again, eager to enter and face the men, and yet doubting whether the right moment had yet arrived. And our hero was to discover again to his cost that indecision does not always pay. In fact, that the man who can make up his mind on the spur of the moment, in a flash as it were, and act upon it inflexibly, without doubts, without a second's delay, is the man who more often succeeds in this life than he who is dilatory. But expedition in such matters is not to be expected from a lad of Jack's age. It was only natural that he should hesitate. After all, he was suddenly face to face with a dilemma which might well have tried the discretion and courage and steadiness of an elder man. He hesitated.

"If I go now they will get clean away with that silver. If I wait till they are fully engaged, and then wake someone in the house, then they may well be captured. Guess I'll wait. Helloo!"

Another dull footfall had come to his ears, and he swung round to see who had caused it. A big man was stealing up to him along the corridor, a man dressed in nightshirt and trousers, bearing a small lantern, and armed with a club. Jack was thoroughly startled, and, to be honest, lost his head. He was between two fires, and was likely to be singed by both.

"S-s-s-sh!" he whispered, holding up his finger. "In there. In there."

He pointed to the room at the door of which he stood, and again held up his finger for silence. But the man who was creeping down that passage had but one idea in his mind. He had been awakened by a sound, and from his position in one wing of the mansion had caught the flash of a light in one of the living rooms. The instant he saw Jack he took him for a burglar, and, now that he was within striking distance, he disregarded our hero's signs, and, suddenly dashing in, brought his club down with a furious swish. Fortunately for Jack it missed the mark. But in another moment they were locked in one another's arms, the newcomer endeavouring to use his club, while Jack gripped his arm with all his might. They fell to the ground during the struggle, and continued the contest there.

"Leave go!" shouted Jack at the top of his voice. "Can't you tell I'm on the same errand as you are. There are two men in there. Burglars! I've tracked them."

Crash! The club, seized in the man's other hand, came with a resounding bang against his head, and in a second our hero was unconscious. At the same moment the door of the room was torn open, and the lamp, which had rolled to the floor of the passage, but which was not extinguished, showed the two whom Jack had followed.

"Hands up!" shouted the fellow who had so unexpectedly appeared upon the scene, and who had made such a stupid error with respect to our hero. "Yer won't! Then take the consequences!"

He was a sturdy fighter, this caretaker of the mansion and in one brief half-second had broken the arm of one of the men. Then he attacked the second, and no doubt would have done him a like injury with his formidable weapon had not the fellow drawn back. Something bright glinted in his hand; there was a sharp report, which went echoing down the corridor, and instantly his attacker fell to the ground.

"Wall! If that don't beat everything! Dead, is he?"

The one with the broken arm bent over, supporting his injured limb with the other, and looked at the man who had been shot.

"As mutton," he said curtly; "and serve him right. He's broken my arm."

"Who's the other? Seems he must have been following us, and this old fool took him for one of our gang. Turn him over."

Together they rolled Jack over on to his back and inspected his face.

"Gee!" cried the leader, the one who had come to the forge that morning; "ef it ain't the youngster who made the key for me. And I thought he was soft. Phew!

Wall, he's brought it on hisself. Get the sack, mate, and let's be moving. We know the old man was alone in the house, so thar's no hurry. But it won't do ter wait. Someone else might be in the game. Get the sack, and we'll drive."

Without a thought for the man they had shot, or for poor Jack, they decamped from the mansion, leaving the two victims lying on the floor. Ten minutes later their buggy was whirling them away, so that no trace was left of them when the morning came. And it was not till then that the crime was discovered. A gardener found the door open, and, being unable to make the caretaker hear, entered the mansion. An hour later Hopeville's solitary policeman was there.

"Hm! A burglary," he said knowingly; "and the old man came in at the right moment. Is he dead?"

"Left for dead, but still breathing ever so gently," answered the gardener. "I've sent for the doctor."

"And t'other fellow?"

"Head pretty nigh bashed in. Insensible, and likely to remain so for a day," was the report. "Reckon Davy caught him nicely. What'll you do?"

"Note the surroundings first. Then, when the doctor arrives, get 'em to bed. Reckon the thief couldn't be moved yet awhile."

It was an hour before surgical aid arrived, and very soon afterwards Jack was put into a bed in one of the attics, with a groom to watch him, and make sure that he did not escape. As for Davy, he was carried to a sofa, the movement nearly shaking the slender thread of life still remaining out of his body. He rallied slightly, opened his eyes, and in a feeble voice gave an account of the burglary. Then he closed his eyes, and died within ten minutes.

"Which makes the case worse for that young blackguard upstairs," said the man of law. "To think that James Orring's man should take to such ways. I've sent along for him, so as to ask a few questions. Guess he'll be mighty put about. It was only yesterday that he passed me on the road, and got to talking about young Jack Kingsley. It'll be a case of——" He jerked his head back, and indicated a hanging.

"Y-e-e-es," agreed the other doubtfully, "ef it's proved. In the States a man ain't guilty, and don't hang in consequence, till he's proved to have done murder."

"Proved! It's a clear case," exclaimed the policeman. "Clear as daylight. Here's the young blackguard discovered on the premises, knocked silly by Davy's club, and Davy himself dyin'. Ef that ain't clear, what is?"

His familiarity with the law, the necessity for showing greater knowledge than the gardener, caused the policeman to sniff with indignation. To his legal mind Jack was not only guilty of the offence, but was already condemned. Indeed, looking at the evidence clearly, things wore a black aspect for him. Now that

Davy was dead there was no one to give evidence but himself, and the poor fellow who had so recently died had definitely stated that Jack was one of the burglars, believing that to be the case himself.

Let the reader imagine our hero's feelings when at length he regained consciousness, and was taken to the station-house.

"Taken for one of the burglars, just because that poor, stupid fellow made the mistake! Surely not," he groaned. "That would be too cruel! I can prove that I was not. I can describe what happened—how I met them on the heath and followed. I can speak about the key, and——"

He broke off with a groan, for as he reviewed the matter he realized that he could but make a statement of what had happened, but that there was no one to bear it out. After all, facts were glaringly against him. Indeed he realized that to the full when he was brought up before the sheriff and judges.

"The prisoner states that he was at work in the forge when a man entered and desired to have a key made," counsel for the prosecution announced, when summing up the case. "That may or may not be the case, though we can believe that it happened, for there were footmarks in the mud outside the smithy which correspond with others on the lawn outside the mansion. But we maintain that those marks were those of an accomplice. The prisoner made the key to match a wax impression supplied by this accomplice, and carelessly left the impression in the smithy. Now let us follow the prisoner's movements. He shuts the smithy and goes off in the evening, as he has done many times before. But let us bear in mind an important item of evidence. On ordinary days he would have to be back by nine o'clock at the latest. But on this particular evening he owns that he walked so far that a return at that hour was impossible. With that we place the fact that James Orring and his wife were lured away from Hopeville for the night. Is that not very suggestive of prisoner's complicity in this crime? He lures his patron away, so that his absence shall not be detected. And why should he walk farther on this particular occasion? To meet the buggy with his two accomplices. The tracks on the heather are clear enough to show that three men were about the buggy. It stands to reason that one man could not have been spying, for he would certainly have been detected.

"And now we come to the mansion. Davy declares that this man was one of the miscreants, though he did not say who fired the shot. That is his dying deposition. Is it probable that he would have thrown himself upon a defenceless youth? Highly improbable. Unbelievable. Contrary to common sense. And had he done so, is it possible that he could still have persevered in his error? No, a thousand times no! Davy, at death's door, gave us his honest conviction."

23

Terribly black was the evidence, and it may be imagined with what a sinking heart our unfortunate hero listened to it all. There was no one to speak for him, save honest James Orring, who sturdily maintained that his apprentice was innocent.

"Find the weapon with which he shot the man Davy," he asked savagely, "and then talk of the lad's guilt. A steadier boy never worked in a forge. Him a burglar! Not much! And ef he was, do yer think I shouldn't have spotted it, with him under my eyes day and night?"

Jack's case stirred the countryside, and filled the columns of the paper. Discussion as to his guilt or innocence waxed loud and furious, and was responsible for many incidents. People took up the cudgels for him in the saloons, and often enough that led to angry words and to broken heads. Even the jury wavered. Looking at Jack in the dock they were bound to confess that a franker face never before was seen. The prisoner faced his terrible position with a courage and fortitude which were commendable, while his answers were so direct, so evidently spontaneous and sincere, that even with that damning evidence before them the most experienced of the jury felt a qualm, hesitated a little, and was inclined to give some benefit to the prisoner.

"It'll be manslaughter," said James dolefully, "as he discussed the matter with his wife. They'll never hang Jack, even though the evidence is so black against him. He'll be given ten years, ten long years, in prison."

Mrs. Orring wept, and was joined by Jack's mother, who had come to stay with them during the trial.

"Ten long years," she moaned. "He'll be an old man by then. To think that a bonny fellow such as he must be shut up for the finest years of his life, must be treated like a wild beast. Oh, it is horrible!"

"He shan't! I tell yer he shan't!" cried James, banging his fist on the parlour table till the whole floor shook. "Even though I war the victim of a hoax that cleared me away for the time being, I ain't never had ought but a friendly feelin' for young Jack, and I'm dead sartin that he's as innocent as a babe. If them skunks who were in it had the pluck of sparrows, they'd come forward and declare theirselves. But they won't—trust 'em! And they'll see this young chap nigh hanged and put in prison, while they're free ter burglar other places. Jack's up against it hot and strong, and I'm his friend. I say again, he shan't go to prison."

His vehemence was remarkable, and stirred his listeners.

"Not go to prison! You won't——" commenced Mrs. Orring.

"Silence, woman!" thundered James, his brows knit close together, his eyes staring at the opposite wall. "Ye've heard what I've had to say. Then silence! Not another word! Don't breathe a syllable to a soul. Good night!"

The usually pleasant and easy-going smith got up and left the room abruptly, while the two women stared at one another, half-laughing and half-weeping.

"This is how I look at it," said James, when he was well away from the house. "I can't get to think in there with women round me, but here a man can see things clearer. Jack's done. If he ain't hanged, he'll be put away fer ten solid years. And how's he ter prove his innocence when he's cooped up within four walls? He can't, and thar's no one else to do it fer him. And supposin' he goes fer the ten years, he's branded as a felon, and won't have the spirit or the energy ter try to clear himself when at last he gets free. I don't, as a rule, get advisin' a man as is innocent ter skip before his trial's finished. It makes things all the blacker agin him. But here's a case where no good can come with waitin'. He's branded, sure, and he'll stay branded if he goes to prison. I'll go and see Pete."

Pete was an old friend of James's, and because of help he had had at a critical time, from the owner of the smithy, he always had an indulgent ear for James.

"Ef yer could get ter chat along with the policeman, maybe I'd be able ter take a look at Jack," said James, accosting his friend, and passing him a wink. "Not yet awhile, though, 'cos I'm busy. But after tea. Jest about sevin o'clock."

Pete looked up quickly, and a sharp glance shot from his eyes. He was a man of sixty-five, perhaps, though he looked older, and was already as white as snow as to his hair and beard. But he was no fool, was Pete, and his glance showed that he half-understood James.

"You aer thinkin' that boy's innocent?" he asked, as he sucked at his pipe.

"Dead sartin," replied James. "Sit down and have a smoke. Try mine."

He handed out his tobacco skin, and Pete filled from it gratefully.

"Up!" he remarked, as he pulled at the pipe; "and you was thinkin' maybe that Jack——"

"Yer know what I was thinkin', Pete," exclaimed James bluntly. "Look ye here. Have yer ever been dead down on yer luck, right clean hard up agin it?"

Pete nodded, his ferrety little eyes watching the smoke curl up from the bowl, and his whole expression denoting satisfaction.

"I've been dead down on the rocks, with the pinnacles comin' clear through," he admitted, as if the recollection caused him enjoyment. "I've had fortune play me so scurvily that I couldn't see a crust anywheres, and hadn't but one friend ter turn to. Yes, James, I've knowd what it is ter be clean up agin it."

"And yer didn't want help?"

25

"Ye've struck it wrong. Every man wants help some day. It may be only when he's old and tottery, like me——" he stopped to smile, and watch the smoke again—"jest like me," he repeated. "Sometimes he don't want it even then. But there's others want it, soon and plenty, when they're just cuttin' their teeth. Guess Jack's one of 'em."

"And he's jest got one friend," said James slowly. "That's me."

"Then you've struck it wrong agin. Jack's got two. Jack's friend is my friend. I don't forget the time when I was up agin it."

The shrewd, sharp look came again from the old man, and James noted it. Taking his courage in both hands he blurted out his news.

"I'm goin' to fetch him out of that ere jug of a prison," he said curtly. "Help me with the policeman, and—and——"

"Why, bless us! what am I doin'," cried Pete, suddenly taking his pipe from his mouth. "It's five o'clock now, and I must be goin'. I've got a 'pointment with the constable at sivin, jest to do a bit of talkin'. So long, James."

"And bless you," thought the owner of the smithy, as Pete departed. "Now ef I don't fix it, my name ain't James Orring. First thing's an aliby."

He stood thinking for a few moments, and then hastened back home. Tea was ready, and after that, and a smoke, it wanted only a quarter to seven.

"Missus," said James suddenly, "I'm agoin' to bed. I've a headache. Jest come in and put the light out, will yer."

Mrs. Orring was not gifted with a brilliant wit, and stood for a while regarding her husband with questioning eyes. For James certainly did not look to have a headache. If ever a man looked in robust and absolute health it was he. But Jack's mother saved the situation.

"I think I should go and do as he says in a few moments, dear," she whispered. "You see, to-morrow you will be able to tell the people that James went to bed, and that you left him there, sick with a headache."

It dawned upon Mrs. Orring that this manœuvre of her husband's might have something to do with Jack, and promptly she carried out his wishes.

"And jest sit right there in the front parlour," said James, as the light was put out. "Then I shan't be disturbed with the talking. Yer can come in and see how my head's doin' when I call. Not before, 'cos I shall likely be sleepin'."

He yawned, turned over, and drew the clothes well across him, as if disposing himself for sleep. But within a minute of Mrs. Orring's departure, James was out of bed. To open the window and leap out was the work of a moment. Then he went straight to the smithy, procured a file and a hammer, and, covering his face with a scarf, set off towards the prison, choosing a path at the back of the houses.

"Better see as Pete's got the constable in tow," he said to himself as he went. "Now's the time to work a liberation, 'cos this jail ain't by noways strong. But after the trial's over, and the verdict's given, guess Jack'll be taken to a place as strong as could be wanted. Now what in thunder aer we ter do with him when he's out."

The difficulty almost floored James, and for a time he sat pondering.

"Got it!" he cried at last. "Thar's bound ter be a hue and cry, and a dickens of a fuss; and the country-side'll be searched high and low. Guess I'll help ter put 'em off the tracks."

Some ten minutes later he was close to the prison, and had safely hidden himself in the angle of a house from which he could watch the street. Hopeville boasted of a town hall and a jail, both perched at the edge of a square, which, now that the township was a dozen years old, had become the fashionable promenade of the inhabitants. It was lighted by some half-dozen swaying oil lamps, and was provided with a few benches. On one of these, some distance from the tiny prison, Pete was seated as James looked, smoking quietly, and engaged in earnest conversation with the only constable that Hopeville possessed. And if that conversation could have been overheard, it would have appeared at once that the artful Pete was playing on the constable's vanity.

"Good for me! Good for Jack!" thought James. "Now, I won't lose no time about it, and I'll go at it like a man."

Being the only smith in the place, he was thoroughly acquainted with the ins and outs of the prison, and knew the solitary cell it boasted. James was no believer in half-measures. He clambered on to a wall at the back of the prison, made his way along it, and gained a roof. The grilled window of the cell looked on to this, and in a twinkling James was at it.

"Hist!" he called through the bars. "That you, Jack!"

He had to repeat the summons before our hero put in an appearance.

"What is it?" he asked sleepily. "You! James!"

"Fer sure. Look here, Jack! Ye're innocent, and we knows it."

Our hero nodded curtly. He had heard the same tale from James before, and had blessed him for his support. But the iron of this terrible time had seared his mind; his feelings were dulled; he felt that he was already branded a thief and a murderer.

"And I've made up me mind ter give yer a chance. Look here, lad! Ef yer go to prison it'll be fer ten solid years, and thar'll be no one ter clear you."

"Well," asked Jack, his eyes brightening a little.

"Ef yer bolts, people can't say more than they have done. Yer ain't more guilty than yer wur afore, but yer have a chance ter get hold of that chap and make

27

him clear yer. Savvy? Wall, yer can take yer liberty or leave it. It's right here, outside the windy. Will yer have it?"

Jack thought for a moment. He realized that to leave was practically to declare his guilt. Then he looked at the other side, the prison side: the impossibility of being able to show his innocence—the hopelessness of his future life. Rightly or wrongly he chose liberty.

"I'll take it," he said breathlessly. "How'll you manage the bars? I'll leave 'em to you, while I scribble a note."

He went across to the far side of the cell, where light entered the place in a thin stream from a candle placed in a niche in the corridor outside. Pulling out a pocket-book, he wrote boldly and in large letters:

"This is to declare solemnly, on my word of honour, that I am entirely innocent, and that every word I have uttered is true. I have to face death or imprisonment under the brand of a felon, and without hope of justice reaching me. On the far side of my prison bars I see liberty: if I can gain it, the chance to clear my good name and bring the right men to justice. I choose the last, whether it stamps me guilty or not. I will return when the time arrives, and will deliver myself up again to the law."

He scrawled his name boldly beneath the words, and left the sheet of paper on the tiny table. Meanwhile James had stripped off his coat, had wrapped it into a thick buffer, and, placing this against the bars, had broken them with a few lusty blows from his hammer. In a minute Jack was free, shaking himself like a dog just emerged from the water.

"And now?" he asked.

"Jest come along with me, and doggo aer the order. Do yer remember the store of scrap, back of the smithy? Then ye're goin' thar. Thar's a place pretty well built all ready for yer. I'll look after things when ye're hid, and send 'em off on the wrong scent. But doggo it's got ter be. Yer must lie as quiet as any mouse."

James led him swiftly from the broken cell and took him to the smithy. At the back, in the open, was a mass of odds and ends of iron. Axletrees, plough-irons, swingle-bars, rods and hoops, and old horseshoes galore. The heap was piled high, and leaned against the side of the smithy. But James was a tidy man, and for a long while had insisted on piling his old horseshoes wall-fashion, and in course of time quite a big wall had been formed.

"Thar's room and plenty for yer," he whispered to Jack, indicating the heap. "Get along in, while I sling a few bars up agin it. And not a word till I give the signal, not even if you're starvin'."

Jack crept into the hole, which, by the way, he had never noticed before in the scrap heap, and James threw a number of bars and hoops up against the opening.

"Ter-morrow there'll be shoes and sichlike to sling," he said. "So long, and don't forget it, it's doggo."

Running as fast as possible, James made for the river, and in ten minutes had beaten in the boards of an old dinghy which had once been Pete's, and which was now old and useless. He cut the painter and let the wreck drift.

"It'll be down ten foot and more in a jiffy," he said, "and in a while it'll reach the bottom, or get broken up and float away. Anyway, it'll give 'em a scent. They'll turn to the river, or the far shore."

Satisfied with his labours he retreated to his house, clambered in through the window of the bedroom, and presently called loudly for his wife.

"Wuss," he said as she entered, sitting up and treating her to a broad wink. "It's wuss, that head of mine. Feels like a swollen pertater. Can't think. Can't even sleep. What's the clock?"

"The time? Why, ten," answered Mrs. Orring. "You've been asleep, sure."

"That's likely. I thought it war somewhere's in the neighbourhood of sevin. Good night!"

James threw himself flat again, and grunted, while Mrs. Orring retired.

"He's been fast asleep all this while, I do believe," she said, addressing Jack's mother, and nodding significantly. "Poor dear, I've left him to it!"

Having safely established his alibi, James Orring fell into a deep slumber, and indeed was still snoring heavily when the constable appeared and insisted on searching the premises.

CHAPTER IV

The Road to California

Jack Kingsley's escape from the jail at Hopeville caused a huge sensation, and the hue and cry raised by the constable and by the officials in charge of the case extended into the country on every side. It was clear that he had been aided by some outside individual, and, as was perfectly natural, suspicion fell upon James Orring.

"He's been the one all through that's stuck up for the prisoner," reported the constable, at his wits' end to provide a tale which would clear himself from blame, "and I can't help thinking he's done it. But he's too clever."

"How?" demanded the official who was interrogating him.

"Just this way. James has witnesses to swear he was at home from after tea till I went round to inspect and search the premises. I went to his house the instant I learned that the prisoner had escaped, and found James fast asleep."

"Or kidding," suggested the official.

"No; right down fast asleep, and no mistake. And Mrs. Orring, whom I've known all my life, declared he'd gone to bed with a baddish headache soon after tea, and had been there ever since. He'd wakened once, and had called her."

"Is there anyone else whom you suspect of complicity in the escape?" he was asked.

"Nary one. Jack Kingsley was a stranger, so ter speak, and hadn't any friends. That's why I'll stake my davy James was in it."

"Well? And have you any news as to the direction he took?"

"Down stream," answered the constable emphatically. "I searched James Orring's yard thoroughly, yer bet, and then someone told me that a boat was missing. Later on it was reported stranded on the far shore, with the planks kicked in. So the prisoner is at large over thar."

"Where we shall lay our hands on him," said the official. "I will send his description to all the stations."

But a week passed and still there was no trace of the prisoner.

"Yer must jest lie low and doggo a little longer," said James one early morning, standing at the door of the smithy, and speaking apparently to the air. "Find it comfortable in thar?"

"Been in a worse spot," sang out Jack cheerily, for he was still ensconced behind James's scrap heap. "It's a little cramping to the legs, that's all."

"And had enough to eat?"

"Heaps, thanks!"

"Then stick it out a bit longer. That 'ere Simpkins, the constable, can't get it outer his mind that I war the one to free yer. He's got a sorter idea you're here, and he comes slinking round most times of the day. So don't yer show so much as a finger."

Jack, fortunately for him, obeyed these instructions to the letter, never emerging from his retreat even at night-time. For one evening the constable put in an unexpected appearance, coming from the back of the houses. He found James Orring washing before a bucket placed in the yard standing between the smithy and the house, and his wife holding a towel in readiness for him.

"Why, it aer the constable!" said James in surprise, as his face emerged from the pail and he stretched out for the towel. "What in thunder aer he come along fer? Say, Simpkins, will yer come and have a bit of tea with us? I knows ye've been a trifle put out over this affair, and have got it stuck into yer head that I'm the man that's done it. Jest try to get the idea put clean aside, and let bygones be bygones. Come and have a bit of tea and a smoke afterwards."

But Simpkins was not to be beguiled. He strode into the smithy, and afterwards carefully searched every corner of the yard, climbing on to the top of the scrap heap. Evidently he disbelieved James, and thought he was being hoaxed. His attitude vexed Mrs. Orring till her patience gave out.

"Look ye here, young man," she called out at last, "ef yer want to come searching round here most hours of the day and night, yer'd better by half come and take up yer quarters here altogether, so as to save trouble. Trade's not been that good that we'd sniff at a lodger, and we'd make yer comfortable. Then yer could sit right at the smithy door, and count the people what comes during the day. Or yer could sit right thar in the parlour, and make sure as sure that we ain't feedin' young Jack. More shame to yer to hound after him so! A wee, young chap such as he."

James Orring laughed heartily, while Simpkins looked confused, and reddened. He had a very great idea of his own importance, and banter irritated him. Moreover, cases in Hopeville being few and far between, he had made the utmost of this one of burglary and murder. He had been so energetic, in fact, that he had won the commendation of the sheriff. And now the escape of his prisoner at the eleventh hour had brought ridicule down on his head. People joked him in the street, and his wounded dignity was ready to blaze out at anything. If Mrs. Orring had been alone he would have given her a piece of his mind. But James was there, looking particularly formidable, and laughing heartily, thereby showing he cared not a fig for the constable.

"If I was you I'd jest git," said James. "This here smithy ain't a healthy place for sech as you. Don't yer take my missus serious. She don't want you ter stop up here; not at all."

"I'm open to lay anything that you helped the prisoner to escape," blustered Simpkins; "and I believe that if I searched high and low I'd find him."

"Then why not get to at it?" asked James with a bantering smile. "One would have thought yer had already done it pretty thoroughly."

"Then I haven't. I'd like to pull the smithy down and see what's behind those bellows, or up in the loft Besides, there's that heap of scrap. Fer all I know you've hidden him there."

James Orring went off into a peal of gruff laughter while his wife turned away to hide her dismay. As for Simpkins, he walked to the tumbled heap of iron rusting against the smithy, and began to pull portions of it away.

"Say, constable, you'll be the death of me," gasped James, doubling up with laughing. "Why, if that ain't Seth and Piggy Harten! Say, boys, what do yer think's the latest? This here Simpkins guesses as Jack Kingsley's hidden up somewhars here, and he wants a man or two ter pull the smithy about, tear down the bellows and sichlike, and cart away that heap of scrap. He's jest took on that heap. He believes as Jack's lyin' there at the bottom."

It happened that Seth was not on the best of terms with the constable, and at James's words he giggled audibly, and turned a scornful face to Simpkins.

"You're jest about right," he cried. "Jack's 'way down below that heap o' iron scrap, and yer'd best get a horse or so to pull it about. Reckon he'll be no use as a prisoner though."

Simpkins turned an enquiring look upon him. He was a stubborn fellow, this constable, and all the banter only made him more determined.

"Why no use?" he asked.

"'Cos he'll jest be as flat as a pancake. Jest like a sheet, you bet. There's three ton o' iron there, man, and it'd squeeze the life out of even a constable."

Seth went off laughing, while the constable again reddened. Turning on his heel, he gave James one quick, vindictive look, and then departed.

"He means mischief," said Mrs. Orring. "That man suspects something, and he'll not be satisfied till he's rummaged the smithy and every corner. Jack'll be found."

"Ef he's here," answered James cunningly; "ef he's here, missus. Jest yer hop right in and tell Mrs. Kingsley as her son'll be at the back door a bit after sevin. He'll be sayin' goodbye. Ef she's got a trifle for him, she'd better have it ready."

It was already getting dusk, so that there was little fear of being disturbed. James went promptly to Jack's hiding place and dragged away the odds and ends of iron he had thrown against the heap so as to hide the opening.

"Yer can hop out right now," he said. "Now, ye've got ter git, and precious slippy, else Simpkins'll have yer. How aer yer off for brass?"

"I've saved fifty-eight dollars," answered Jack promptly.

"And here's another fifty. On loan, lad. Yer can pay me back some o' these days when things have shaped a little differently. Now, what aer yer going ter do?"

Jack had been thinking it over during his enforced idleness in his retreat, and answered promptly. "I'll make west to California," he said. "Once there I shall be perfectly safe. It's the getting there that will be difficult. There's this red head of mine to tell tales everywhere."

"To be sure there is. But yer ain't no need ter fear. Mrs. Orring and me thought of that. We've sent down river for a bottle of hair dye, and guess it'll change yer nicely. Come along into the smithy, and we'll try it right now. So you'll make for Californy? And how?"

"By road. If I tried the rail I should certainly be detected. I'll make down by road somehow. Perhaps I'll get a job on the way. If not, I'll walk at night and hide up during the day."

"That's a cute idea; and say, youngster, when you gets there jest send a line. We've took your mother's address, and we can post on to her. Don't give no proper address, and don't sign a name. Savvy? Now fer the hair."

An hour later our hero was well outside the township of Hopeville, on the road to California, hundreds and hundreds of miles to the west. He was glad now to have said farewell to his friends and to be alone; for he felt that he could think better, that he could shape his actions for the future, and decide what course to follow. Uppermost in his mind, swamping all other considerations, was the overwhelming desire to prove his innocence. That was a task which he would never neglect nor forget. But for the moment he must get clear away from Hopeville, and be lost, as it were.

"In a year or so I'll be able to grow a beard," he said to himself. "By then this matter will have been forgotten, and so long as I do not come to Hopeville I shall be secure. Yes, I must get away, and wait till my appearance is changed. For the present I have a long walk before me."

All that night he trudged on in a westerly direction, traversing a road which was hardly deserving of the name. It was little better than a cart track. And the following night found him some thirty miles from his starting-point. He had met no one, and so far as he knew no one had seen him. As the evening of the third day from Hopeville closed in he ate the remainder of his provisions and took the road again; for he had slept during the day hidden in a small wood.

"To-morrow I shall have to show myself," he said. "I must buy food, or I shall be unable to stand the walking. I'll try some farm. That will be better than going to a town."

It was, indeed, the only sensible course to pursue under the circumstances, for, had he but known of it, the constable at Hopeville had supplied a description of the runaway to all towns within a hundred miles, while so greatly had the trial preyed upon Jack that, in spite of the change in his complexion, he felt nervous of discovery, as if the first woman or child who met him would recognize him at once. It was a horrible feeling, and not to be conquered till time had elapsed.

Jack had covered some five miles of his tramp that night when his ear detected sounds in the distance. He moved forward cautiously, and presently discovered a cart and horse halted in the roadway. A man was walking to and fro beside the cart, talking to himself excitedly, and kicking the ground as if he were in a temper. Our hero took as close a look at him as possible, for now and again the stranger crossed before the beam of light thrown out from a solitary lantern. He was ridiculously short, and ludicrously dressed. On his head was a black wideawake, from beneath the brim of which rolls of hair descended till they trailed on to his shoulders. He wore a short frockcoat, the tails of which came little lower than his waist, and served to accentuate his lack of stature, while a massive chain flashed across a rather ample waistcoat. The face was neither ugly nor handsome, while at the same time, in spite of the temper in which this individual undoubtedly was, it gave promise of kindliness. Jack took his courage in both hands.

"Goody!" he said, striding up. "Anything amiss?"

The stranger started back at first, and looked not a little frightened. Then he took the lamp and inspected our hero carefully, while it was as much as the latter could do to return his glances. That odious accusation, the fact that he was an escaping criminal, had almost robbed his youthful face of its refreshing frankness.

"My word! Thought you was that villain George at first," said the stranger. "Jest see here. I hired him out to look after the hosses and act the professional man. He took good wages too. And he's jest bolted. Said as he'd follow, and hasn't. Met him on the road?"

Jack shook his head. "Seen no one," he said.

"Wall, that jest proves it. He's done a bolt, and my tin box has gone with him. Guess it's lucky I cleared the cash last night. What might you be doin'?"

"Travelling west," said Jack.

"Business?" asked the stranger.

"N-n-no. Just travelling west," answered Jack. "I'm making for the diggings."

"Oh!" exclaimed the little man. "Likely enough you're goin' to meet friends there."

"I haven't any," said Jack, shaking his head, and thinking rather bitterly of his position.

"Then you ain't in a hurry, and you ain't fixed for a job. P'raps you've no need fer one."

Again Jack shook his head. He was not going to be communicative to this little man, and yet at the same time he could not afford to throw away a chance of help. If this stranger needed a man, why should he, Jack, not accept the post?

"I'm ready for a job when I find one," he said quietly. "But I'm bound for the west."

"And so am I, and I need someone to accompany me. See here," cried the little man, "you're a fair height, and would make up splendidly. I'll tell you what I'll do. I'll give you ten dollars a week and your food to come with me. You'll have to feed and mind the horses, and clean out the van. Then, when we set up shop at the towns, you'll have to dress up fine and come on the stage."

"Stage!" exclaimed Jack, somewhat bewildered.

"Jest so. I'll explain. I'm a travelling conjuror and mesmerist. I have to have help. Wall, to be candid, there are tricks that can't be worked without a second man. You'll have a beard and moustache, and will dress in a frockcoat, and all that, to look professional, and you'll hang about till I call for one of the audience to come on the stage. That'll be your chance. You'll hop up, and the trick will go like fire. And for the job, ten dollars a week, your grub, and lodging in the van. It's as snug as any house."

It was a tempting offer, and Jack decided to accept it at once. But he asked another question.

"How about California? I'm bound there, and must go. I warn you I could not stay very long in your service."

"And no need. I'm makin' west, and you and me'll be strangers wherever we go. Leastwise, you will, for I've been along the route before. Wall, now, you'll get known, and ef on the return run the same man appears, and walks up on the stage, the people would spot something wrong and funny. You can leave at the end of the trip, and I'll pick up another man."

"Then I accept," said Jack.

He had been thinking keenly all the while, and saw in the offer now made him an excellent opportunity of obtaining work and a disguise at the same time. One thing, however, he did not like entirely. He asked himself whether he was to be a dupe, whether the post he had accepted would entail behaviour likely to gull the public. If that were so, he decided offhand that he would leave this little man promptly; for, though his position was critical, and arrest stared him in the face at any moment, Jack was not the one to lend himself to dishonesty.

"I'm innocent, Heaven knows," he thought, somewhat bitterly, "and I have to clear myself of that crime for which I was about to be condemned. But I will not begin the task I have set myself by acting dishonestly in any way."

"What name, please?" he asked.

"Amos Shirley, at your service from right now."

In the feeble light given by the solitary lamp the little man pulled off his huge hat with a theatrical gesture, and bobbed in Jack's direction. Indeed, looking at him there, he was, without doubt, a comical little man, full of his own importance, with plenty of humour and kindliness, and, if the truth be told, given not a little to pomposity.

"Amos Shirley, conjuror, clairvoyant, mesmerist, known up and down the country. And you?"

"Tom Starling," answered Jack, reddening under Amos's gaze, a fact which the little man noted, for he coughed significantly.

"And I wish to say that I reserve the right of giving a week's notice at any time, and also that while I will help you willingly, and to the best of my ability, I will not lend myself to any underhand tricks, any sort of subterfuge, likely to gull your public."

Amos Shirley gave vent to a shrill whistle.

"Then the job's off," he said promptly, watching our hero closely. For this conjuring business was no easy one to manipulate, particularly with the intelligent people to be met with in America. Amos had before now discovered that an audience of miners, for instance, not wholly convinced of the genuineness of a trick, were apt to insist on embarrassing conditions, and were not above pelting the conjuror, or even perforating the stage with their bullets. He had, indeed, found before now that miners and cowboys required clever humouring; and while they were ready to pay liberally, and, indeed, to throw dollar notes on the stage if pleased in some particular, that they were at the same time a merry, high-spirited lot, apt now and again to become playfully reckless, and attempt a counter attraction, which chiefly took the form of showing how easily they could shoot the front lights of the stage away, or puncture the broad-brimmed hat of the conjuror with their bullets without doing any real harm.

"I'm sorry," replied Jack. "Goody!"

"Hold on. Say now," said Amos, feeling that he was about to lose a chance. "Who said there was any gulling?"

"No one," answered our hero. "At the same time I gathered there might be some sort of wish on your part. I'll help in every way when it's a case of conjuring, for we all know that sleight of hand is required, and general smartness. But in mesmerism, or anything of that sort, I'll not take a hand."

"Gee! That's straight. Say now," cried Amos, "I'll take you on those terms. You're a queer fish, you are, sticking out about such a trifle. But we won't quarrel. You will learn what's expected, and I've sufficient good tricks to play without overstepping your decision. Let's git along. Had any food?"

For five weeks in succession our hero travelled west with Amos, and the two became excellent friends. He found the work to his liking, and the post an excellent passport. No one, unless well acquainted with Jack, could have detected in Amos's helper the escaped prisoner from Hopeville. The hair die disguised him well, while the beard and moustache he donned, as soon as the stage was erected before the travelling wagon, made him even more secure. But it is always the unforeseen that happens. One evening, when he had stepped on to the stage, dressed in top hat, frockcoat, beard, and moustache, to help his employer in some conjuring trick, his eyes, roaming over the faces of the collected audience, met one which was familiar. It was Simpkins, the constable from Hopeville, sharp and alert, closely inspecting his neighbours in the audience, and every person within his vision.

CHAPTER V

On the Railway

As the constable's eyes travelled round the audience watching Amos Shirley's conjuring performance, and finally alighted on the stage, Jack felt as if he would have given anything if the rough boards beneath his feet would open. He sat in a chair, holding in his hand a handkerchief, in which his employer had, a moment or so before, wrapped a silver dollar, before the eyes of the gazer.

"You are sure it is there, ain't yer, friends?" said the little man, stepping to the front of the stage, and wagging his head in a peculiar way he had. "Did I hear someone say it was not there? Yes, I guess so. Then will you please to open the handkerchief, sir, and show the audience whether it contains something or nothing."

He tripped up to Jack, tapped the handkerchief with his wand, and displayed to the eyes of all the dollar he had placed there.

"And now to proceed with the feat," he cried, in his most pompous manner. "We wrap the coin so, and thar ain't no mistake about it. That dollar's thar solid. Yer can hear the tap of the wand. It's thar, and in a moment I'll transfer it to the audience. Now, one, two, three. There she goes."

He waved the wand again, and then caught the handkerchief from Jack's fingers.

"Say, did yer feel it fly?" he asked.

Simpkins's eyes were now on our hero, and for the moment the latter felt as if the constable were a snake whose gaze fascinated him. Jack was almost trembling. In his mind's eye he saw the cell from which he had so recently escaped, that sombre court in which the trial had proceeded, and in the near distance the prison to which he would be sent to spend ten solitary, hopeless years of his life. He could only shake his head to the question.

"Yer didn't feel it fly. But it's gone. Ye're sure of that?"

Jack nodded his head vigorously, while for one brief second he looked squarely into Simpkins's eyes. Did he see suspicion there? Or was that only a morbid fancy? The doubt was terrifying, and to speak the truth Jack Kingsley was at that moment as near to acting foolishly as ever in his life. The impulse was with him to leap to his feet, to jump from the platform, and race away for his life. For there was suspicion in Simpkins's eyes. Every man he regarded while on this special journey upon which the officials had sent him was a suspect, the prisoner who had escaped from Hopeville. Even the same man with the black beard and moustaches who had clambered on to the stage at the call of the conjuror might be the man he was searching for. And in consequence the constable regarded him with a fixed stare, and struck by something, the height perhaps, or some unconscious pose of Jack's, moved a trifle closer. A moment later a movement on the part of Amos arrested further advance.

"Ah, there is no mistake, my friends! That coin is gone, flown, as I said it would. And already I can see it. Pardon me, sir, but you have it."

The wand pointed direct at Simpkins, much to the latter's annoyance. He attempted to move away, but the crowd wedged him in, and, moreover, all eyes were on him. A chorus of laughter greeted his attempt.

"He never made a dollar easier in all his life," cried one of the audience. "Stop him! That ain't his money."

The sally drew another roar from the crowd, and set Simpkins scowling. Amos, with all his showman's instincts, made the most of the occasion.

"Say, sir," he called out, "if I may trouble yer. That money ain't yours altogether, though yer happen to have it on you. Would you jest mind stepping along this way and handin' it over? I wouldn't trouble yer, but then, if I was to come down myself, the gentlemen here might think there was some faking, and that I'd jest dropped the coin right where it is. Jest a moment, sir, and thank ye."

Simpkins could not draw back, and, finding that his scowls only made merriment for the crowd, he came forward unwillingly, shaking his head all the while.

"Ye're mistook," he called out. "There's not a stray dollar about me. Yer can hunt if yer like."

He mounted to the platform, and stood there awkwardly, within three feet of Jack, and directly facing him. Would he stretch out his hand and take the prisoner? Did he actually recognize the young man sitting there apparently so cool, and yet in reality quaking?

"Excuse me," said Amos. "Yer said you hadn't got that 'ere dollar, and I call the audience to witness as yer added that yer hadn't a stray dollar anywheres. But if that ain't a silver dollar, why——"

"Good fer you! He's got it," came the same voice from the crowd. "Didn't I say he was fer walkin' off. Hold on to it, siree. We're all able to swear as it's yours."

The reader can imagine the confusion of the constable, as Amos, standing on tiptoe, reached for his hat, and, having removed it from Simpkins's head, showed a dollar resting in it. And still more so, when, as if not yet satisfied, the conjuror discovered a second in the lining of the hat, a third in his handkerchief, and others elsewhere, not to mention a variety of objects from his pockets, such as silk neckcloths, a toy gun, and last of all a live rabbit. Then indeed was the constable overcome. He dashed from the stage and away from the audience, followed by their shouts of merriment. But he left his mark behind. Never before had Amos found his assistant so unsympathetic. His carelessness was remarkable, and more than one trick was almost spoiled. For our unfortunate young hero was more than perturbed. The chilling influence of the law was on him, and, do what he could, he failed to drive from his mind that ever-present dread that his disguise was discovered.

"I shall have to bolt again," he thought, as he sat in the chair facing the audience. "There is nothing else for it. Simpkins will be asking questions all round, and the instant he hears from Amos that I met him back east on the road, he'll know that I'm his man. I must go the instant this business is over."

It seemed an eternity before the performance was ended, and he was able to retire to the wagon. Then, at once, he accosted his employer.

"I want to say something," he said quietly, "and I hope you won't think badly of me. But I must leave you at once. Never mind the reason. I must go right now without another minute's delay. I know it will put you out a little, for you will want someone else. But I am willing to hand back half the wages you have paid me."

Amos regarded his young helper with an expression of surprise and concern. He had come to like his right-hand man very much, and indeed treated him now more as if he were his son.

"Gee!" he cried. "What's this? Leave right now, but——"

"I am sorry. It must be, though," said Jack. "Here's the money. Half of what I have earned. Shake hands and let me go."

There was a moment's pause while Amos regarded him critically and with a kindly eye.

"Ye've acted straight and willing by me all through, yer have, Tom," he said at last, "and if yer must go, why yer must. But you'd better by half trust a man who's to be trusted. I ain't a fool. I've seen all through that yer had something hard on yer mind, and I've often felt sorry for yer. It does a chap good sometimes to find a real friend who won't give him away, and who'll be right alongside to lend him some advice. What's it all about, lad? Yer can trust me as you could yer own mother. What's the trouble? If it's bad I may be able to advise, fer after all these years I'm a knowing old bird. In any case I'm sound. Your secret stays with me safe as if it was locked up in a bank."

He held out a friendly hand, and Jack gripped it, gulping hard all the while at the lump which filled his throat. He, too, had become much attached to Amos.

Indeed, they had been more like father and son. And in his employer he had long since discovered a man who lived on no bed of roses, but who had to work hard for a living. But with it all he was a good fellow, by no means grasping, ready always to lend a helping hand. More than that, too, he was trustworthy, and sufficiently a man of the world to be able to look at two sides of a question. "I'm an escaped prisoner," he said suddenly, blurting out the words. "I was taken at Hopeville, and broke out of my cell. The charge was one of burglary in which a murder was concerned."

"Wall?" asked Amos coolly, still gripping his hand.

"I can't tell the whole tale here. I haven't time."

"And no need, neither," came the answer. "I've seen it in the papers, and all about the escape. What else?"

"I swear I am innocent. As you know the whole story, you will remember how I was taken. I swear that I had followed those men to warn the people of the house. James was the only one to believe me—James Orring of the smithy at Hopeville. I hadn't another friend, save his wife and my mother. So I made up my mind to bolt, for outside a prison I have a chance of finding those men and of clearing myself."

"Guess you have," came the reply. "Guess, too, that yer did right, and Jim Orring aer a good man to help yer."

There was a smile on his face now, and it increased as Jack regarded him with a startled expression.

"Yer see," he explained, "Jim and me aer friends, and have been since we were nippers together at Hopeville. That 'ere place is where I war born, and reckon I know every man, woman, and child thar. But I've been away a heap, and have seen so many people that I begin to forget. For instance, I didn't quite fix that 'ere Simpkins when first I set eyes on him. Jim Orring aer an old friend, and now that you tell me he's yours too, and that he was one of few to believe in you, I ain't surprised he helped yer to break out. Yer needn't get startled," he continued, for Jack showed his concern at the last statement, for he was anxious that no harm should come to the smith. "I've jest guessed the last part, and reckon I'm dead right. It's the sort of handsome thing Jim would get to doin'. But you haven't any need to admit that he helped yer. Don't say a word. Wall, now, I suppose it is Simpkins that's disturbed you?"

Jack nodded. He was so taken up with thoughts of his escape that he could scarcely speak, and, in spite of Amos's kindness, was anxious to flee.

"I recognized him after a bit," went on Amos, "but I didn't connect him with you. I thought perhaps that he meant trouble with me, for six months ago, back there close to Hopeville, there was a ruction round my stand one night. A rough in the audience wouldn't give me a fair show to get on with my performance. Wall, it came to blows, and jest when I saw Simpkins I thought he was here on that concern. Seems he ain't; but I took the pluck out of him anyway. Now, let's think. He's a nasty fellow is Simpkins, suspicious, and all that; and, as sure as eggs are eggs, he'll be round here asking me where I've been, who's my man, and where I got him; for of course he knows I always have a man to help in the show. Yes, Tom, guess ye've got to git slippy. I won't stop yer. Yer hop right off, and jest put that money back in yer pocket. I'll get another man easy, and no bother. Jest remember this, ef you're in any trouble, Amos is the one to call on. He's alongside of Jim. He believes that you're as innocent of that 'ere crime as any baby."

He gave Jack's hand a firm and kindly squeeze, and put courage into him. Indeed, those few seconds did a great deal for our hero. The fact that another man believed in him put heart into the lad, braced him for the work before him, and lifted a load from his mind. He seemed at once to be able to look more clearly and resolutely into the future.

"Thank you, sir," he answered gratefully. "Then I'll go, and go all the happier for what you've said."

"And how'll yer move?" asked Amos curiously.

"I don't know one bit. I want to get out of the town, and then I can think."

"Wall, I ain't going to ask more, but a nod's as good as a wink they say. Supposin' you was to make fer the station. We ain't at the end of the rail yet. It runs on another hundred miles easy. Wall, supposin', I say, yer was to make for the station, and found a train likely to leave for the west. It ain't difficult to climb aboard when she's under weigh. That means yer havn't booked, and no one here'll be the wiser, specially Simpkins. Twenty miles out you get down and buy a ticket. To-morrer you'll be as safe as a house. Goodbye, lad, I've been pleased to meet yer."

There were tears in Jack's eyes as he bade farewell to his employer and sped from the wagon. Somehow or other the fear of arrest, the consciousness, ever present with him, that he was under the ban of the law, that he was a criminal at large, had undermined his natural resolution and courage. The feeling was so strange to him, and in course of time had so mastered the lad, that he began almost to feel as if he were actually guilty. But a few moments' conversation with Amos had done wonders. Jack's head was set well back on his shoulders again. As he left the wagon he walked like a man conscious of his own uprightness, ready and willing to face the world frankly and courageously.

"I'll take his hint," he thought, as he threaded his way through the streets. "But let me take one last look to see that I am not followed."

He cast his eyes down the road, and saw at the end the wagon which sheltered Amos. A man was walking towards it from the far distance, and our hero watched as he stopped at the wagon and finally entered. It was Simpkins, the constable.

"And likely to hear a tale which will put him off the scent," said Jack, now by no means dismayed. "Here's the station. I'll get into a corner and wait till it's dark."

There were a number of men lounging about the place, for the station was a sort of no-man's land where the idlers and curious gathered. There was no platform to be seen. Only a wooden flooring under a barnlike roof, while the train lying in the station was composed of rough carriages, which bore no resemblance to the magnificent vehicles now plying to and fro on American railways. At the tail of the train was an open truck with deep sides. Jack looked at it longingly.

"When does she start?" he asked one of the idlers.

"Sevin, sharp," was the curt answer. "Goin' west."

"Then she'll suit me," thought Jack. "I'll go along the line and look out for a spot from which I can board her."

It was already getting dusk, and by the time he had walked half a mile it was almost dark. He had traversed a level stretch of rail till now, but was delighted to find that he had reached a steep up gradient.

"It is a heavy train," he thought, "and will be sure to slow down here. I must manage to get aboard."

He sat down and waited patiently, wondering the while what Amos was doing, and what had happened during his interview with Simpkins. If only he had known it, that interview had been more than humorous. For the astute little showman had been suddenly afflicted with forgetfulness. He could hardly even remember Simpkins, much less the fact that he was a constable. As to his man, well, he might be wandering in the town. In any case Simpkins might see him when he cared to call. Yes, he was a good young chap, had been with the van quite a time, but how long he wasn't altogether certain. In fact, Amos threw abundance of dust in the eyes of the constable. But he did not smother his natural suspicions.

"I believe the old hound knows a heap more than he will say," growled Simpkins as he walked away. "And I can't help thinking that thar was something about that man on the stage which struck me as being sort of familiar. Ef it was young Jack Kingsley, whew!"

He whistled loudly, for he realized that re-arrest of the prisoner would mean commendation for the constable, and promotion to a certainty. The very thought stimulated him in his efforts. He went straight off to the station, and was just in time to inspect the train about to leave, from the engine right back to the truck trailing at the end.

"Not here," he said as he walked away, having seen the train run out of the station. "He'll be in the town, I expect. Now that I come to think about it, that fellow on the stage was jest about the right size for the prisoner, and, in spite of the beard he wore, about the same age. Gee!"

There was something else which struck him, something again to do with the pose of the man he had in his mind's eye. And now he remembered that he had often and often watched Jack as he sat in the court under trial. His pose there was precisely that of the man he had so lately seen on the conjurer's stage. In a flash it occurred to him that this must be the prisoner he sought, and he went off at a run to speak again with Amos. Meanwhile the train had run from the town at a smart pace, which, however, dropped as it ascended the rise.

"It will be a job to clamber aboard, all the same," thought Jack, as he saw it coming. "I suppose it is doing seventeen miles an hour. But I have got to get aboard somehow, if I have to dive for it."

He stood back from the rails, so that the engine lamps should not show him to the drivers. But the instant it thundered past he stepped briskly forward. Yes, the long line of heavy vehicles was pounding along at a smart pace, and, more than that, their height above the rails was greater than he had reckoned for. He watched the carriages like a cat, seeking for a handy rail. But one after another they swung past till the last was near at hand. It was a species of conductor's van, and the step descended close to the ground. There was a strong rail beside it, and to this Jack clutched as it came level with him. In spite of the fact that he had begun to run with the train, he was jerked off his feet; for the vehicles were gathering pace every second. But Jack was not to be easily beaten. He clung desperately with one hand to the rail, while he gripped the step with his other. Then he managed to swing his body till it leaned on the step, and, later, to lift himself clean on to it.

"So far so good," he thought. "Now I make back for the truck behind. I'll wait till I have gained my breath, for there is no hurry, and no bridges likely to strike me. The train does not stop for twenty miles, and, as it has to ascend a long gradient, it takes a time to do the work and cover the distance. Gee! That dragging knocked my boots about."

Five minutes later he felt able to undertake the remainder of the task before him, by no means an easy one, namely to clamber along the outside of the coach, and cross to the truck trailing behind the train. It was getting chilly on the step, and he felt that if he did not move soon he would perhaps become too cramped. Clambering to his feet, he gripped the rail overhead, which ran horizontally to the back of the coach, and felt his way along the footboard with his toes. Presently he discovered that, whereas the rail continued to the end, the boards did not. They were cut off abruptly.

"Which makes it a trifle more difficult," he thought. "I shall have to swing my way along."

But to cling to a rail and swing one's way along it when a train is tearing away at thirty-five miles an hour, and swaying horribly, is no easy matter; for the wind tears and grips at one dangerously. Jack found it required all his strength to maintain a grip, and presently drew his legs up and felt desperately for some foothold.

"I'm still a couple of yards from the end," he thought grimly, casting his eyes over his shoulder, "and I'm dead sure I can't hold on like this all the way. I must try—ah, here's something!"

His toes lit upon a beading of the carriage work, and the support he thus obtained helped him wonderfully. Then, in the gloom above, he discerned a second rail, and reaching up with one hand managed to grasp it and haul himself a little higher, with his toes still on the bead. And now his head was on a level with the windows of the coach.

"Three men," he said to himself, withdrawing his head, for a hasty glance told him that the coach was occupied. "No, four. Whew!"

A second glance told him that there was a fourth person; and once he had seen him our hero dropped down again, and gave vent to a low whistle. Surprises seemed to be ever in store for him. The fourth individual he had seen was huddled in a corner of the coach, and the glimpse Jack had caught of him showed that he was bound hand and foot.

"Gee! Now what on earth is the meaning of that?" he asked himself. "Three men sitting at the far end, with a lantern at their feet, and the fourth a prisoner!"

It was not the most comfortable place in the world in which to puzzle about such a knotty question, and, think as he might, our hero could come no nearer a solution. Obviously he must reach some point of safety and then cogitate.

"I'll get along this beading somehow," he thought, "and then take a look round. There's queer doings in that coach."

Inch by inch he wormed his way along the coach, his feet on the beading and his hands on the rail; and in course of time he gained the end. Swinging round it, as the vehicle gave a tremendous lurch, almost tearing his grip away, he found himself close to the buffers. A moment later he was seated on an iron step secured to the coach.

"So far so good," he said to himself. "Now, up I go. There's a lantern on top, and through it I'll be able to see what's happening."

45

It required very little energy to reach the roof of the coach, so that in a couple of minutes he was spread out on it, the air sweeping past him in a perfect hurricane. But he had a firm hold of the lantern, while his face was pressed closely to it. And once more the shrill, low whistle escaped him. For one of the three men below had moved. He had dragged the individual who was bound, into a sitting position, and had placed the lamp so that it threw its light full upon him. As our hero stared down into the interior of the coach, the man pulled a revolver from his belt and levelled it at the head of the prisoner, while his two comrades approached nearer, and, taking up their stands close at hand, began to question the unfortunate man they had bound.

Jack ran his fingers over the lantern, and pulled gently at the framing nearest him. It moved noiselessly, though a little sound made no difference, for the roar of the train drowned anything. Little by little he contrived to open the lantern, till the window provided in it was standing at right angles from the main framework. Then he dragged himself forward, and slowly inserted his head. In two minutes he was in such a position that he could see the interior of the coach clearly, while he was directly above the four men. More than that, once his head was through the window the roar of the wind ceased entirely, while the rumble of the train was no greater than those below had to contend with. They were shouting at the prisoner, and Jack opened his ears wide to listen.

CHAPTER VI

A Hold-up

As Jack looked down into the coach with his head thrust through the window of the lantern, the view he was able to obtain of the contents was infinitely clearer than that he had had when a dirty pane of glass intervened between him and the interior. Almost directly beneath him was the man holding his revolver levelled, while a little to the left, his back propped against the side of the coach, was the prisoner. He was heavily-moustached, and his clothes bore witness to the fact that he was a railway employee. Farther off were the other two, young men to look at, and from their general appearance hardly the class of individuals to lend themselves to violence. But good looks are not always a criterion of good manners. It was very clear that both were unscrupulous ruffians.

"Now yer can jest listen here, conductor," one of them was saying in loud tones, so that the roar of the train should not drown his words, and with a menace in his voice which there was no mistaking; "ye've got ter weaken right now, and without any more bobbery, or——"

He wagged his head at the revolver, while the rascal who held the weapon squinted along the sights.

"Or what?" demanded the prisoner, his voice calm, his courage unshaken.

"Or get what yer deserve. Yer've heard tell of us before, I guess; but if yer ain't, why, we're Bill Buster's band, and that'll tell yer what to look out for. Now all we want is an answer to a little question. Whar's the strong box? Even if yer don't tell us, and we have to put lead into your carcass, it won't make much difference, 'cos, we'll have the whole train easy, and then it ain't hard to find the box. By tellin' us, yer jest make the thing easier and quicker. Now, whar is it? Number three coach? Eh?"

"Go and find fer yerselves," came the bold answer. "I ain't goin' to say. Look for yerselves."

Sturdily the prisoner faced his captors, and it seemed that he would remain stubborn. But a revolver held at the head of a defenceless man has a way of persuading; for the threat these rascals had made was no idle one. It was clear they would shoot the conductor without the smallest compunction.

"Wall, a man has only one life, and so you'd better have the answer," said the conductor at last, after a painful pause. "Number four's the wagon."

"Good! Thought you wasn't a fool," said the spokesman for the bandits. "Now for the amount. It war clearin' day back thar, and the bank has sent all the stuff it could spare. How much?"

"Guess it's not far short of twenty-five thousand dollars," said the conductor grudgingly. "But thar ain't nothin' definite on the way-bills. One jest gets ter kind of hear."

"Twenty-five thousand," cried the leader of the men below, a note of triumph in his voice. "And thar's fifty-six passengers in all. Take 'em at ten dollars a head, which is a small allowance; that means quite five hundred dollars more. But they'll have a heap, some of 'em. They're goin' down to buy farms, and stock, and sich like. Now look ye here, conductor. Ye're a sensible man, as yer've proved, and we ain't got no grudge agin yer, so long as yer don't get up ter no tricks. Ef yer do, my mate here'll have a talk with yer slippy."

"Yer ain't got any cause ter bother," came the answer. "Do I look as if I could do anything?"

The conductor cast his eyes down at the cords which bound him hand and foot, and then laughed harshly.

"Reckon it'll mean a lost job to me," he said. "But give me a smoke. One of yer may happen ter have a weed."

One of the conspirators produced a cigar promptly, bit off the end, and, having placed it in the conductor's mouth, held a light to the weed.

"What I call a sensible man," said the leader of the ruffians. "Now we can git ter thinking serious of this affair. Number four's the wagon. Jim, ye'll make along fer that, and stand up at the far end. Tom here'll drop to the rails and run to the engine. I'll be with Jim before the train's stopped. She'll begin to go steadier soon, fer we're about at the foot of the long draw-up, and the incline soon tells upon her. When she's going slower you two can slip on to the footboards and make along to the first coach. I'll jest bring her up with the screw brake. That's clear? Then best have a look to see how the boards lie."

From the manner in which the rascals set about their work of raiding the train it was clear that they were old hands. The two told off to go forward did not trouble to wait till the pace had diminished. They threw open the door of the coach and swung themselves out on to the footboards. Then they moved along them with an ease which put Jack's efforts to shame, and, having reached the second coach, sat down on the boards. By then the train was well on the incline, and the pace was getting less. Half a mile farther on she was making only twenty miles an hour.

"Jest the moment fer me," said the man who had remained in the coach. "I'll give her the brake. Now mind it that yer don't interfere, conductor. Ef yer do, it'll mean a case of shootin'."

As cool as an icicle the man stepped across to the big wheel which controlled the tail brake of the train, and swung it round till it was hard on. Instantly the screech of the slippers on the wheels could be heard, while a line of fire sprang from the surface of the rails.

"That'll do it in five minutes or less," said the man, thrusting his head out of the open door. "No engine will be able ter pull agin it. So long! and don't git interferin'."

He, too, swung himself out of the coach, leaving the prisoner alone, with Jack still staring in through the lantern. And let the reader imagine for a moment the struggle going on in our hero's mind. Once before, but a short while ago, he had endeavoured to thwart a crime, to come between robbers and their prey; and he himself had been accused of the crime he was attempting to put a stop to. The bitterness of that bitter experience was still with him. It had clouded his young life, till he could think of little else. And here he was face to face with a similar experience, a crime about to be committed, and he alone to stand between the passengers on the train and the ruffians about to rob them. It was, indeed, a struggle. Jack was not naturally indecisive. He could make up his mind when he liked, and quickly too. But it must be owned that he hesitated. Fear of another terrible misunderstanding haunted him. Then he thought of the passengers, of the man below, and of his responsibility. In a moment he was clambering in through the window in the lantern, and a second later dropped down into the coach.

"My! What, another!"

The conductor had taken him for one of the gang, and looked at him with scowling face.

"No," cried Jack emphatically. "I heard all they said, and I've come to help you. There!"

He drew his knife and cut the cords, setting the man free.

"Now," he said, "I've taken the first step. I'm willing to do what you may suggest."

"But—but how on airth did yer get thar, up in the lantern?" asked the conductor. "Aer you a passenger?"

"Yes and no," answered our hero boldly. "I climbed aboard when the train was going, and got on the back of this coach. But I'd seen you tied up when I looked in through the window. I thought I'd help."

"And so ye've risked bein' shot by those villains. Lad, ye've grit in you. Shake a paw. Now, what's ter be done? The train's almost stopping. Ah, swing that wheel back! My hands and arms are too numbed to do it. That'll let the pace git up agin, and possibly leave one of the men behind. Next thing is to make along to the other coaches. Pull that er drawer open. Thar's a couple of shooters thar, and they're ready loaded."

Jack followed the man's orders swiftly, and felt the train gathering way already. Then he brought the revolvers.

"Get a grip of one yerself," said the conductor. "Now jest rub these arms of mine. That's the way. There's a bit more feelin' in 'em already. In a little I'll have a grip, and then we'll give them rascals sauce. Aer yer afraid?"

"No, I don't reckon I am," answered Jack. "I'll help you."

"Then come along. Stick the shooter in your pocket and grip the rail. But I forgot, yer've had experience jest lately. One warnin' though before we move. Ef yer get a sight of those fellers, shoot! Don't wait. Shoot!"

Our hero nodded, and made up his mind to do as he was told. He waited for the conductor to get on to the footboard, and followed promptly. Very soon they had gained the next coach.

"Next's Number four," shouted the conductor. "Let's get on the roof. We can make along there easier, and reach 'em better. Did yer hear that? They're at it."

The sharp sound of a pistol shot came to the ears of the two, and after it a shrill cry. They scrambled to the top of the coach as quickly as possible, and then went on hands and knees, and made their way along it. At the far end they descended by means of the iron steps and rails, and again took to the footboards.

"Now get ready fer shootin'," shouted the conductor. "Thar'll be a man posted at this end, and I'm going to fire through the window at him. Jest be prepared to hop right in and take a shot at the others."

Jack hung to the step, closely hugging the coach, and watched the figure of the conductor as he scrambled farther along. He saw him stand to his full height and peer in through a window. His revolver was raised swiftly, and then there came a sharp crack from the inside of the coach. The conductor dropped from the footboards without a sound, and Jack caught a fleeting glimpse of his body bounding over the side track. He was alone now, and the safety or otherwise of the passengers depended upon him.

"I'll do it," he said to himself, his blood afire, and all hesitation gone. "If I break in through the door I shall be dropped for a certainty. And if I attempt to shoot through the window I shall meet with the conductor's fate. I'll try the roof again."

He went scrambling up, and within a minute had reached one of the round lanterns through which the lamps were dropped. Lifting the lid, he found he had a fair view of the interior, for there was no lamp in this lantern, and in those days the apertures were very large when compared with modern fittings. Directly below him he detected a carpeted floor and one end of a seat, while a pair of legs stretched over the carpet. They evidently belonged to some unfortunate individual who had been shot.

"Likely enough the one whose call we heard," thought Jack. "Now, let me think. From his position he fell on to his back. He didn't tumble face downwards and then roll over. That means that the man who shot him is somewhere underneath me. I'll lean over and get a better view."

He was in the act of thrusting his head into the wide lantern, when sounds at the side of the track caught his attention. Even in spite of the roar of the train he heard shouts, while an instant later the darkness was punctuated by red flashes. At the same time he became aware of the disagreeable fact that the spluttering, hissing sounds round about him were caused by bullets. Then he grasped the significance of the situation.

"Gee!" he cried. "Then they are the friends of those three rascals who boarded the cars. Now I see through the whole business. They were to tie up the conductor, and then put the brakes on. That would bring the train to a halt on the incline, and those men out there would ride up and support the robbery. Ah! They're done nicely! We've run through them. We shall see what's going to happen."

If Jack was elated one cannot blame him. But if he thought he was going to master the difficult situation without further trouble he was much mistaken. He thrust his head into the lantern and took a careful survey of the interior of the coach. Now he could see the complete figure of the man lying on his back, and saw that he was dead. There were four other persons near him, crouching on the seat, and two were ladies. Just a little farther back, almost beneath where his own feet lay, a man stood with arms folded. He was tall, sunburned—for that Jack could see, since he was bareheaded—and had a pair of fine flowing moustaches. His arms were crossed on his breast, and his whole attitude was one of resolution. A further effort on our hero's part showed him the muzzle of a revolver, held within six inches of the tall man's head, and finally of the figure of one of the robbers.

Should he fire now? Was he to shoot the man down in cold blood as it were, though to speak the truth Jack's pulses were tingling. Was that fair play?

Who will blame the young American that he hesitated to take life? He waited a second, and that wait nearly proved his undoing. The robber caught a glimpse of him, and at once sent a stream of bullets through the roof. They tore through the boards on every side, sending the splinters flying, and drumming against the ironwork of the lantern, and by the merest chance they missed Jack.

"But he'll have me if I ain't extra smart," thought our hero, determined more than ever now to get the best of the man. "Ah, here's something to give me a hold! I'll try through the window."

He gripped a short smokestack which projected through the roof, and holding firmly with one hand leaned over the side of the car. A window was directly beneath, and well within his reach. Jack broke it with the butt of his revolver without the smallest hesitation. Then, quick as lightning, he returned to the lantern on top. One glance told him that the man inside was standing prepared to fire, either through the window or through the lantern.

"I'll make him think of the lantern," thought Jack. "It's my only chance now."

Stretched full length on the roof, with his head depending downwards, he once more gripped the smokestack, and leaned over the edge of the car. Then he deliberately kicked the lantern with his feet, and continued to drum his toes against it. Now was the time. He stretched over till he could obtain a clear view of the interior of the coach through the window, and at once caught sight of the robber standing in the same position as before, his eye half-fixed on the lantern, and half on the tall man standing so close to him. Up went Jack's revolver, though aiming was out of the question considering his inverted position. His finger went to the trigger just as the rascal within caught sight of him. And then Jack pressed unconsciously, while at the same instant the cracked glass to his right was shivered into thousands of fragments and a cloud of cutting dust was blown into his face.

"Gee! Got him! But I do believe he's managed to hit me. Seems mighty like it. Ugh! My shoulder!"

"HE SAW THE RASCAL CRUMPLE INTO A HEAP"

As if in a dream he saw the rascal within the coach crumple into a heap, and watched the tall man dart forward and bend over him. Then a sharp, burning pain shot through his own shoulder, and for one brief instant made him feel faint. But it was no safe place in which to encourage weakness, and with an effort Jack braced himself to the task still before him. He scrambled back on to the roof, slid to the end, and descended the swaying steps. Then he clutched his way along the footboard, and gained the door of the coach. It was opened by the man he had seen standing with his arms so resolutely folded.

"Come right in! come right in!" he cried, extending a hand. "Now, where are the others?"

Jack was winded with his exertions, but managed to answer. "One was to have gone forward to the engine," he said quickly, "and one was to make for this coach, where the third would join him. Where they are now I don't know. The conductor was tied hand and foot, but I released him. But he was hit, and dropped from the train. I think we ran through the men who were waiting to help them."

"Then we've had a fine escape," came the answer. "But we've got to take those men, and the sooner the better. Get a pull on that cord, and then be ready to shoot. They'll drop from the coaches the first chance they have, and git for their lives."

Jack tugged at the alarm fitted just outside the window, and presently the brakes began to grind and the train to slow down. As it did so two figures dropped from it and raced away, Jack and his companion firing at them, while a number of passengers in other coaches did the same. Then lamps were brought, and an inspection made.

"Guess we're lucky, down right lucky!" exclaimed the man whom Jack had spoken to. "Thar's one man killed in this coach. He swung round when this rascal entered, and put his hand to his shooter. That was quite enough to bring a bullet his way. Reckon there wasn't a move left in the rest of us. The fellow had it all his own way. A chap can't grope for his shootin' iron when a revolver's grinnin' at him. What's the news elsewhere?"

"Much the same as yourn," came from a passenger. "We were kind er dozing, and I'd jest begun ter wonder why in thunder the chap behind had put on his brakes so hard, specially when we were on a sharp incline, when the door bursts open, and a young chap climbs in smart. 'Hands up!' he says, just as quiet as may be, and 'hands up!' it had ter be. We was cornered. That young chap was Bill Buster, as he'd got to be called hereabouts, one of the expertest leaders of railway breakers and thieves that's ever been. What's the driver say?"

"I ain't heard nothing," came from the latter, who stood inside the coach rubbing his dirty hands with a piece of waste. "I wondered why the conductor had put on his brakes, 'cos it ain't too easy a job to pull out over the rise, particular when thar's a heavy train like this. But he took 'em off quick, and so we was able to pull along. Seems thar's been shootin'."

"Shootin'! Rather! And it ain't the fault of the rascals as came aboard that thar wasn't more," said the tall man. "We owe it to this here young stranger that things ain't worse. How'd it all come about? Didn't see you climb aboard way back there."

"Because I climbed aboard down the road," answered Jack boldly, the old frankness in his eyes, his face flushed with delight and triumph. For success had at last come his way. Though he hesitated to interfere at first, frightened by the cruel disappointment of that other experience, he had in the end undertaken what was clearly his duty, as it would have been the duty of any other person similarly placed. And success had come his way, though in gaining it he had incurred danger. His head was well set back on his shoulders, his eyes flashed, and Jack Kingsley looked his old, bonny self as he answered:

"I got aboard after she'd started, and managed to reach the conductor's coach. When I took a peep inside, there he was, tied up like a sack, with three men sitting over him. That's one of the fellows."

He nodded towards the body lying on the floor, and wondered vaguely whether it was his bullet which had struck him, and, if so, where. Then, leaning against the woodwork of the coach, he continued:

"So I climbed to the roof," he said, "and managed to hear what was going on. You see, there's a large lantern back there, and it has a window in it. I learned all about the attack, and saw the robbers separate while the last put on the brakes hard. Then I slipped in quick."

"Yes," came eagerly from the assembled passengers.

"There ain't much more," said Jack lamely. "The conductor led the way along to coach Number four, and I followed. He was shot. Guess he's way back there on the track, and needs our help. I climbed right up on to the roof, and—and the gentlemen here knows the rest."

"Gee! I do. This young chap never'll have a nearer shave. There's many a grown man who would have funked it," exclaimed the tall man, "funked it, I say. But he bamboozled that fellow. How'd yer manage?"

Jack explained, lamely, that he had gripped the smokestack and kicked the lantern with his feet.

"Smart! real smart!" exclaimed the tall passenger, while a chorus of approval came from the others. "Say, siree, who may yer be, and where aer yer goin'? Yer ain't fer the plains?"

"I'm a smith," answered Jack limply, for his wound was very painful, and the carriage excessively hot.

"A smith, and—here, what's the matter with the lad? Let him sit down. Did the rascal wing yer?"

The big man gripped our hero in his arms as if he were a child, and laid him on the seat. Then he bent over him and spoke softly.

"Whar's the hit?" he asked. "Ah, thar ain't no more need ter ask!"

Suddenly his eyes had detected the dark stain trailing down Jack's sleeve, while he noticed how limply the arm hung. Then his whole attention was attracted to our hero, for Jack marked the occasion of this success of his by fainting. He fell back heavily on the seat, and lay there as deathly pale as the man from whom he had received the bullet.

CHAPTER VII

Friends and Hunters

"My, now, you've given us quite a fright! Feel a bit queerish? Eh?"

As if in a dream, Jack heard the words and struggled to answer. But for some reason or other, which his disordered mind could not fathom, and which distressed him greatly, the words would not come to his lips. Moreover, he could not concentrate his wandering thoughts on any one matter. Now he was in court, under trial for robbery, and a moment later he was on the stage with Amos, helping in some conjuring feat which drew roars of applause from the assembled audience. His thoughts even swept back to that eventful ride on the railway; but they never reached finality. The train ran on and on, while he clung to the rail and the footboard, immovable, desperate, unable to creep forward or back.

"Say, now, yer ain't feelin' quite so bad? A bit shook up and so on? But better, ain't yer?"

Jack opened his eyes, and saw a bearded face leaning over him. He shut them again promptly, as if the sight had been too much for him, as well it might, for the individual who had stared so closely at our hero was not prepossessing, to say the least of it. He was gently pushed aside by another individual, and a woman's gentle voice spoke.

"Leave him to me a little," she said. "He is still very weak, and not fully conscious. Leave him, please. In a little while he will be better."

Jack felt a warm pressure on his hand, and sank once more into oblivion. But it was a pleasant unconsciousness on this occasion. No longer was he distressed with views of the court, with counsel for the prosecution standing before the jury and encouraging them to find this young fellow guilty. No longer did he cling desperately to the rail of the train. He sank into a dreamless, comforting oblivion, which held him securely in its tender grip for another half-hour. And then he suddenly opened his eyes.

"Well, now," he exclaimed, somewhat feebly, for his tongue seemed to be heavily loaded, "where on earth am I? And what has been happening? Coming, sir, coming."

Back wandered his mind to Amos, and he fancied he heard the conjurer calling to him.

57

"Lie still and you'll feel better. Sip this," said someone, and at once, obedient to the command, too weak to be over curious as to why it was given or by whom, our hero sipped at the glass placed to his lips. And the spirit there revived him wonderfully. It was as if a spur were needed to stimulate his flagging energies. The cordial given him seemed to have acted as a strong fillip, and in a minute he was sitting up, pushing aside an arm which endeavoured to hold him down.

"Here, what's this?" he asked indignantly. "I'm not a baby! I—halloo! Where am I?"

"Still in the train, recovering from the wound you received," said the same gentle voice. "Now lie down again."

But Jack was stubborn, and had a horror of illness or of any show of weakness. He let his legs slide from the long seat on which he had been lying, and sat bolt upright. He looked round in a dazed fashion, and then gave a cry of recognition.

"Ah, the train!" he said. "Guess this is where that robber lay. What happened?"

"A heap," said someone standing near at hand, and, looking at him, our hero discovered the man who had stood with folded arms whilst the robber's revolver was pointed at him. "Jest a heap, young sir. But there ain't no further call to fear the robber. Guess he's rubbed out clean."

He pointed to the far end of the coach, where, under a piece of sailcloth, rested something which had the form of a body. Jack shuddered and turned away.

"And no need to blame yourself neither," came from the man. "It was done in fair fight, and thar warn't no favour. 'Sides, he managed to wing you. How's the arm?"

"I had forgotten it," answered Jack, looking down and discovering that his arm rested in a sling made from a scarf. "It hurts just a little, but nothing to what it did at first. Is the wound severe?"

"Enough to cripple yer for a time, I guess, but not so baddish. A young chap like you'll be able to swing the arm within three weeks, and work with it in six. The bullet jest went a bit high. Or low, was it, seeing as you was kinder upside down? It clipped the bone, I reckon, but thar ain't a break. Ye'll do nicely. Now, if yer feel up to it, jest tell us how it all happened."

Jack felt wonderfully better already, though a little bashful, for the coach was half-filled with passengers, all of whom were looking at him and listening eagerly. He stared back at them for a time, for the men here were in many cases of a different class to those he was accustomed to. They were sunburned, with but a few exceptions, and these latter were obviously commercial men, travelling for some trade. The others looked more like settlers, or cowboys, or even miners. They wore rough, highly coloured shirts, broad belts, and riding-boots and breeches. Each one carried a revolver, and some a hunting-knife.

"Kinder surprised at the look of us, eh?" smiled the tall man with the big moustaches. "Wall, we're ordinary enough out this way. Yer don't get folks out in this part dressin' as if they was in New York, not much. We're ranchers, or miners, almost to a man. Now fer that 'ere yarn."

Very quietly and modestly Jack told how he had boarded the train, and recounted his subsequent actions.

"Reckon it was the only thing I could do," he wound up lamely. "They'd have shot me as well as anyone else."

"I dunno," came hotly from one of the passengers. "I dunno so much. Excuse me, young stranger, but I'll ax a question. Yer was right aft thar, close to the truck, warn't you? And yer could have boarded that as easy as possible? Eh?"

Jack nodded, colouring visibly, for he began to wonder whether he would have to declare to all present that that was actually his intention.

"Then them skunks wouldn't have found you. They was huntin' for the car what carries the gold. Yer hadn't no call to enter the conductor's crib, none at all, siree, and yet yer did. Yer cut him loose, and then come along the footboard. There war something else you could ha' done. Yer could ha' layed there snug, and not cared a jot. Reckon ye've saved a pile for the owners of that 'ere money."

There was a loud chorus of approval, and immediately afterwards the tall man with the fine moustaches stepped forward.

"That isn't all," he said slowly. "Ladies and gentlemen, many of you know me. I'm Tom Horsfall, from down Colorado way, and I've made this trip many a time, and scores of others. I've been through the Indian country, and have seen fighting. Then every mother's son of us has used his gun to save the outfit we've been along with, and to keep our own scalps. Reckon we hadn't a show here. Those varmint were on to us too quick, and a man has to weaken sometimes when he hasn't had time to lift his gun. This young stranger didn't save the gold alone. Guess he saved a goodish few of us."

Once more there was a chorus of approval.

"Ye've put it neat and handy, Tom," sang out the one who had spoken earlier. "He's saved lives as well as money."

"And as a mark of our appreciation the passengers on the train, as well as the staff, have made a collection. I have much pleasure in handing you three hundred dollars."

The big man smiled—a comprehensive smile, which took in all the company present, and Jack in particular. He stepped up to our hero, and handed him a skin purse which was heavy with dollars.

"Ye've earned it fair and handsome," he said. "Take it, my lad."

To say that Jack was delighted and somewhat overcome would be to describe his condition incorrectly. Tears were in his eyes as he took the money, and he attempted vainly to return thanks. But the big man helped him out.

"Yer ain't no call to say a word," he said kindly. "We all understand, and we don't want thanks. Now, stranger, jest yer lie down again and sleep. We'll talk later on."

"But the conductor?" asked Jack, suddenly remembering the man he had released, and who had fallen from the train.

"He's jest as comfortable as may be," came the reassuring answer. "The bullet that ruffian fired went slick through his wrist and made him let go. He's a bit shook, and no wonder; but thar ain't anything worse with him than a hole in his wrist, and that'll mend as soon as your wound. Now, git down and rest."

The order was peremptory now, and Jack obeyed it. A delicious sense of comfort and security came over him, and, better than all, the feeling that he had friends. A while ago he was a hunted criminal, with none to look to for help. Now, in the pocket of his jacket, he had solid evidence of good friendship; for the dollars chinked loudly when he moved, while all who looked at him smiled or patted his hand. Meanwhile the train was proceeding, and when in the course of seven hours Jack awoke, he found houses about him, and lights flickering through the morning mist. The passengers were descending from the cars, gripping their luggage, and everything pointed to the fact that the end of the journey was reached.

"The rails don't go any farther," said Tom Horsfall, coming and sitting beside him. "From here those who live farther afield have to go by caravan, and there they are, hurrying away, as if they hadn't a moment to lose. Where are you going, lad?"

Jack sat up suddenly and looked at his questioner. From the very first he had taken a liking to Tom, and knew intuitively that he was one who could be trusted. Still, he reflected, he must not say too much. The constable might even now be following.

"To California," he answered steadily.

"To dig?"

Jack nodded his head. "Partly that, partly to earn money at the forge. I've done a course of smith's work, and am fairly handy."

An exclamation of pleasure escaped Tom promptly.

"Do yer want a job?" he asked swiftly. "'Cos I've one ter offer."

To do Jack full justice, he hesitated to accept the post, and felt troubled. For common sense told him that the place was offered because of what he had done. It was, in a measure, a reward for his services. But there was another aspect of the matter. When he had accepted Amos's offer it was at a moment when he was sorely pressed, and when, because of his haste, he had little time to consider other matters. But Jack was honest to the core, and he had made up his mind to work for himself at his trade rather than to accept a post and leave his employer ignorant of his past history. And here he was face to face with the dilemma. He must either refuse what might turn out to be just the thing for him, or he must declare himself and hold nothing back.

"Yer ain't got no cause to fret about the arm," said Tom, noticing his hesitation, "'cos we've a long march before us. It'll be three months before we reach Nevada, and another before we hit upon a spot at which ter dig. Long before then ye'll be fit again, and it's when we're at the diggin's that ye'll come in handy. We've been lookin' out fer a smith, and, yer see, we're off to Californy like you, so the thing seems kinder ter fit."

"It isn't that," exclaimed Jack quickly. "I want to say something. You don't know anything about me. I might be anything at all."

"Now, look ye here," cried Tom hotly, "don't yer jest take me fer a fool. No one out here knows what his mates are, nor cares either. 'Tain't no business of no one's. Reckon out thar at the diggin's and on the plains yer kin meet men as was dukes in Europe, others that's thieves, and crowds that has as shady a history as yer could well think of. That ain't no one's concern. But you!—with that honest face and frank look—don't yer try ter get telling me that you've got a history marked up against yer. Yer may have met trouble, but I reckon it come from someone else's fault; or it was a monkey trick that any lad'll get up to. Don't tell me. I've been out these ways boy and man, and I ain't easily took in."

"Listen a moment," said Jack quietly. "I am an escaped prisoner, under trial quite recently for burglary, and under suspicion of having killed a man."

If our hero expected Tom to give vent to a whistle of astonishment, and to make some sort of demonstration, he was disappointed. Tom sat down coolly, pulled out a cigar, and bit the end off.

"Jest you fire ahead with the yarn, young 'un," he said, between the puffs, as he held a match to the weed. "Tell me jest as much as yer like, and jest as little. I ain't no policeman, I'm a plain man; and where I've worked, though thar's been a sheriff, he's mostly lived a hundred or more miles away. Consequence is, we've jedged matters fer ourselves. Reckon we don't make many mistakes, neither. If a man's a horse thief or a train robber, or something of that sort, he has a fair show to clear himself. Ef he can't, he's shot. What's the row been about?"

Jack told him frankly what his trouble was, and how he had fled from the prison. Then he described his work with Amos, and finally his dash for the train. Tom listened coolly, taking deep pulls at his weed, and filling the carriage with smoke. Not an observation escaped him. But his brows were wrinkled, and his eyes almost closed, seeming to point to the fact that he was thinking deeply. He rose and went to the window to toss the ash from his weed, and sauntered back again.

"Do yer smoke, young 'un?" he asked curtly but not unkindly. Then, as Jack shook his head, he went on. "Ah, more's the pity jest now, for a smoke kinder helps a man. He gets something between his teeth, and grips tight at it. Ef he's got a plaguey business on hand, somehow or other the thing between his teeth, and the smoke bubbling up into the air, lets him get down to the bottom of that 'ere business. Jest tell me. Could you recognize that 'ere chap as came to the forge for the key?"

"Anywhere!" exclaimed Jack emphatically.

"Then yer ain't no cause ter worry. And I'll tell yer why. All the train robbers and sich like that works out east has to make tracks sooner or later. Things gets too hot for 'em, and they have to move or be nabbed. Wall, this here fellow has made things hot. A murder's a murder, and it don't help matters even if the papers tell him that someone else is standing his trial for the crime. The truth will out some day, and that some day may be sooner rather than later; so the chap clears from the east. And whar does he make for?"

Tom looked steadily at Jack, and, seeing that he shook his head, went on promptly. "I'll tell yer. He goes slick west, to the diggin's, whar thar's miners to swindle, and gold trains ter hold up. That's whar the ruffians get to; and seeing that that's the case, ye're like ter meet this fellow out Californy way sooner than in New York direction. That's a good solid reason for yer to come west yerself, and though yer may have thought, and rightly too, to throw off pursuit quicker in that direction, ye've chosen at the same time the one place in all the world whar you're likely ter get evidence that'll clear yer. Do I believe you did it?"

Tom looked at Jack as he asked the question, and then burst into a loud guffaw.

"Shucks!" he cried; "thar ain't no sense in the noddles of them stay-at-homes. Anyone could see with half an eye that sarcumstances was dead against yer, and that before jedgment was given, your age, your past life, everything should be taken into consideration. But that jedge and jury seemed ter have made up their minds, without even setting to work to learn if other men had been handy, if a cart had been hired, or other burglaries committed in them parts by two men. Reckon that friend of yours you call James did well ter advise yer ter skip. Once ye'd put your nose into a prison, ye'd have been done. Ye'd never have cleared yourself. Now ye've a goodish chance, and I'll help yer. That job's still open, youngster. And, by the way, what's the name?"

"Jack Kingsley. Tom Starling when I boarded the train."

"Then Jack let it be. Thar ain't no call ter have a second name. One's good enough, and heaps. Will yer come?"

"Rather! and ever so many thanks for helping me," cried Jack, his lip a trifle tremulous, for such kindness moved him.

"I ain't done nothing," came the prompt answer, "nothing compared with what you've managed fer me. Reckon that rascal near let lead into me. Jest remember this, lad. Ye're as good as any hereabouts, and no call to hang your head. And thar ain't no fear of arrest. Thar ain't a soul as'll know yer, save the villain that did that burglary and left yer to face the trial. Ef yer meet him ye'll have ter act, and afore yer get to the diggin's ye'll have learned how. Now jest a word about myself. I've been everything—cowboy, rancher with my own ranch, storekeeper, and miner. I ain't no wife nor chicks, and so a wandering life suits me. And I've been lucky. Two years ago come Christmas time I struck it rich and plenty way west in Californy, and me and my mate cleared out with a handsome banking account. We agreed to separate till this time, and then ter go partners again ef both of us wished ter have another turn. Wall, we're both for the diggin's again, and we're going to do it big this time. We've each put three thousand dollars into the thing, and I've with me on the train an outfit that'll wash gold of itself. It'll want a bit of fixin', and now and again a little repair, without a doubt. A smith's the man for that, and so you're jest rightly fitted. Yer ain't got no tools, perhaps?"

"None," Jack admitted, and then with a smile, "you see, I left so hurriedly. There wasn't time to bring much away, and an anvil is rather heavy."

"And perlicemen have a way of skipping along precious quick," laughed Tom. "But we'll fix the whole matter. My mate meets me here at the rail head, and we buy a wagon and some mules or hosses. Then we set off across the plains, choosing some convoy to go with, ef that's possible. Ef not, we'll have to risk the Indians. In any case we shall have a long trail before us, and ef you're fond of shootin' and huntin' thar'll be heaps of both for yer. Why, ef that ain't Steve!"

A short, spare man entered the car at this moment, and stepped lightly towards Tom. There was the merest smile of recognition on his face, while the eyes lit up for a moment. They gripped hands for an instant, and then Steve crossed to the window, and looked out sharply, craning his head so as to see in either direction. Tom laughed heartily.

"Steve's the silentest man I ever chummed with," he said. "And he can't get that 'ere backwoods trick out of his mind. Don't matter where he is, he's lookin' round, p'raps for enemies, p'raps for somethin' ter eat. Lookin' round's become a sorter habit with him. Howdy, Steve?" he shouted out. "Jest come and larn to know our new hand. This here's Jack, smith to our outfit."

The little man strode from the window, faced Jack openly, and gripped his hand till our hero could have shouted. He liked the look of Steve. He was the very image of those hunters and scouts he had so often read about; the silent, lean hunter who went his way into the wilderness, and whose every hour called for courage and determination.

"Howdy, stranger?" said Steve. "Kin yer shoot?"

"None," answered Jack promptly.

"Nor ride?"

"A very little."

"Then ye'll do. Most every tenderfoot that comes this way is clean off the finest shot and the best ter sit a horse that was ever seen. They git to teachin' the old hands. Ef yer ain't used to neither, reckon ye'll shape mighty soon. I ain't one who holds with side. Deeds is worth a hull wagon load of boastin'."

"And words ain't much in your line," laughed Tom. "I never heard Steve make a longer speech. He's took well to yer, Jack. Now then, listen here, mate. This Jack's begun his shootin' already. We got held up back thar down the line, and he cleared us proper. Jest cast yer eye up there at the roof."

Steve strode beneath the lantern, and rapidly surveyed the punctures which the robber's bullets had made. In a flash his eye took in the general disorder, the broken window, the stained carpet, and the long form lying beneath the sailcloth.

"It war warm while it lasted," he said, returning. "Whar was you?"

Jack pointed aloft. "On the roof," he said quietly. "He'd have had me there I expect. So I held on to a smokestack, and shot him through the window."

Steve strode to the side of the car, and once more surveyed the surroundings. He leaped to the ground, and they saw him clambering along the footboard. Then he returned as suddenly as he had gone.

"Ever pulled a trigger afore?" he asked bluntly.

"Never."

"And yer was upside down, so ter speak?"

"That's so," admitted Jack.

"I'm glad ye're comin'."

Steve was a character. He was as taciturn and as silent as a man might well be. But honest to the core. A stanch friend, a bitter enemy, for his had been a rough life; and a man so sharp that nothing escaped him. His last words were high commendation indeed, and Jack, realizing that, reddened.

"We'll be startin' right away," said Steve, addressing Tom. "A town ain't no fit place fer a scout. One can't kinder breathe, with all the smoke and the houses. I've palled with six boys as is goin' west."

The news was excellent, especially when Tom had persuaded his partner to be a little more explicit. The boys turned out to be old hunter friends of Steve's, accustomed to the plains, and their addition to the party would make it possible for Tom and Steve and Jack to push on promptly, and not wait for a larger party. For in those days the wide tracts of plain separating the east from California were infested by cut-throat Indians, and many was the massacre for which they were responsible. Indeed, hundreds of unfortunate men and women, making their way across to the goldfields, fell foul of these red demons, and were slaughtered and scalped unmercifully.

"Then to-morrow we'll move," said Tom. "It won't take more'n two hours ter buy up an anvil and sich like things. Hosses ain't no difficulty. Thar's always plenty of 'em. Now, Jack, let's be movin'. Ye'll come right along with us to the camp, and start in as our man from this moment."

CHAPTER VIII

Out on the Prairie

Shouldering their baggage, Tom and Steve led the way from the station, and, having traversed some few hundred yards, came to a single wagon, halted by the roadside. It was a large affair, covered with a big canvas tilt, and mounted on four strong wheels. A single shaft protruded in front, to which the wheelers of the team of horses could be attached. In fact, beyond a few minor particulars which followed the custom in vogue in this part of America, the wagon was very similar to those huge conveyances, sometimes called the "ships of the veldt", which are to be found in South Africa.

"A tidy weight it is, too," said Tom, as Jack remarked on the wagon when approaching. "But it's jest the thing for the plains. Yer see, ter do any good way over in Californy a man wants a heap of tools and sich like. Wall, they're to be had from San Francisco, or Sacramento; but, gee! ain't the prices tall! It pays handsome ter buy a wagon back here and fill it with stuff. That's what we're doin'. Me and Steve's put a sight of earnin's and savin's into the matter, and we'll have ter strike it rich way over thar to git the money back. Thar's something else. Ef bad weather comes on, we kin shelter of a night under the tilt—leastwise, we kin at first. After a bit thar won't be the chance. Them skunks of Indians'll make us look out fer trouble, and any man as has a care fer the haar on his head don't get sleepin' too heavy once he's come into their country. Guess them's our mates. Scouts Steve called 'em."

By now they were close to the wagon, and Jack noticed that quite a little camp had been formed round it. At a little distance some ten horses were grazing, while one man mounted guard over them. Close at hand a dozen more were tethered to pegs, and nibbled the grass in a circle round their pegs. A fire was burning just outside the wagon, and over it a pot was suspended on an iron tripod. Steve gave a shout, and promptly five men, who were seated near the fire, rose and lounged forward.

"Gee, now! Ef that ain't Seth, Tricky Seth, as we called him," shouted out Tom, waving his hat above his head. "Howdy, Seth? Didn't know yer was this way. When last I set eyes on yer it was way down in New Mexico. What's brought yer here?"

A short, heavily built man stepped forward from amongst his comrades. He was so tanned by wind and exposure that one might have been excused the mistake if one had taken him for an Indian. His eyes were a steely grey, his chin and upper lip covered with thick, bushy hair, while the backs of his hands, and his arms, which were exposed to the elbows, were also thickly clad with the same material. He wore a wide-brimmed hat, which decidedly had seen better days, a shirt which had once been red, but which frequent washings and much exposure to a hot sun had bleached to a mottled brown, while his nether limbs were clad in cowboy overalls fringed with leather tassels. A picturesque fellow he looked, and something more. His keen eyes, the resolute set of his features, hardly needed the addition of the huge belt he wore, in which reposed a big Colt, to tell a stranger that Seth—"Tricky Seth", as Tom had called him—was something more than picturesque. He came forward with sparkling eyes and with hand outstretched.

"Why, so it war," he cried, speaking with a very pronounced twang; "so it war. And I jest reckon I was as s'prised as you to find myself up this way. But New Mexico's that full of horse thieves and Injun skunks that an honest man can't live. Fact is, I got into a muss with a gang of robbers. I come up against 'em accidental at first, and that got their danders up agin me. They was fer shootin' right off whenever they seed me."

"And that ain't healthy fer any man," burst in Tom, "though I guess as Seth ain't easy ter frighten."

"Not as a general thing; but this here case were special. I stood it fer a while, yer bet, and by keepin' out in the plains and mountains, trappin' and huntin' managed ter hold 'em clear fer a bit. But it got precious onreasonable ter have bullets flyin' whenever I went into town ter sell the skins I'd been collectin'. What with one meetin' and another I got a matter of three holes drilled through me, and that warn't pleasant. I give 'em snuff in return, I jest did, but that don't help ter mend holes in a fellow's carcass. So I comed away. Then I struck along o' Steve, and hearin' yer was goin' partners, and was off to Californy, why, me and my mates here agreed ter go. We was thinkin' of earning a bit by acting as sort of escort to other convoys makin' across to the diggin's. But, bless yer, the crowds that's goin' don't think of danger; they thinks of gold only."

"And believes they'll find it in handfuls, the poor fools," cried Tom. "Thar's many a hundred as has lost their scalps crossin' the plains."

"And many more'll meet with the same," agreed Seth. "But they don't reckon to meet nothin'. It's goin' ter be a picnic all the way across, that's what they say and think, and so they don't want no escort. Me and my mates fixed then that we'd try a little diggin' ourselves, and as yer was goin', why, it seemed jest the chance to make across together. Who's the stranger?"

Tom introduced Jack to Seth promptly, and then handed him over to the latter, who made him acquainted with his comrades. Nor was it long before all became familiar with the story of his behaviour on the train.

"For a fust shot it war good, precious good," declared Seth. "I've let off a gun in most positions, but never upside down, as I reckon you was. So, without offence, youngster, I should say as how that 'ere shot weren't altogether of yer own doin'. There was a bit of flukin, in it. Howsomever, that ain't the point. Yer had the grit to lean over and hold fast to the gun. That's whar you came in. Yer held fast, and drew trigger jest at the right moment. Reckon the gun did the rest. And he managed to wing yer?"

Jack nodded. "He put a ball through my shoulder," he said. "It hurt a bit, but someone seems to have bandaged it, and it's quite easy now."

"Then yer ain't no cause to blush and 'low folks to say as you're a green 'un," laughed Seth. "Reckon a chap as has had daylight put through him has seen something. But yer'll have to set to at shootin'. My advice is to buy a hull heap of ammunition. Me and my mates most always jest carry a dozen rounds. That's heaps under ordinary sarcumstances; but when yer get to shootin' with a revolver, the ammunition melts away, as it war. And a man ain't nothin' of a shot till he's fired thousands of rounds. So buy up a supply, and set to in earnest when we gets clear of the town."

Jack made a mental note of the advice given him, and decided to invest some of his savings in a thoroughly good revolver and gun and the necessary ammunition. Nor had he any reason to fear the expenditure, for he had saved a good deal when in Amos's employ, and had hardly touched the money he had brought away from Hopeville. In addition, that same evening, when Tom and his friends were making their final preparations for leaving camp at an early hour on the following day, two officials of the bank to which the money on board the train was consigned approached, and handed our hero no less than fifteen hundred dollars.

"As a reward for saving our consignment," they said. "We had a very much larger sum on board the train than was supposed, and had those robbers succeeded in mastering all the passengers, and in stopping the coaches, our loss would have been a very severe one."

They left the camp within a few minutes, expressing the hope that Jack would soon recover from his wound. But that young fellow was almost too elated to recollect the fact that his shoulder was damaged. He was more than delighted at the gift, and at once fell to wondering what he would do with such riches.

"I shall return James and Mother the sums they lent me," he said, "and for the rest I suppose I'd better bank it. I'll ask Tom."

"Yer can jest do one o' two things," replied the latter, when Jack had spoken to him. "Ef yer bank it here the money'll be safe, and yer can arrange to have a draft on a bank way over near Sacramento. Then, once we get to Californy, and yer've had time to look round, yer can set up some sort of business for yerself. Buy a plot in one of the towns that's springing up like mushrooms, and set up as a smith. That'd bring in dollars quick, for there ain't many smiths handy, and ironwork aer well paid. Five hundred dollars should see yer started, with the rest and your savings while working fer us safe in the bank in case of illness or failure. Not that yer want ter think of failure. That are a word no young man should allow has a place in the language. Seems to me ef a youngster jest kind of pins 'success' up in front of him, and sets to to gain it by steady, hard work, he's bound, sooner or later—and the steadier he is the sooner it'll be—to find he's got to the thing he's aimed at. But I was sayin' there's two things yer could do with that money. I've mentioned one."

"And the other?" asked Jack eagerly.

"The other aer a proposition of my own—mine and Steve's; and mind yer, ef it don't seem right and likely to you, jest refuse, 'cos no offence'll be given. We've put jest three thousand dollars apiece into this scheme of ours, me and Steve have, and a goodish part of the money has gone to buy the wagon and outfit. Still, thar's a tidy few dollars left, and that'll be workin' capital for when we reach the diggin's. Wall, now, more workin' capital are always useful. Yer can buy up appliances that'll make the diggin' and windin' easier, besides employing more hands, and so gettin' down to the gold quicker. Ef yer like the proposition yer kin buy a share in this consarn of ours, and come in as a partner instead of a hired man. Yer'll stand to lose along with us; but ef we strike it rich, why, ye'll gain, jest as we shall, in proportion to the amount ye've put into the partnership. Now, jest yer get away by yerself fer a while, or talk it over with Seth and his mates. They're straight, and ef the consarn ain't worth it, or the proposition ain't a fair one to you, they'll say so for sure. Come back agin in an hour's time. I'm goin' into the town jest to finish a little buying."

Jack needed very little time for consideration, for he had already practically made up his mind. There was something transparently honest and straightforward about Tom and Steve, and he felt he could not do better than throw in his lot with them. To be sure, if their efforts to discover gold were not successful, he would lose all the money he subscribed. But then, they might meet with good fortune.

"I'll do it," he said to himself, and that, too, without discussing the matter with Seth and his friends. "I'll send along the money I borrowed from Mother and James Orring, pay a thousand dollars to this partnership, and bank the rest against a rainy day. Who knows, I may be glad to have the use of it later on."

His determination to become a partner in the little firm of gold diggers delayed the departure of the party for a few hours.

"Things has to be done fair and square," said Tom, when Jack announced his decision. "We'll get into town, as soon as it's light, and rouse up a lawyer. It'll take him an hour to prepare a draft same as Steve and I have. Then the sheriff'll have to sign it, and me and Steve too. When the document's ready, you'd best hand it over to the bank, and give 'em instructions to transfer it to their branch at Sacramento. They'll send it *via* New York and Panama, and thar ain't a doubt but that it'll reach. The lawyer'll make a second copy, so that in any case you'll be able to refer to the agreement if you want to."

"And we'd best put something into the draft that'll fix it right ef one of us partners wants to clear," exclaimed Steve, who, though a silent man as a rule, was not backward in making suggestions when his experience told him they were needed. "Seems to me it might happen as one of us would want to leave fer New York or somewheares else. Wall, his money's in the firm, but he don't work no longer. And, sense work aer the thing that's mainly wanted, why, ef he leaves, he ain't no longer of any use."

"Agreed," cried Tom instantly. "I'm ready to stand by that."

"And I also," added Jack. "We might put in a clause giving the remaining partners the right to buy up the share of the one leaving, and to do that they might sell it to an outsider if they hadn't the money themselves."

"Which'd be better than givin' the retirin' partner the right of bringin' in someone as was his friend, and who mightn't hit it off with t'others," said Tom. "Now, that's a fair and square proposal, and ef we're all willin', why, it won't take more'n a few minutes longer fer the lawyer feller ter stick in them extry clauses. While he's doin' the thing, we'll get to the doctor's and have thet shoulder seen to, young 'un. When you was took bad in the train, and lay thar as if you was dead, this doctor man fixed the wound nicely for you. Lucky he jest happened to be aboard. Wall, ter-morrer he'll take another look, and we'll get him to fix us up with bandages and sich like. Now it's time to be turning in."

Jack Kingsley lay awake for some time on this his first night with his new comrades. His surroundings were so entirely different from those he was accustomed to, while even the accent and the language of the scouts was so strange, that his brain was too full to allow of sleep. The stamp of the horses outside, and the gentle whisper of the breeze as it blew against the canvas tilt, all served to keep him awake. Then, too, his wound became distinctly painful, while he himself felt burning hot and icy cold in turns. However, at length he fell into a troubled sleep which lasted till the early morning.

"How aer yer?" asked Tom, who lay in a bunk on the other side of the wagon. "Fit as ever, youngster?"

Jack rose from his blanket couch and shook himself. After such a night he was not at all sure whether he did feel as fit as he should do. But within ten minutes he was laughing and joking merrily; the keen morning air, the brilliant light of the rising sun, and the appetizing smell wafted from the steaming kettle all serving to rouse his spirits.

"Ye'll do, yer will," cried Tom some few minutes later, as he watched our hero. "Guess yer hadn't the best o' nights. I sleeps light always, 'cos where I've lived my days a man has to be easy waked, and ready at a moment fer action. I heard yer a-heavin' and a-tossin' in yer blankets, and I reckoned as the shoulder war a trifle troublesome. But ye've took to yer breakfast. I never seed a fellow eat heartier. Seems as ef the air hereabouts agreed with yer."

"And as ef bein' shot war a thing as give him an appetite," laughed Steve. "But we'd best be movin' slippy into the town. I knows these lawyer fellers. They're all jaw, and thar ain't no makin' them hurry. Let's skip in thar right now, and the sooner we reach the chap, the sooner we'll be able ter git altogether."

Leaving Seth and his mates to clear the camp and make all preparations for their march, Tom and Steve and Jack walked briskly into the town. A call was made at once on a lawyer, and, having given him the necessary particulars, they left him to prepare the agreement which would make Jack a partner in the firm.

"And now fer an outfit fer you, youngster," said Tom. "Ye're wantin' a rifle and a revolver. Wall, ef yer go to a proper gunsmith, he'll fix yer up with anythin', but it'll cost money. Thar's fellers in these towns as buy weapons from hunters who aer in want of money, or from miners returning east. They're the men to go to."

He led the way past the better part of the town, and dived into a smaller street built at right angles to the one they had just left. Then he stopped at a little shop, in the tiny window of which were displayed an assortment of articles.

"Jest leave the tradin' to me," he said. "Likely enough, ef yer was to try and fix the deal, the fellow would ask double his price, for these men aer wonderful cute at spottin' newcomers. Leave it ter me; I've bought off him afore."

Tom indeed made an excellent bargainer, for within half an hour Jack found himself possessed of a fine rifle, and a revolver which appeared never to have been used. Also, Tom bought for him a large quantity of ammunition.

"The whole dirt cheap at a hundred dollars," he said as they issued from the shop. "Now, all we've got ter buy is an anvil and sich tools as ye'll want, 'cos that'll be your work in the partnership, besides diggin'. In a firm like ours each of the partners'll do what he kin, and as much as he kin, to get things going and to make dollars. Steve, thar, has the best eye fer locatin' a likely corner fer gold as ever I came upon. But he ain't no good with the pick and spade; he's built too light. Last time we was partners, 'way in Californy, guess me an a hired man did most all the diggin'. But Steve did more'n his equal share of work for the firm, 'cos it was he who went nosin' round till he finally hit upon the spot that panned out rich and gave us gold in plenty. Ha! here's the general stores. They'll likely enough have all we want."

They had, in fact, no difficulty in purchasing all the tools Jack was likely to require, and arranged with the storekeeper to have them sent to their camp at once. An anvil of moderate size, a bag of fuel, the necessary tools, and a small portable forge were bought; and, that done, the trio returned to the lawyer's.

"Ready, gentlemen," he said, meeting them with a smile. "I know how impatient you scouts and miners are, and I made a special effort to press on with the document. It is here, and we can go across to the sheriff right away. There the document can be duly signed and sealed, the money can be paid over, and the exchange duly witnessed."

Within an hour Jack found himself a member of the firm, with Tom Horsfall and Steve as his partners, and, as he left the sheriff's office, could not refrain from silently contrasting his position then with what it had been a few weeks formerly. Then everything seemed to be against him, while a long imprisonment stared him in the face. But two days ago he was a hunted criminal, seeking to make good his escape; and now—so stimulating was the effect of the success his bold action on the train had met with, and the few kind words with which he had been greeted—he feared to face no man, no, not even Constable Simpkins.

"I feel for the first time as if I had taken a step in the right direction," he said to himself, "the direction which will lead to the discovery of that ruffian for whom I have suffered so much. I have met with a stroke of amazing fortune, and have earned enough money to give me a start. Well, I'll do my utmost to turn it to good account. I'll slave to make this partnership a success, and if it prove to be that, then I'll use what money I gain in tracking that criminal. For clear my name from this slur I will, even if it costs me every dollar I possess, and takes years and years to accomplish."

A visit to the doctor was made on the way back to camp, and having had his shoulder dressed, and careful instructions given for the future care of the wound, Jack returned to the camp with his friends.

"We didn't rightly know when you'd be returning," said Seth, "and so we didn't hook in the beasts. But everything else is ready packed, and in ten minutes we'll be movin'. That youngster had better climb into the wagon. It won't do that shoulder of his'n any good jolting on a mustang."

Let the reader imagine the party as they marched from the town. In front of the wagon rode three horsemen, such horsemen as are not to be met with in any other country; for these hunters had the free-and-easy seat which comes from long custom. They rode, in fact, like others in different countries who use their legs so seldom that walking is a labour, and who climb into a saddle, even if they only wish to pass from one tent to another. A fine picture Tom and Seth and Steve made as they led the march. After them came the wagon, its team blowing, for they were soft after a long rest and plenty of feeding, while beside the beasts walked a negro, wielding a long whip, which cracked like a pistol shot when he flicked it. On the front sat Jack, radiantly happy, while in rear rode five more scouts, alert and watchful even here; for such is the force of habit.

And so they turned their faces from the towns and moved off into the plains—those long flats of country which stretched, with a break here and there, right away to the mountains of Nevada.

"And by the time we reaches 'em yer'll be a scout same as we are," said Tom, riding his horse close beside the wagon. "As soon as that 'ere shoulder aer better yer'll be able to mount and ride same as us, and then Steve'll set to with yer. Thar ain't another in Americky like him to larn a youngster all the ways o' huntin', and how to track and follow a trail. Yer've jest to sit thar tight and get well, and out here on the plains, whar the air's pure, a fellow mends in no time."

This proved to be the case. The air of the plains is notoriously healthy, and very soon Jack was able to use his arm. In three weeks he was mounted, and then his real enjoyment of the trip began. Long before that he had become bosom friends with his mates, and found them more than kindly. Tom alone knew his secret, but the remainder guessed that their new mate was a fugitive from justice.

"And why?" asked one of them with a laugh, as they sat round the camp fire one evening. "'Cos Jack aer changed his colour. When he comed along to the camp his haar war as black as a coal. Now it's carrots. If that don't point ter something, my name ain't Jacob."

73

There was a hearty laugh, and then the conversation was turned; for in those parts no man enquired too closely into the past history of his mates. A man was judged for himself. If he was a good and true friend that was enough. So Jack settled down amongst them, and quickly answered to the name of "Carrots".

As to his companions on this long and venturesome journey across the plains which stretched between the point of their departure and California, they were without a shadow of doubt far more interesting than those one usually met. Already the group of hunters had come upon parties of would-be miners journeying to the land of gold, and Jack was forced to confess—it was brought home to him accidentally as it were, but forcibly for all that—that the men they had met were poor specimens for the most part. Often enough the bands were composed of clerks from the cities, of storekeepers who had lost their all in their venture at trading, and sometimes, mixed up with these men of the towns, who, to say the best of them, were by their previous lives and experience wholly unsuited to the new career at which they aimed, were men from a higher sphere—dentists, doctors, soldiers, sailors, and even an actor or two. Poorly developed for the most part, the glaring sun beneath which they marched, and the open-air life which their journey forced them to lead, had given them a colour to which many no doubt had been strangers before. But no amount of exposure could give them experience of the plains—that experience which could be learned only after years of travelling, and which was so essential to them.

"It makes a man ache, so it do," said Seth, after they had bade farewell to one of these bands, which was hopelessly delayed by the loss of their draught horses. "Them poor critters would be better off back in the towns instead of coming out here. In course they're delayed. Chances are thar's some of 'em never had ter do with a hoss till now, and they ain't a notion when ter feed and water him, when ter work him fer all he's worth, and when ter give him a rest. In course out here a hoss mostly feeds hisself. The grass is that good he'd get fat ef he warn't worked, and worked hard too. But thar's sech a thing as resting the critters in the heat of the day, of grooming them occasionally, and of giving 'em a feed of corn when thar's a settlement handy. Them men we've jest left ain't no more notion of a hoss than they have of an Injun, and the wust of it are fer them that in the fust place the delay aren't all they've got ter suffer, while in the second it are generally a case of bein' clean and regular wiped out. Huh!"

Jack could not help but contrast his friends with these unhappy and inexperienced men the party had come upon. He looked about him as he jogged along, and was fain to confess that there was essentially a business air about his mates—an air of the plains, an atmosphere which spoke of independence, of courage, of that resource without which no hunter or scout in those days could have survived for long. Ahead of him rode the burly Tom, the first man to befriend him. Jack could catch a view of the tips of his long, flowing fair moustache blowing back at either side of his cheeks. What a seat the man had! He seemed to be a part of the animal he rode, and yet there was no effort about his horsemanship. To look at him he simply lounged in his saddle. Yet, as many an incident had proved, Tom was not to be easily shaken from his seat. A sudden start of his animal, a plunge, a trip over some hidden hole produced the same result. The burly Tom sat still at ease, the picture of contentment. And beside him jogged Steve, the wiry little man who has already been introduced to the reader. Taciturn and silent as a general rule, this little man, so fine drawn and lean, could on occasion be almost garrulous. But his features seldom wore other than a serious look. His keen eye was always watchful.

"Jest as I told yer," remarked Tom one day. "Steve aer always lookin' round. He aer always expecting something, and fer that reason thar ain't a scout as I'd sooner ride with. Ef you're dull and sleepy yerself, thar's Steve to watch fer yer."

Let the reader glance at those others who had banded themselves with Jack and his mates. Seth, Tricky Seth, a picture of good health and manliness: sunburned to the last degree, scarred across the forehead as the result of a toss from a horse when much younger, bearded and moustached, and as handsome a man as one could meet in a week's march. Yet how simple the man was! In spite of his good looks, of his obvious power, of a frame which was magnificently put together, this Seth was like an overgrown boy—jolly the day long, friendly with all, however humble, and ready to lend a hand to the first who needed help. There were no airs and graces about this scout.

Then turn to Jacob. Heavy and dull of feature, more taciturn than Steve even, if that were possible, this silent scout seemed to be permanently occupied with his thoughts. Of huge proportions, he moved as a general rule with a sluggishness and a want of celerity which were in distinct contrast with the sprightliness and alertness of Steve. But the man knew the plains by heart. He had been born, one might say, with a gun in his hand; and where horses were concerned there was not another to be found who could teach him.

"He aer got the appearance of a parson or a teacher," laughed Tom, "but Jacob ain't always thinkin'. Reckon he kin be lively when he likes; and ef he took to runnin' yer or me for a mile, guess we'd come in last by a goodish bit. And yer should jest see him when he's got a grip of the ribbons. I've seen a hull heap of men runnin' teams, and sometimes it's mules, and t'others it's hosses. Wall, it don't make no sorter difference ter Jacob what the beasts aer. Reckon ef they was buffalo he'd fix 'em jest the same. It aer a treat to see him steering a team across bad country, and when we comes ter settlements, and he aer conducting the outfit, why, guess it makes them city folks open their eyes. Jacob aer a man fer hosses."

Then there was Black Bill, laughing and full of fun, but a thorough man of the plains for all that. Dusky of complexion, of medium height, Bill could hold his own with anyone when it came to the management of cattle, for he had spent some years in the stockyards. And it was reported that even Steve himself had seen no more of the Indians. Bill had experienced a deal of fighting.

Of Tom Langham and David there is little to report. The one was as lean as Steve, but lankier, and amongst his friends was a reputed yarner. There were few who could tell a fireside tale as Tom Langham could. David was more of Jacob's stamp, with little to make him distinctive. And yet, put all these men together, with our hero Jack accompanying them, and even a novice in those parts, a city man, would have found something to hold his attention. It was that subtle air of business which these scouts carried with them wherever they went, the air which warned ruffians of the road to leave them severely alone, and made Indians cautious of attacking them. No wonder that Jack considered himself lucky. He was in the very best of hands, and if only his journey to California turned out as favourably as the beginning augured, then he promised himself success. Who could say? Perhaps in that country of glorious skies, of sunrises and sunsets, he would discover more than gold. It might even happen, unlikely though it seemed, that there amidst the miners he might come upon that evidence for which he sought, that man whose word alone could clear his character, could make of him once again a respected citizen of that town from which he had so lately fled.

CHAPTER IX

Only a Youngster

"We've a longish day before us," said Tom one afternoon, just after the sun had mounted to its central position, and the heat was at its height. "Them pals of ours has gone off huntin', fer it stands to reason we must have fresh meat to keep us in good health. But, as I was sayin', we're here, you and I, in charge of the team and the wagon; and sense we dursent sleep, for there ain't never no sayin' when something won't turn up, why we'd best settle down fer a jaw. I was thinking of that business of ours in the train, when yer climbed on ter the roof. I wonder what made yer think of that?"

Our hero was troubled by the question. When he came to review his movements on that eventful evening, and this particular one more especially, he found it hard to say why he had clambered to the roof of the railway coach.

"I suppose I saw in a flash that that man would shoot me if I went along the footboards," he said. "I had seen the conductor wounded and forced to let go, so I suppose, without thinking, I realized that the roof was the only place."

"Jest as I thought," remarked Tom, nodding his head, and busying himself with his whip, which he seemed to crack on every spare occasion. "That 'ere fight reminds me of a time same as this, when I was jest a slip of a youngster. It was down Mexico way, not in California, whar we're goin', and thar was gold in the question, same as thar was with you the other day. Yer see, my uncle owned a team of beasts. In fact, he owned several teams, and made a fine living by carting stores down to the Mexican mines, and returning with gold. He'd been extry lucky, too, and hadn't been held up more than once. Then my father died, and Uncle Jim took me under his wing. I used to march alongside the team, help feed and water the beasts, and lend a hand at anything that war wanted. I war jest about thirteen years of age, I reckon."

"Young," remarked Jack. "But I suppose many boys are to be found with the mule teams as young as that?"

"Sometimes they're regular kids," came the laughing rejoinder. "I mind one kid as war jest twelve, and he'd already had a turn agin the Injuns. Boys in this country don't get so much schoolin' as they might elsewhere—in England, fer instance—though I've no doubt, when America's settled, the youngsters will get all the schoolin' they want, and more besides. And so it ain't nothin' outer the ordinary to meet kids out on the plains. Wall, I was a regular kid, and Uncle Jim and I did many a march together. We'd been down to a mine located well in the south, though I can't get hold of the name at this moment. We'd dropped all our goods thar—hard tack, picks, and spades, and what not, and had filled chuck-full with gold. Reckon there was twenty-thousand dollars worth of dust on board—a fortune that wanted taking care of! And take good care of it we did, Uncle sleeping by day, while I drove the team. At night he'd fix his pipe in between his teeth, and keep watch wherever we were camped, while I turned into my blankets. It war jolly while it lasted, and yer may bet that I war a proud kid, takin' care of that 'ere team and all the gold by my solitary self durin' the day."

"And then?" asked Jack eagerly. "You were held up by a gang of robbers?"

"Hold hard," sang out Tom. "We ain't got thar yet. Things was goin' smoothly enough, when Uncle took ill. He war mighty queer. To this day I ain't sure what ailed him. But I've a notion he'd got a kind of heat stroke. Anyways, he war as hot as fire, and fer a time wanderin' in his head. I remember it war somewhere's about this time of the day when he went queer, and, sense I couldn't drive the team and look to him at the same time, I formed camp jest beside the bank of a river, whar the road ran down to the ford. I watered the beasts, pegged them out to feed, and then set to work putting cold cloths, wrung out of river water, on Uncle's head. Reckon I kept at it all that day, and right into the night, till I was that weary I was falling asleep the instant I set down in the wagon. And in the end I went right fast off beside Uncle, and lay there snorin' till the sun was up, and it war nigh ten o'clock. It war a shout that waked me."

Tom looked over his shoulder to see that Jack was listening, and then threw the tail of his whip lightly over his leaders, sending his team bounding forward.

"A shout," repeated Jack. "Yes."

"From over the water," said Tom. "I lifted the tilt of the wagon, and looked across the river. There was four men, mounted, wavin' their arms.

"'Whar's the ford start?' one of them sang out, when he seed me come clamberin' outer the wagon. 'Does it run straight over thar from whar we're standin', or whar in thunder does it begin?'

"Wall, I war that green I was jest on the point of singing out that it cut clear down stream from whar our wagon was located till you was in line with a tree on the far side, and a kind of little bay on ours. Thar was shallow water on top of a ledge running to that point. Perhaps it war deep enough to come to the floor of the wagon, and in bad weather it might be an inch or two deeper. But it warn't never more that I ever knowed. On either side the ledge shelved off gradually, and in course the water got deeper and deeper. From the point I jest mentioned one had to swing the team right across stream, drive 'em fer ten yards or so, and then swing their heads up stream again. It war the stiffest ford as ever I crossed, and I can't make no shape to guess how it war first located. But thar it was, I'd been over it a dozen times, and was game to take the team myself, with the load of gold dust, Uncle, and all. I war sayin', I war jest on the point of singing out directions to the strangers over the far side, when Uncle jest pops the tip of his nose outer the wagon.

"'Hold on, Tom,' he says. 'Who aer they?'

"I didn't know one bit. They was travellers I supposed. But Uncle had been on that road for seven years, and guess he knew everyone for miles up and down.

"'There's four of them,' I said. 'Guess they're going down to the mines.'

"'Guess they're bound for gold anyway,' he says. 'Sing out as there's another ford six miles up stream,' he says. 'That'll give us a breather. Don't tell them on any account that they kin cross here.'

"You may reckon I got wondering whether Uncle were still wandering, and off his head. I looked at him precious hard, and axed him ef he meant it. 'They kin guess there's a ford here, and we know it,' I said, 'else we shouldn't be camped by the entrance.'

"'Let 'em guess it, then,' he kind of snapped. 'Better they should think we was fools than we should tell 'em the ford and have 'em takin' every dollar we've got on board. Sonny, those four strangers aer a gang that's been watchin' fer me more than once. I've give them the slip three times already, and I'll do it agin this time ef I'm able. Ah, thunder! I can't even stand.'

"He'd climbed to his feet inside the wagon, holding on to the tilt, and jest as I looked across the river again I heard him fall with a bang. Then the man who'd shouted from the far side sang out again: 'We're making south,' he hailed. 'We've been directed to this here ford, and sence you're meaning to cross yer must know it. We was told it war tricky. Whar does it start, and whar does one have to turn?'

"'Bluff 'em,' calls Uncle from the wagon. 'Ef yer don't, it'll be a case with both of us, youngster.'

"Wall, I war only a kid," said Tom, gathering his reins in a bunch, "and I don't mind agreein' that I war in a mortal funk. I'd heard of Uncle's escapes, in course, and I knew that thar war men out on the road who'd take every dollar we had, and shoot us into the bargain. In my fright I was nearly telling them the ford. But Uncle war at the tilt again, glaring at me, and calling to me not ter be a fool. And I reckon I war more afraid of Uncle when he was in a rage than I war of any other man under the sun. I warn't fer telling a lie anyhow, but I 'low as all aer fair in love and war, and thet was a case of war. So I plucked up some sorter courage and called back to the men: 'Uncle's ill,' I shouted. 'He's too ill to come out and show the ford. But thar's another, six miles higher up. Yer can't miss it when you get thar. It's easier than this one.'

"Wall, that didn't please 'em. I could see the critters putting their heads together, and perhaps they guessed that Uncle could ha' told me, even if he war too ill to shout to them. So they tried to scare me into telling them.

"'This here's a case of life and death,' sings out the rascal as had shouted before. 'We're going south ter see our mother. She's thet bad she ain't expected ter last over long. So we're pushing down as fast as we can. Ax yer uncle ter tell you the road.'

"'Ax him the name of his mother,' growls Uncle from the wagon.

"Wall, thet did it," said Tom with a grin, looking into Jack's face. "In course they seed that they was being bluffed, and one of 'em made up his mind to find the ford for himself. He rid down the bank, spurred his horse on into the water, and was ten feet out in no time. By then the water was jest washin' his boots. Reckon he war on the ledge that carried the ford on the far side.

"'You kin come along, mates,' he sang out. 'Ef that imp don't care ter ax his uncle, or ef his uncle's foxin' ill, and won't say, why we'll get across all the same, and make south all the sooner.'

"Guess he thought he was safely over," laughed Tom; "but he warn't. One of his mates joined him, while the other two rode jest behind. Then suddenly, afore you could have expected it, the two who were leading, plunged into deep water. In course their horses started swimmin', but the jerk, and being unused to thet sort of thing perhaps, upset their riders, and reckon them two had a fine sousing. They turned back to the bank, and went climbing outer the water, shoutin' and cussin', and sayin' what they'd do ter me ef they could only get across. Then they turned their hosses' heads and rid like mad fer the other ford!

"'Get them mules in quick,' sings out Uncle, squintin' outer the wagon from beneath the tilt. 'Them critters'll be here afore yer kin look round, and ef we ain't slippy they'll have us. Cut the ropes, lad, and let yer blankets and sich things lie as they are. Ef we're alive we kin come back fer 'em. Ef we're dead, guess we shan't want 'em. Quick aer the word!'

"Yer could see as he war anxious, and in course I set to ter fix the team into the wagon jest as slippy as I could. But I war a boy, yer must remember, and it aer a man's work ter tie a hull team into their places. Then, what with thinkin' of them critters, and the funk I war in, every trace I touched got hooked to the wrong bar. There was Uncle, too, squintin' at me from under the tilt, his face a fiery red, and his dander burnin'. I wonder now thet I war able to fix 'em all. But at last the mules were tied in and we was ready.

"'I'm to drive 'em over?" I axed the old man. 'Clean slick across?'

"'You aer soft!" he sings out in a kind of shriek. 'That's what they want you to do. It's jest what we ain't meanin' ter carry out. Kin yer guess why?'

"I couldn't," said Tom, making a grimace. "I war a thick-headed kid, and the bustle had scared away all the sense I ever had.

""'Cos them critters'll have divided,' shouted Uncle. 'They know that I'm queer, and they guess a kid ain't much ter be afraid of. Ef they'd happened to have known this ford they would have ridden clean across, took the gold, and riddled us with bullets. As it aer, two of 'em will cross, the other two's hid up thar over the far side of the river. They reckon they're bound ter have us either way. Boy, aer you game ter fight 'em?'

"'I'll try,' I says. 'What am I ter do?'

"'Send yer team into the water, and cut out along the ford. When you've reached the point whar, in the ordinary course, you'd swing 'em up stream, jest pull 'em in. It ain't over deep thar, and sense it's hot these days the mules won't mind it. Hold the critters thar till you see how things aer workin'. Ef the two men who have crossed ride out to us, we must try and shoot 'em. Ef the others come riding out to join them, then we've two things we kin do. One is ter send the team along the road fer the other bank and chance the shootin'. T'other is to drive 'em into deep water till the cart is out of reach, cut the traces, and leave the mules to swim ashore.'

"Wall, that fairly staggered me," said Tom. "'Drive the wagon into deep water, Uncle?' I axed, and I reckon my eyes was nearly starting from my head.

"'Yer've got it,' he answers, as if thar warn't nothing outer the way in the order. 'This cart's heavy. It are got enough dust aboard to keep it on the bottom till the whole of the tilt is covered with water. I'd sooner sink the hull thing, and myself too, ef that war necessary, than see them critters get the gold. But we ain't goin' ter do that. Drive the wagon off the road till the mules are off their feet and swimmin'. By then we shall be deep enough. Then cut 'em free and wait fer them critters. Yer've got to shoot, young un.'

"We was in a bad muss anyway," said Tom, his face assuming for the moment a stern aspect; "and what with the bustle of puttin' in the mules, and headin' them for the ford, I kind of forgot my fears. I was that busy I hadn't time to think what might happen when those villains reached us. So, somehow or other, I grew out of the funk that had set my teeth chatterin' and my fingers shakin', and, rememberin' that the team was in my hands entirely, I made up my mind to bring 'em through. The leaders was enterin' the water before yer could think, and before five minutes had passed, we were well out in the centre.

"'Now pull 'em in,' says Uncle. 'Them critters'll be here in ten minutes, and by then the mules will be wantin' to move on. Yer'll have ter hold 'em tight, lad. Jest remember that you are in charge of yer old uncle and of the gold. Ef yer pull us through it'll be the making of yer.'

"From being in a funk I got quite lively, and as proud as a peacock, and sat there at the front of the wagon, same as I am here, holding the reins, and fingering my shooter every now and again. I'd never let one off before that, except sometimes Uncle would give me a shot when we were well out on the plains. But I 'lowed as I could try, and by the time them critters turned up I'd fixed it that I would shoot every man of 'em sooner than lose the wagon and Uncle.

"Wall, in course of time two of the men that we'd first seen on the far side of the river came galloping up along the bank we'd jest left. Reckon they and their mates had been lying hid, waiting fer us ter get across, and they set to howlin' when it war clear that we had taken to the river ter get protection. The two who had stayed up on the other bank came over a hill some four hundred yards away, and thar ain't a doubt but that they had been watchin'. Anyway, they knew the route we'd taken. There warn't, neither, any more doubt as to what their business was. One of the critters let his shooter loose, and in a second, flick! goes a bullet through the tilt of the wagon close behind my ear.

"'That ain't nothin',' sings out Uncle. 'A bullet don't hurt till it hits, and the range are long for 'em. Hold them critters steady, lad, and ef I tell yer, whip 'em up and swing 'em fer the far shore. Thar's this in our favour: we've only two a side to deal with. When they was on the far bank there were four. Now we kin be more even.'

"The two on our side rode their horses right down into the water, and then we larned that we wasn't to have it altogether our own way. Uncle had forgotten that two of the critters had been watchin', and these two stood with their hosses' feet in the water and called across to their friends, giving them directions how to move so as to follow the ford. They meant business, there warn't a doubt, fer in two seconds the men on our side were edging their beasts slowly into the stream, kinder feelin' the ridge beneath them, and making out to where we were stood. It began to look ticklish, and a lot wuss when the two varmint on the far side rid their mounts farther into the river, and, as ef they'd guessed that the ledge must make in a line to whar we were, began to push on towards us.

"'It aer a case of facin' the hull crowd or of sinking the cargo,' sings out Uncle.

"Ef he'd been strong enough ter get to his feet I reckon he would have faced the crowd alone, fer he had fine courage; but he war as weak as a child, and could only lie there raging at his helplessness.

"Kin you tackle the lot alone, Tom?' he asked after a bit, when them critters was close handy.

"I suppose I looked what I thought. There warn't a chance that I could manage the team and fight them four.

"'Then whip 'em up and run her into deep water,' cries the old man. 'Ef the cart sinks fer good, then at any rate they won't have had the gold. Ef she holds the bottom we'll be able to get a rope on to her later on, and an extry team will pull her out. Swing 'em over, lad, and get ready to cut the critters loose. It wouldn't do to leave them tied by the traces. They'd drown like rats in a trap."

"Yer should ha' heard the row them fellers made when the cart got moving suddenly," said Tom, laughing loudly at the recollection. "I war a boy, yer must recollect, and thim shouts fairly scared me fer a moment, and kind of driv all my courage outer my elbows. I mind the fact that, fer months after, when I happened to dream a little, it war always about those men, and the shout they gave used ter set me awake, sitting up in my blankets and quaking. But thar was Uncle close handy, and, though he was helpless, I feared him a goodish deal more than the robbers who were riding out into the stream. Also, and yer kin believe it, seeing as you're young, I had a sort of feeling that kept me going. I knew that I was responsible fer the safety of Uncle and the gold. There wasn't another soul handy to help me, and ef I went down through funk then everything was lost. I may be right—Gee! I'm sure I am—when a young chap knows that others are relying on him, that he has a sort of duty before him, why it's in his nature, it's human nature ef yer like, fer him to buckle to, ter get savage and stubborn, and ter swear to hisself that he's going ter get through with the job and win out whatever happens. Anyway, that's how I felt. I didn't give a how of chips for the thought that I might be drowned. I jest picked up the reins hard, flicked my whip-end over the leaders, and sent 'em forward. In two yards I should ha' swung them to the right ef I wanted to follow the ford. Ef I swung 'em to the left they would drag the cart into deep water, and pretty sudden too, fer the ledge carrying the road over the river broke off on that side rather abruptly, and thar was ten foot of depth within six yards of whar we were standing.

"'Git at it, lad!' sings out Uncle. And git at it I did. I drove the mules clear to the left, and in a few seconds the leaders was swimming. I made sure that in another moment or two I should be in water up to my neck. But jest then one of the robbers sent a bullet in our direction. It missed me by a hair, and, flying on, struck one of the wheelers. And thet 'ere bullet seemed to finish the case fer us. It sent the mule it struck plunging right and left, and scared the other beasts. Instead of pulling the cart out into deep water, the leader of our team swum round fer the place they knew would give 'em footing. And once they had got it, there they stood, sweating in spite of the water, ready to break away at any moment, and refusing to answer to the reins. It war a fix. Thar war the cart in deeper water, to be sure, but still on the ledge, and easily get-at-able by them robbers.

"'Give 'em the whip. Swing 'em over, Tom,' shouts Uncle. 'Them critters will get us here. Push the team on!'

"It war easy ter order, but hard ter carry out the work. The mules were that scared they wouldn't budge one way or the other. They jest stood thar, with the water washing all round them, their ears thrown back, ready ter do something extry silly the next second, but refusing blank ter do what war expected of them. And all the while thar was them four robbers riding out, feelin' their way carefully, and gettin' nearer. In fact, they was at that moment within twenty paces, close enough to make fair shooting. I know that, 'cos one of the varmint lifted his shooter, took a careful aim at me sittin' there on the box, and let off his gun. It war lucky that them leaders give a jerk just then. It made me swing over to the right, while the bullet ripped past my shoulder and cut a neat little hole in the tilt.

"'We're done,' I heard Uncle groan. Then the corner of the tilt that he had been holding up, so as to be able to look out, fell back into place, and by the bump I heard I reckoned he'd fallen back in a faint. Thar war I left all alone ter face them critters."

The very recollection of such a position made Tom hot. He drew a huge, red handkerchief from his hat, where he was in the habit of carrying it, and mopped his forehead.

"It war a teaser," he said.

"It was," admitted Jack. "What happened?"

"I expected to be shot any second. I gave a slash at my leaders again, and did my best to move them. But they wouldn't budge. Then one of them villains let off his gun so close that I reckon the smoke and the flash scared me, though why the bullet didn't hit me is a puzzle I ain't going to try ter explain. I war scared right enough, and the start I gave caused me to roll from the seat where I was sitting splosh into the water. Yer should ha' heard them critters yell again. Guess they took it fer granted that the trouble was over, and that the gold and the cart was theirs. But it warn't. I had got something more to say in the business."

"How?" asked Jack, who was more than interested. "You fell from your seat into the water."

"I did that. The cart war left on the edge of the ledge, as I've already said, and the river was jest about washing the floor boards. I floundered under the surface for a bit, and then got my feet safe on ter the ledge. But when I lifted my head to take a breath it came bump up agin the floor boards. I war clear under the wagon, and, as luck would have it, there was jest enough space there to allow me to breathe. Guess them four critters thought I was drownded, fer they rid up to the wagon laughing fit ter bust.

"'That 'ere shot cleared him out fine,' I heard one of them shout. 'Git to their heads, mate, and take them along the ford. We ain't out of this muss yet. Joe, ride ahead, and make sure ye're on the ledge. Now that we've got the gold it won't do ter lose it. I'll keep close handy to the cart. The old man'll want shootin'.'

"That's the sort of ruffians they was," explained Tom. "They didn't think no more of shootin' a man then I think of eatin' dinner. And it didn't make no difference to them whether it war a boy their bullets hit, or a man. But I war under the wagon, and though I had been scared I warn't done with, not by a heap. Yer must understand that gold dust are heavy stuff to carry, but it don't take up a heap of room, so thar was plenty o' space left fer us in the wagon. Then, same as we have here, some of the boards was kept loose on purpose. Yer see, out on the plains, when ye've a load, yer often want to carry odds and ends slung to the wagon. Thar's a pail fer watering the mules, a cooking pot, and sich like things. Sometimes they're jest slung to hooks screwed into the bottom boards. But Uncle had his own ideas of comfort and of doin' things, and I reckon he ought to know what was right, seem' he'd been on the road so long. His idea was to have a tray slung under the centre of the wagon by means of four short lengths of chain, and the bottom boards above carried loose, so as you could haul up anything you wanted from the tray. Wall now, in course, seeing that we had to cross the river, I had removed every stick from that tray. It come bump up agin me as I crouched below the wagon, and, as those men moved the team along, I jest climbed on to the tray and rose my head through the boards of the wagon. It war as good as a play. There were them critters thinkin' that I was floatin' down the river. And there was me, half in the wagon, extry lively, wonderin' hard what ter do. It war Uncle's shooter that decided the matter. He was lying close handy to the opening, as pale as death, with his revolver on the boards beside him.

"'Yer own's drenched by the river,' I said to myself, feeling for the shooter I carried in my belt. 'His is all right. Take it, and go fer them critters.' Wall, I hopped clean into the wagon then, waited a bit till we were getting close to the far bank, fer the robbers war guiding the team all the while, and war going forward as slow as ef it war to a funeral. Then I lifted the edge of the tilt, took aim at the chap riding nearest, and pulled the trigger. Reckon he war killed outright. Anyway, he plumped into the water, and none of us saw him agin. But you kin guess that thar war a ruction. Them fellers thought that they had the thing all to themselves, and then, all of a sudden, one of their number was wiped out. They wasn't cowards, to say the best of them, and the three who war left gave up minding the mules and came ridin' their hosses back to the wagon, sending a bullet or so to show that they war coming. Yer don't think I waited for 'em, do yer?"

Tom asked the question with a knowing wag of his head.

"Not much," he proceeded, as Jack showed his doubt. "I knew ef I stayed in the wagon they'd riddle me before I could wink: same as you guessed that thet fellow in the railway carriage would shoot yer ef yer rose your head above the window. Thar was Uncle, too. Ef I got shot where I was, he was certain ter be found and an end made of him. I kinder guessed the whole thing in a flash, and then dived through the boards of the wagon, on to the tray below, and then into the river. There was eight inches or more of air space beneath the boards by then, fer the ledge was rising, and ef a man had stood in the river and stooped, so as to get a view, he could have seen me fer certain. But them critters was on horseback, and I reckon they never gave a thought to the under part of the wagon. Anyway, they rode up with every intention of pulling the tilt aside and shooting me the moment they could clap eyes on my figure. And I disappointed 'em. I jest waded to the edge of the wagon, fixed myself inside one of the wheels, and when they was within five feet of me let go with my pistol. It fixed 'em sure. They wasn't expecting anything from underneath the wagon, same as that critter in the train warn't expecting nothing from the roof. My bullet must have struck one of the hosses, and the mad plunging of the beast didn't help matters for them. Then a second bullet winged one of the men, and in a moment they went flying. Gee! It makes me laugh now to think of the muss they got into. The bank war on our left, and a short cut to it took yer into deep water. They war properly scared, and, like people in a similar condition, they made fer safety by what seemed ter be the quickest route. In two seconds their hosses was swimming, and before they managed to reach the bank one at least of the villains had had a narrow squeak fer his life. As fer me, I climbed on to the box, took up the reins, and sent the mules flyin' to the bank. But I didn't stay there. I turned 'em, and came back over the water. Yer see, the three robbers was left on the far side, and ef they wanted to attack again they had to cross the ford there in full view, or had to gallop up to the other ford. In any case it would give me time to fix matters up a little, and pay some attention to Uncle."

"You saved him," said Jack enthusiastically. "He must have been proud of you. You were only a boy, I must remember."

"He war a peppery feller," laughed Tom. "He came to his senses five minutes later, and fer a time I guess he thought the cart and the gold were taken. Then he reckoned he'd had a baddish dream. It warn't till the following day thet I told him."

"And then?" asked Jack.

"He war a regular father to me. He's an old man now, living in New York State; but his home's mine, and his money too ef I wanted it."

CHAPTER X

A Buffalo Hunt

"Them's buffalo without a shadow o' doubt," said Steve, one afternoon, six weeks after the little party had set out on their long journey to California. "Ef yer shade yer eyes and look close yer can see a dark line that ain't never still. Them's buffalo."

The little hunter spoke with an assurance born of long experience, and sat his horse with one hand above his eyes, and the brim of his hat pulled low. Jack followed suit; but though he could distinguish the dark line away on the plain, he could make nothing more of it.

"There is a line, right enough, Steve," he admitted, "and as you say it's buffalo I'm bound to believe you; but I can't see a single animal."

"No more yer would ef yer was to stare for half a day," came the answer, "'cos they're packed as tight as herrings in a barrel. But the cloud above the line tells a hunter the right tale. That aer dust, and them beasts is moving pretty rapid. How'd yer like ter try a shot at 'em?"

Jack was all eagerness at once, for he had been practising diligently with his weapons during the days which had passed, and wished now to show of what he was capable. Indeed, the injury to his shoulder had in a measure been for his good; for in place of mounting a rough horse immediately on joining the party, and thereby risking perhaps a heavy fall, he had been obliged to take a mount which was known to be quiet and well trained. And from the back of this animal he had been able to use his weapons without fear of a sudden movement which would have unseated him.

"I'd much rather have taken my chances like any other newcomer," he had said to Tom one day, as they jogged along; "but I'm bound to admit that this steady practice in the saddle, and using my rifle and revolver, have done much for me."

"Yer bet," was the answer. "Thar's a sight of green 'uns comes out this way, and thinks they're goin' to show the boys right off how to ride. Wall, that leads to falls in general, sometimes to broken necks. Thar are some, I 'low, as comes through fine, and shows heaps of grit. But others weakens, while not a few gets broken up, legs or arms smashed, or somethin' of that sort. From what I knows of yer, young 'un, it's natural yer'd ha' liked to show yer grit like those others.

But that shoulder aren't to be played with. Yer've got ter take it easy, and take care not to risk a fall. But yer've got one big advantage."

"And what is that?" asked Jack, wondering.

"I'll tell yer. Most every man larns to shoot when on his legs. There ain't nothin' to prevent yer doin' the same. But with that quiet horse yer kin set to with the guns on the trace, and there ain't nothin' like the man as can shoot as quick and as straight when on a movin' horse. 'Sides, you can practise both hands. 'Twon't hurt the shoulder."

And so, thanks to constant practice, Jack was now by no means a duffer with rifle and revolver, while he could shoot with the latter equally well with either hand.

"Them buffalo are making east," said Steve, as he watched the distant line, "and sense the wind's from that quarter thar ain't nothin' to prevent us comin' up behind 'em. Mind yer, none but a downright fool would ever attempt to head 'em, 'cos thar ain't no stoppin' buffalo on the move. Ef you was to build a wall in front of 'em, they'd push it over. Thar's thousands as a rule in the herds, and them as is in the back lines don't know what's happenin' away in front. And so they goes on pushin' and shovin', and squeezin' the ones up in the front, till they're bound ter move forward. Hundreds and hundreds of the beasts have been known ter go head over ears over a cliff before their mates behind got to reckon what was happenin'. Guess we'll cut dead across. That'll bring us near level with the last of the herd, and then it'll be a poor day ef we don't manage to cut one of 'em out."

Slinging his rifle at Steve's bidding, Jack shook up his horse, a more spirited one now than the animal he had at first ridden, and cantered along beside the huntsman.

"A gun aer no use fer this job," sang out Steve. "Thar ain't no fetchin' a buffalo down unless he's hit heavy, and to do that yer've got ter ride in close. The Injuns kill 'em with arrows, and I've seen their hunters ride up behind a herd and stand on the back of the beast they've chosen. Then, with an arrow drawn to the head, the chances are it'll go clean through the buffalo's heart. A shooter are the weapon for 'em, and when yer fire, aim just behind the shoulder."

A sharp canter took them rapidly closer to the herd, and very soon the dark line resolved itself into a mass of moving beasts, over whom hung a cloud of yellow dust. Steve turned his horse a little, and cantered on till the tail of the herd was passing.

"Now's the time," he sang out. "Keep along beside me till we're well behind 'em. Then ride forward till ye're almost in the crowd. That'll allow yer to select a beast and shoot him. Don't fire at more than one. Guess two beasts altogether will keep us in food fer a month. And jest one more warnin'. Keep clear of their horns. They're the ugliest things fer diggin' I ever hit across."

Gripping his reins firmly in his left hand, Jack followed Steve until they were right behind the centre of the herd. The beasts seemed to have scented their enemies; for the pace of those behind increased of a sudden, while those in front, pressed on in spite of themselves, soon broke into a fast gallop, which taxed the fleetness of the horses. Watching the mass of struggling beasts, our hero soon picked out a huge animal, floundering along in rear, and when Steve shouted, he turned his horse and rode him up beside the buffalo he had selected. And it seemed at once as if the beast realized his intentions, for it increased its pace, and, shouldering its way amongst its fellows, soon placed a couple of rows of buffalo between it and Jack.

"I've chosen him, and I'm going to bag him, whatever happens," thought our hero, as he raced along. "I'll follow in after the beast."

Pressing his horse with both knees, and urging him forward with voice and spur, he managed to wedge himself in the last line of moving buffalo. Another effort and he passed right through it, and was almost within shot of the animal he wanted. Then he heard a sharp report on his right, followed by a shout, and, turning, saw Steve riding hard towards him.

"Yer've got to be careful in thar," shouted the hunter. "Mind their horns, and jest see that when he falls the others don't come tumbling on ter yer. Now, let him have it."

Steve was within a few feet of Jack now, for the hunter felt anxious for the safety of his young friend.

"I never seed a new 'un with more grit," he was saying to himself. "The most of 'em would be content to ride up behind, and fire from a little distance. But Carrots ain't like that. I've noticed he's a way of doin' a thing proper or not at all. He's bound on making a point-blank shot."

That, in fact, was Jack's intention, and, careless of the tossing heads about him, of the horns turning this way and that, and of the angry bellows, he pressed his horse still more forward, till he was right up against the beast he had selected. And there, jammed in the press, and going hard all the while, our hero stood up in his stirrups, watched for the right moment, and fired his weapon, aiming just behind the moving shoulder.

"Pull out!" shouted Steve, "Pull out or they'll carry yer along."

To retire from the position he had taken up was not an easy task, as Jack soon found; for behind him a solid wall of buffalo swung along, while the animal he had fired at still galloped forward as if it had received no wound. It seemed, indeed, as if our hero had failed. But he was not the lad to give in easily. Food was wanted for the camp, and this was the very first opportunity he had had of showing his prowess. Once more he spurred up beside the beast and sent a second bullet crashing into his body. And then there was a sudden change in the situation. The buffalo dropped like a log, while the animal immediately behind tripped, fell on his nose, and in doing so knocked the legs of Jack's mount from under him. In an instant there was a scene of dire confusion. Jack went flying far ahead, over the ears of his horse, while Steve, who was riding just behind him by then, came a terrible cropper. Clouds of dust were thrown into the air, and dimly seen through it were struggling beasts, feet lashing here and there, and frightened eyes. Never had Jack heard such a bellowing. It seemed as if all the buffalo in that country were round him, and then, as suddenly, they were gone. The beasts who had fallen got to their feet and charged madly by him, leaving him alone with the one he had shot, stretched just a foot away from it, while farther behind was his horse, looking at him, as if the poor beast still wondered what had happened. As for Steve, he lay very still, one boot remaining in his stirrup, while his well-trained beast stood close beside him, grazing, as if buffalo had never existed, and as if such a thing as a catastrophe had never occurred.

Jack clambered to his feet and ran to Steve, to find him conscious, and lying with eyes wide open.

"Jest lift my foot out of the stirrup," he said cheerfully, but in a voice little above a whisper. "We was goin' fast, I guess? and I wasn't lookin' for a fall. Reckon my back's badly shook, 'cos I ain't got no power over my legs. Pain? No. I ain't any, but it's queer fer me to be lying here unable ter move."

Jack gently disengaged his foot from the stirrup, and made his friend comfortable. Then he turned to look about him, and at once an exclamation escaped him.

"Look!" he cried. "They're returning. Something seems to have caused the herd to swing round, and they're chargin' back this way."

A flush came to the hunter's face as he heard the news, and with an obvious effort he managed to turn his head. Then he called to Jack, and spoke quietly.

"Yer'd best be going," he said earnestly. "That mob's less than half a mile away, and ef they're coming along as they was a few minutes ago, they'll be here afore yer can look round. Ef they find yer still on this spot yer best friend won't know yer when they're gone. Best git, slippy. So long!"

"And you?" asked Jack, casting another glance towards the herd, which, for some unexplained reason had undoubtedly turned, and was charging back over the ground it had so recently covered. "And what about you, Steve?" he asked.

"Would your best friend be able to recognize you any better than mine would be?"

"Shucks! Ye're talkin', and wastin' valuable time," growled Steve. "Yer kin see it's a case with me. I'm done fer, and I don't mind if no one can recognize me. Ye git, and precious slippy. Yer ain't got too much time ter clear even now."

"And desert you, the man who has been so friendly to me," said Jack. "Never! I'll do my best to carry him off. Can you hold anything, Steve?" he asked, kneeling beside the helpless hunter.

"Yer bet. Give us yer hand. Thar. So long!"

Steve gripped Jack's hand firmly, and then thrust him away. "Didn't I tell yer to be goin'?" he cried angrily. "The chances aer ye'll not do it even now. Them beasts is coming quicker'n yer kin gallop. Aer yer a fool?"

"Get a hold round my neck," cried Jack, bending lower over him. "Quickly! You're only wasting my time and yours by hesitating. There! Grip hard. I'm going to get into my saddle."

"Yer ain't! Git as quick as yer kin, and leave me to it. Ain't I warned yer? Jest quit foolin'?"

Steve blazed out at Jack as the latter again bent over him, and with an emphatic shake of his head refused to do as our hero suggested. For the little scout knew what he was talking about. Already it was doubtful whether either of them could escape that rushing herd, even if well mounted. But if he in his unselfishness was determined not to ruin Jack's chances of escape, the latter was equally determined not to leave Steve to be trampled into the dust by the charging buffalo. He could never face his other friends if he returned with such a tale of cowardice, and in spite of Steve's obstinacy he made up his mind there and then that he would save him, or stand and face the beasts by his side.

"Quit foolin' and git off!" shouted Steve again. "Yer ain't got a moment to lose."

"And you won't take a grip of my neck and let me lift you?" asked Jack.

"I won't. I ain't goin' ter spoil the chances of one fer the sake of savin' myself. Git, and have done with the talkin'."

"Then you've yourself to thank. I'll do as I know to be proper."

Jack stooped once more over the little hunter, and with one big heave threw him over his shoulder. Then he hurried with him to his horse, placed the injured man in front of the saddle, and with a bound was up behind him. Leaving Steve's mount to follow as it liked, he dug his spurs into his own beast and sent it galloping forward. Then began a desperate race, for already the herd was within a hundred yards, sweeping along over the plain in one dense mass, which stretched for a quarter of a mile on either side. Indeed, it might have been more; for in those days, before railways had come, and the march of civilization had driven the animals away, herds of twenty and more thousand buffalo were often to be encountered. Whatever its proportions, this particular herd came thundering along, a dense mass of dust flying in the air above it, while the earth beneath trembled with the thud of so many hoofs. It was as much as a horse could do to keep in front of the maddened animals, and very soon Jack found his own mount flagging.

"We're bound to go down before them if I can't find my way to one side," he thought. "Let me see how much ahead of them I am."

Gripping Steve firmly, so that he could not be shaken off, and digging his knees into his mount, Jack swung his head round and looked behind him. There was a sea of tossing manes, of flashing eyes and terrible horns, within twenty yards, and the thunder the animals made would have drowned the ordinary voice. And on either side the line stretched till it seemed to be interminable. Then Jack looked ahead, and, seeing some trees growing on a rising knoll away on the right, he swung his horse in that direction, and applied his spurs again, calling upon the noble animal to make one last effort. As for Steve, our hero could feel him wriggling, and even heard his voice as he endeavoured to expostulate with his saviour. But the words came jerkily. The movement of the horse shook the breath out of the little hunter's body.

"We'll do it! Stick to the game!" shouted Jack, stretching out one hand to pat his horse's neck. "Now, a little more, and we shall be there."

But safety was not yet accomplished, and for some minutes it seemed as if both he and Steve must go down before the mob and be trampled to death, when of a sudden there was another movement amongst the herd. Imperceptibly at first, and then with a swing, the leaders faced away from the rising knoll for which Jack had been aiming, and, pressing their fellows on the left farther to that side, galloped off on a line at a tangent to that which had previously been followed. This unforeseen movement at once gave the fugitives an advantage, for those beasts directly behind them and farther to the right were placed even farther behind.

"Forward!" shouted Jack, applying his spurs again. "We've just a chance still."

But it proved, before the matter was ended, to be a close escape for both of them, for before the right-hand margin of the herd was reached many of the animals were thundering along immediately in rear, while on the very outskirts of the crowd some of the buffalo had actually passed ahead of Jack. He watched his opportunity and then suddenly swung his horse well to one side, pulling him in a minute later amongst the trees for which he had been aiming. And there, as he dismounted and lifted Steve to the ground, he watched as the whole herd rushed past him, watched for five minutes as the thunder of their hoofs drummed on his ear. Then he sat down to rest and wipe his forehead.

"That aer the nearest thing yer'll ever have, nor me either," said Steve suddenly, when the noise had died down. "Jack, jest pull in that critter and place him well behind the bushes. There ain't a chance of our bein' seen, for ye've chose a proper little hollow, and no one could easily see us from outside on the plain. Gee! That war a near thing, and I ain't so sure that there ain't more to follow."

Despite his helplessness the little scout managed to prop himself up against a tree, and lay there staring out into the plain, while Jack followed out his instructions. Taking the horse, he led him amidst the trees to a spot where a dense mass of bushes grew, and left him there to blow and regain his wind. As for Steve's mount, he had fled for those trees at the very first, and, being unencumbered by a rider, had reached them well in advance. Jack slipped his reins over the fork of a tree and returned to Steve.

"I war sayin' we was mighty lucky," exclaimed the scout, "and I war advisin' yer to keep well down and hide the horses. Do yer know the reason?"

Jack shook his head. He was beginning to wonder if the fall had in some manner upset Steve's reason as well as damaging his back.

"Wall, I'll tell yer. What sent them varmints back on their trail so onexpectedly?" he asked. "Yer don't know, and can't guess. But I had a notion from the very fust, and I reckoned that ef we got clear of the herd we'd have somethin' else to face. It was Injuns, Jack. Buffalo don't face about fer nothin'. I've seen twenty and more hunters trying to turn a pack of 'em smaller than this here by a heap. They've fired their revolvers into the face of the herd, and shouted, and rid across. But it ain't done nothin'. The beasts has come along solid all the same. But when thar's a hundred painted Injun varmints a-shriekin' in front and shootin' their arrows, why, even buffalo'll turn then."

"But——" exclaimed Jack, his eyes wide open with amazement.

"Yer didn't see any of 'em," cried Steve. "No more yer did, nor me neither at first. The dust covered everything. But jest you look thar."

He pointed after the herd, and, following that direction, Jack's eyes fell upon a number of horsemen who must have swept by the spot where he and Steve lay, directly in wake of the buffalo.

"Indians!" he cried in amazement.

"Them's the red-skinned varmints, and a fine time they'll give us ef we drop into their hands. Aer yer sure ye've hid up them hosses?"

"Certain. I couldn't make out what you meant by giving such directions, and began to wonder whether you were all right in your head. But I hid the horses right enough. No one would see them from outside."

"Then we're right fer the moment," said Steve, "but it'll be only fer the moment. Them varmint'll see the beasts we killed, and'll know in a minute as white men ha' done it, 'cos they're shot with bullets. That'll tell 'em we were behind the herd before it turned. They'll be proper bothered after that, 'cos there ain't a trace left now to follow. Every mark has been stamped out of the ground. But that won't beat 'em. They'll send out parties to ride round till they strike our tracks, and a glance'll tell 'em whether we were goin' or comin'. Wall, they'll see, in course, that we ain't rid away. Then they'll set to ter find us. And as far as I can see thar ain't another likely spot, barrin' these trees."

The outlook did indeed appear to be anything but rosy; for, as Jack kneeled amidst the trees beside his injured friend and looked out into the plain, he could distinguish fully fifty Indians, all mounted, and slowly returning from following the buffalo. Had he but known the men were part of a tribe which had camped three miles away in a hollow which hid them completely, and, having ridden from a direction the opposite of that from which Jack and his friends were making, neither party had seen the other. It was the maddened herd of buffalo which had first disturbed the Indians, and, finding it probable that they would charge right across their own camping-ground, they had turned out in force, and by dint of much shouting had contrived to stem the rush, and in the end to cause the whole herd to face about. And up to now they were still ignorant of the presence of white people. A minute later, however, there was a shout out on the plain, and a batch of the Indians galloped across to the buffalo which Jack had shot.

"In course they seed it. I knew they would," growled Steve. "It ain't likely that an Injun could miss a beast like that. And ain't they jest talkin'! Guess they'll know in less than a minute that they ain't the only people hereabouts, and that thar's scalps within distance that's worth the taking."

At any other time Jack could have watched with interest as the Indians gathered round the fallen buffalo and inspected the carcass. For their movements were picturesque, to say the least of it. But he had heard enough already to prove to him that these bands still roving the plains were just as implacable enemies of the white men as their fathers had ever been, while he knew it to be a fact that scores of unhappy people making across the plains for California had been ruthlessly slaughtered by the red man. If he had any doubt of the Indians he was watching it was dispelled in an instant. A fierce shout suddenly broke the silence.

"Didn't I say so?" cried Steve, a grim look on his face. "Them varmint aer hit upon the truth, and they know well that white men has been after them buffalo within this last hour. Thar they go in two parties, while that chap ridin' away by hisself is goin' to the camp to bring along the others. Seems to me we shall have the hull crowd of 'em about us afore many minutes. Lad, seems almost a pity you troubled to bring me out."

The little scout smiled at Jack, and held out a hand.

"Yer ain't no tenderfoot," he said huskily. "I've been round about the plains boy and man, and I've seen a sight of gallant actions, but they was mostly the work of experienced men, not of young chaps new from the towns. Jack, I've marked it up fer yer. Ef we squeeze out of this, t'others shall know, and Steve won't forget what he's owing. Now, lad, jest roll me over and pull off my shirt. Thar's a bit of beef in my saddle bag, and ef yer cut a hunk of fat from it it'll do to rub into the back. Seems the spine's a bit shook up, and is already better. Gee, ef I can't move a toe now!"

He smiled grimly as he pointed to one boot, and showed our hero that he could move it. Then he lay back against the tree and watched the enemy eagerly. As for Jack, he rubbed Steve's back vigorously till the scout declared that he was better. Then, seizing his gun, he lay down to watch, wondering how long it would take the Indians to find them, and whether, in that event, he and Steve could hope to escape.

Nor was it long before his mind was filled with misgiving. As the shades of evening drew in, a party of Indians came to a halt a mile from their hiding place, and pointed eagerly in their direction.

"Didn't I say so," growled Steve, kneeling up, for his strength was fast returning. "Them varmints are hit on our trail, and'll be along in half a jiffy. Jack, thar ain't no use denyin' it, you and me ain't got half a show. Them critters is bound to take us."

Let the reader place himself for one brief moment in the position in which our hero so suddenly and unexpectedly found himself. There he was, young, full of life and vigour, with his outlook upon the world rendered wonderfully more attractive by the friendship and companionship of Steve and his brother scouts, face to face with a danger which the experienced Indian fighter beside him assured him was great—so great that death must almost inevitably follow. The announcement was enough to blanch the cheek of a man, let alone a young fellow of his age. It was enough to unnerve the boldest. Yet Jack did not quake, though, to speak the truth, his heart set to work hammering at his ribs as it never seemed to have done before. He even feared that that rat-a-tat-tat in his ears, the thud of his heart drumming so loudly within his breast, would be heard by the enemy, would reach the Indians and hasten the end at which Steve so bluntly hinted.

"Bound to take us," he repeated, whispering the words.

"Ay, bound to. That is, as fer as I can see. I've been in many a ruction with the critters, and I don't say as I ain't never been as badly up agin it as I am now. But, yer see, sarcumstances is that bad. It ain't as if this here wood was a big one, and we could slip away through the trees, giving them varmint their work to follow. It ain't big. It's small, and, 'sides, thar's these legs of mine. Gee! I've never felt the same before. It ain't often Steve ain't able to get about and lift his shooter. It seems queer too. Here's me, used all my life to carryin' a gun, and findin' as it's saved my life many a time. Wall, here I am, and I guess an Injun kid could come right in and scalp me. It aer enough to make a man swear."

"I will protect you. You have forgotten that I am here."

Suddenly, it seemed to Jack, the thumping of his heart stopped. A moment or two before the drumming in his ears had been annoying, to say the least of it. But now the trouble was gone. He looked steadily at Steve, gripped his rifle, and then turned his attention to the enemy.

"My!" Steve gave vent to the exclamation gently. In the excitement of the moment, with his eyes fixed on the deadly Indian enemy out on the plain, Jack's recent heroism had escaped his memory. He forgot for the moment that the lad had shown unusual grit, and looked upon him as a city lad, brave perhaps, but as helpless as he himself in such a dilemma. Then he suddenly stole a sideways look at Jack, to find the lad watching the enemy coolly, critically, noting every movement. His face was sunburned and held a healthy colour. There was no trace of nervousness about him, and, to Steve's wonder, there was an entire absence of excitement. Jack was cool, and wore a determined appearance, a set of his chin which was strange to him and to Steve.

"My!" exclaimed the hunter again. "Ef I don't believe as ye're ready to tackle all them varmint single-handed. Wall, it do an old hunter like me good ter see sech grit. I've knowed green 'uns face fire for the fust time and seem ter like it. I've knowed old hands get that fidgety when the bullets got whistling that they wasn't able to set or to stand still. And agin I've seed old 'uns and new 'uns get a sudden fit of funks, and then their chances ain't worth buyin'. Reckon, Jack, yer ain't the one to go under without a struggle. Ef them critters want to give yer knocks, you aer goin' ter return 'em."

The idea tickled the humour of the little hunter, and in spite of the dangerous proximity of the Indians, in spite of the death which was so perilously near, he grinned, and once more gave expression to his amazement. "My!" he whispered. "Ef that don't take it!"

"H-h-h-ush! They're moving. What are they going to do?"

Jack held out a hand and touched Steve, drawing his attention to the enemy. And then, for five minutes, the two lay as still as mice. Right before their eyes were the Indians, and during those long minutes Jack had an opportunity of inspecting them thoroughly, of watching their behaviour in their natural haunts, for as yet the band of men was unconscious of his and of Steve's presence. At any other time he would have been filled with admiration and with wonder, for before him were men who, in their own particular way, were as fine, even finer, horsemen than were the hunters. True, time was when a horse was unknown to the Indian of the plain, when he looked upon it as some fearful beast to be carefully avoided. But once the animal had been imported to the country he had been quick to realize its utility. And now he rode, barebacked for the most part, sitting his mount with that easy swing of the body which shows a born horseman. It was fine to see the band of redskins grouped about one another, to watch as the younger men occasionally galloped from the group, only to bring their mounts to the rightabout with amazing swiftness. And then their ease of mounting, the swiftness with which they slipped from the backs of their horses and vaulted again to their seats was a revelation not to be experienced even on a ranch.

"The critters!" exclaimed Steve. "Ef they could shoot jest as well as they kin ride, then thar wouldn't always be so much chance fer us. But this ain't ter be a case of shootin'. It's tracking that's wanted, and whar that's the case thar ain't no one to touch an Injun varmint I tell yer, Jack, we're clear up agin it. We ain't got half a show. As I looks at it, we can't get away from this wood, while them critters can't manage to miss us. Wall, that means jest one thing. They're jest bound ter take us."

CHAPTER XI

Surrounded by Indians

Jack and Steve lay in the narrow belt of trees for another half-hour before either opened their lips again. For the hunter had lifted a warning finger, and had enjoined silence upon his companion. And as they lay there, the band of Indians they had seen collected outside on the plain was increased by the addition of some two dozen more, who rode up from another quarter.

"Guess they're a trifle bothered," said Steve at last, making an effort and managing to kneel; for up till then his lower limbs had been practically powerless. "Yer see, the varmint they've sent riding round has picked up our traces from the point where we left the wagon this mornin', and they've followed 'em right away to the point whar we struck the herd of buffalo. They ain't seen no marks goin' back agin, and so they concludes that we're hid up in this here belt of trees. Wall, now, they ain't sartin."

"And why?" asked Jack, his voice lowered to a whisper, while his eyes were glued upon the Indians. For he was still a novice where these wild men of the plains were concerned, and what he knew already had been picked up by listening to the scouts' tales at night, as they sat round the fire.

"'Cos them buffalo aer done us a right down good turn," said Steve.

"Them skunks out thar has theirselves to thank fer that, for they turned the herd and sent it flying into our faces. And them buffalo fairly smashed out every trace we made coming into these trees. Wall, now, supposin' we was still with the herd: Supposin' our horses happened to have been extry fresh, and not tired after a day of it, they'd likely as not have managed to keep ahead of them chargin' beasts, and, ef they did, we should be miles away by now, and still leadin' 'em. That aer the difficulty. I 'low as it's a small one, and won't take over long fixin'. But thar it is, and them critters has to come right in here afore they're sartin what's happened. That aer a movement clear agin their principles."

"Why?" asked Jack, wondering at the statement; for it seemed hardly probable that, when there were at least thirty of the enemy to each one of themselves, they would hesitate to rush the belt of trees and kill those lying within.

"Why, I'll tell yer. Them varmint out thar aer the cruellest and bravest men as ever stepped the airth. Their trainin' teaches 'em to kill an enemy, and never to go down theirselves ef they can help it. Ef a man's killed, wall, guess to them redskins it's 'cos he's a fool, and ain't been cute enough. That's why yer don't git an Injun creepin' to a place like this when he may likely enough get his skull cracked afore he's seen so much as a haar of the enemy. See?"

Jack did, and for a while pondered the matter. Somehow or other, in spite of his knowledge that he and Steve stood in very imminent danger of losing their lives, he felt no trepidation, no fear for himself, but only a great longing to beat the enemy out there on the plain. As long as the white man fills his present position in the world, and retains his wonderful independence, he will, without doubt, face odds with determination and even some amount of pleasure. A strong fight has always appealed to men of the British race, and to those of America, for the truth of which statement one hardly need turn to the roll of history compiled by each of them. There are examples of heroic struggles, where few were opposed to many, all through the years that have passed, and some are so notorious that one always carries them in one's memory. With that fine record to stimulate him, Jack, too, looked to the coming contest not with fear, but with a certain amount of pleasure. His pulses were beating fast, all his senses were keenly alert, and as he stared out at the Indians his wits were working quickly in the endeavour to discover some scheme whereby he and Steve might outwit them.

"Ef these plaguey legs of mine'll only continue to improve we'll put up a fight that'll astonish them varmint," growled Steve at last. "Yer kin see, they're havin' a palaver, and in a bit, no doubt, the chiefs'll call upon the venturesome young men to investigate this here place. It'll be nigh dark then, which should give us a bit of a chance. Aer yer got yer knife, lad?"

Jack's hand dropped on it, for since he had joined the scouts he had carried the same weapons as themselves. And a large hunting-knife was part of his outfit "It's here," he said. "Right in my belt."

"Wall, ye'll want it. Them critters as comes has got ter be silenced without so much as a sound, and ef yer've any love fer yer own scalp ye'll put away all sorts of skeary notions yer may have had. A man sarcumstanced same as we aer ain't got a look in ef he's too thin-skinned to fight fer his life as best he kin. To live through to-night and keep our haar we've got to kill some of them critters. And a huntin'-knife aer the only weapon. Ef we was to use a revolver, shucks! it'd give the show away. They'd be on to us in a moment Jest look at them young bloods!"

Out in the open there was a good deal of commotion at this moment, and voices, which before had been inaudible, came to the ears of the two hiding amidst the trees and underwood. It seemed that there was an altercation amongst the Indians, for there was shouting, while some of the men urged their horses into the centre of the circle which had been formed, and brandished their weapons.

"Didn't I say as much?" whispered Steve. "Them's the young men of the tribe, and sense they ain't accounted much till they've took a hull heap of scalps, and has done something extry brave, why, in course they're fer rushin' this place agin the advice of the older and cautious ones. Ye'll see as they'll allow two or three to try their hands."

"But why give them a chance?" asked Jack suddenly. "While they're discussing the matter we might get on to the horses and make a dash in the opposite direction."

Steve's grim face showed for a moment a grin of contempt. Then the lines softened as he regarded our hero.

"Ye've got grit right enough, Carrots," he said, "but yer ain't seen much of them varmint. Do yer think as they ain't thought of a dash? Reckon an Injun don't forget nothin'. There's men posted all round this belt of trees, and mounted on the best hosses. 'Sides, ef it did come to a rush, our mounts are that tired they'd break up afore we'd galloped five miles. Then, too, ye're forgettin' my condition. I've never had sich a thing happen to me afore, though I've seen a sight of men thrown heavily, and unable to move for weeks. Yes, and some of 'em never got back the use of their legs. With me it's jest temporary. Reckon the jerk threw something outer gear for a while. But it's mendin' fast, and in a few hours, perhaps, I'll be able to mount and ride."

The same grim look came over the injured scout's face, as much as to say that when those few hours had passed circumstances would make further use of his limbs out of the question. For Steve had not the smallest doubt that nothing but a miracle could save them. He became silent for some few moments, while his weather-beaten face crinkled in all directions, showing big lines across the forehead, which indicated the fact that he was thinking deeply. Meanwhile the excitement amongst the Indians grew even greater. To Jack, as he watched them, it seemed at first as if they would come to blows, and that they were quarrelling seriously. Then the noise died down a little, while five men slipped from their ponies.

"Them's the lads as has been chosen to investigate this here place," said Steve grimly, "and it won't be long afore they're sticking their ugly, painted faces in amongst the trees. Look ye here, Jack, I've been thinkin' somethin'. Yer was rash to stay back there and haul me away from the front of that 'ere herd of buffalo, 'cos ef ye'd rid fer it ye'd have got clear yerself, without a doubt, and could have reached our mates with the start ye'd have had. It war a brave act, and I don't say as I ain't grateful. I am precious grateful, but I'm vexed to think as my poor life are been saved jest fer a few minutes at the expense of yours. Jack, you aer young. The world's dead ahead of yer, and, ef I ain't makin' an error, ye've somethin' real serious to live fer. But fer me, life ain't that rosy. I don't say as I ain't grateful to Him as give it to me; but I've had my day, and am ready to go when the call comes. Yer see, I've lost wife and childer, and when that's the case a man don't kinder stick so fast to this world. But I war sayin' as ye've got somethin' real good to live fer. And I are been thinkin' about them 'ere red-skinned varmints. There aer jest a chance as yer might escape. Ef them critters was all engaged in watchin' the young bloods creepin' in here, I 'low that a man on a fair horse might manage to steal through the fellers hanging around outside, and gallop to his friends. Now, my horse ain't had the doin' that yours has. Yer jest wait a bit, and when I tell yer, creep back and mount. When them young critters aer close handy to these here trees, yer slip out t'other side. It'll be dark then, and the chance aer worth takin'."

For the usually silent Steve the speech was an extraordinarily long one, and once he had finished he let his head drop back against the tree trunk with a sigh of relief. For, after all, even though a man's outlook on life may have faded a little, he still clings to it. And to urge a comrade to escape, and leave one to certain death at the hands of such miscreants, needed not a little fortitude. Even as Steve faced the consequences of his advice to Jack, he shuddered just a little. Somehow or other it required greater courage to face a lonely death, with no comrade at hand to bear him company.

"Ain't yer got ready?" he asked, a minute later, hearing no movement from Jack. "Them varmint aer creepin' nearer, and the night aer fallin' fast. Reckon ye'd best be movin'."

Then, as he turned his head to look at his comrade, a gasp of surprise escaped the hunter. For Jack had not moved an inch. He lay there, hidden from the enemy, behind a tree, his hunting-knife gripped firmly in his hand. Even there, in the gloom cast by the branches, it was possible to observe his face, and Steve noticed for the first time in his life a look of dogged determination. For till that day Jack had shown his new comrades, with the exception of Tom, his lighter side, his merry, good-hearted nature. He was whistling or laughing or singing the day long, and at night listening to their hunter yarns with an interest there was no denying. Suddenly, as it were, he had developed from a boy into a stern man. There was no mistaking his expression.

"Why!" gasped Steve. "Yer ain't moved. Jack, ef yer don't get away to them hosses there won't be any ridin' at all. Jest git, lad, and make no bones about the matter."

"And leave you? Not much!" answered our hero doggedly, just as he had done earlier on when Steve ordered him to ride and leave him to be crushed by the buffalo. "Look ye here, Steve, when I rode from camp with you this mornin', reckon you was in command, 'cos I ain't no great idea of huntin'. But you're hurt. You ain't no longer able to command, so I guess I have to take the job over. I ain't goin' to move away. You can take that as final."

"Yer ain't goin'——!"

"H-h-hush! They'll hear us. Lie quiet!" commanded Jack sternly.

"Jest give us a fist, lad. I ain't angry. A man knows when he meets a real man, and I ain't quarrelin' with yer for it. My! Ef we get outer this thar'll be somethin' to tell the boys!"

Something suspiciously like a sob of relief escaped Steve as he lay back against the tree, and none but the most heartless would have scoffed at him. This grim, courageous little hunter, who had lived his life out on the plains or in the forests, and had become innured to privation and exposure, was, after all, just like any other man possessed of energy and determination. The feeling that he was useless, the very strangeness of being in such a condition, caused the most abject depression of spirits, while the relief of finding that he had a true comrade beside him was almost too much for him. But the determination of the little man soon conquered any passing weakness, and in a few moments he was himself again, the crafty scout, who had fought the Indian enemy many a time.

"Gee! Ef I could get these here legs o' mine to move sensible like," he whispered. "But look ye here, Jack; get on yer knees behind the tree and wait for 'em. Don't so much as move an eyelid till them varmint is close. Then strike. It aer their lives or ourn."

It was indeed a case of self-defence, of taking life to save life, and though our hero's natural gentleness caused him to shrink from the ordeal before him, yet the fact that he found himself suddenly called upon to defend a helpless comrade made him brace himself for the contest, and set his lips firmly together, while a quiet determination came over him to protect Steve, and to come out of the conflict alive. No man likes to be beaten. Jack did not differ from the average individual.

"Separatin'," whispered Steve after a few moments. "They reckon as they've got ter investigate every corner of the place, so they're each of 'em taking a plot. That'll suit us better than ef they came all together. Five of the varmints. Ef I war fit and able to use these here legs, and thar warn't a tarnal heap of their brothers I'd tackle that lot single-handed, and afore breakfast too. It ud jest kinder give me an appetite."

As the moment for action arrived the little scout's spirits revived wonderfully. He was a man who had come through many a fight with the Indians, and had learned never to give up the contest until he was actually beaten. And now, with such a stanch comrade as Jack beside him, he began to look upon their chances as perhaps not altogether hopeless.

"I've knowed wonderful escapes," he said to himself. "And I reckon a chap like this here Carrots ain't goin' under so easy. After showin' grit same as he has done, he desarves to pull through, and, by the 'tarnal, I'll help him."

Stretched full length on the ground, with the branches of trees overhanging them, and brushwood thickly scattered about, Jack and his friend watched the approach of the five young Indians in a grim silence. Where they lay it was now almost dark, so that they could barely see one another. But outside, in the open, it was still possible to perceive objects, though the band of Indians had now become blotted out by the falling gloom. In the gathering dusk five figures could be seen advancing on hands and knees, their eyes fixed on the trees in front of them. Ten yards divided each man from his comrade, and as they came nearer this distance was increased. At length they reached the very edge of the trees, and so that all should enter at the same moment, the one who arrived first lay on his face and signalled to the others.

"Yer hear the critters?" asked Steve in a tense whisper, putting his lips to Jack's ears. "That 'ere aer the bark of a fox, and it tells 'em all that they can push on into the trees. Jest lie as ef yer was dead. That chap out thar'll pass us to one side."

Dimly seen, some ten feet to the right, was one of the Indians; but though Jack listened with all his ears he heard no sound as the stealthy figure crept into the underwood. For the first time he had an illustration of that cunning and cleverness of which he had read and heard, and for which the Red Indian was famous. Though he himself could hardly have advanced a foot without causing a branch to swish heavily, or a twig to snap, not a sound came from the several points where he knew an enemy must be. So, more convinced than ever that deathly silence was essential if he would not be pounced upon before he was ready, he kneeled there like a statue, his eyes peering eagerly into the dense underwood.

Ah! A leaf rustled away to his right, and there was a feeble sound, almost indistinguishable, which told of a branch being set gently aside. And then silence, a deadly, nerve-racking silence, which continued for nearly five minutes. Five minutes! It felt like five hours to Jack. And then a hand caught him by the shoulder.

"H-h-h-ush!" Steve hardly whispered the word. "Jest to the right!"

The hand on his shoulder gripped him firmly and turned Jack a little. Without needing to move his legs, he twisted his body, and found himself looking in a different direction. Then his ears caught a faint sound. A mouse might have made more; a human being could hardly have been expected to make so little. It seemed impossible. A branch dangling just before his face swayed in his direction, and the leaves rustled against his forehead. Then they began to press upon him, gently at first, and then more and more firmly. Someone was trying to push the branch aside and advance. Jack's fingers closed on the haft of his hunting-knife like a vice. He braced his muscles for the encounter, while he held his breath lest the miscreant should hear him, and so gain an advantage. The moment for action was imminent. It was with difficulty that he could restrain himself; but for the hand still gripping his shoulder, telling him that Steve was there, advising him still to remain motionless, Jack would have thrown further caution to the winds, and would have flung himself upon the Indian.

Crash! Away in the centre of the little wood a branch broke with the crisp sound of a pistol shot, and instantly there came that familiar signal, the bark of a fox. It was answered to right and left, and then from a point but three feet from our hero. Instantly the pressure on the branch pushing into his face was relaxed. Those faint, stealthy sounds reached his ear again, and presently subsided.

"Good fer yer," whispered Steve, placing his lips close to Jack's ear again. "I felt yer kinder draw yerself together fer the ruction, and I 'low it takes a heap of grit to lay still when thar's one of them varmint close handy. They've found the hosses, and by the way they're palaverin' it seems to me as if they took it fer granted that we'd slipped from the wood. Do yer hear them calls? They're signalling to the men placed outside."

From the small wood in which they lay, and a little later from the plain outside, came those mysterious barkings, as if a regiment of foxes had suddenly appeared upon the scene. Then voices were heard, as the Indians called openly to one another.

"I think they've gone," said Jack at last, having heard more sounds of breaking branches. "We shall be able to leave perhaps in a little while."

"P'raps," agreed Steve grudgingly. "But ef I know them varmint they won't take their eyes off this place even ef they think we've given 'em the slip. They'll watch it like lynxes all night long, and in the morning they'll know for sure, 'cos there won't be no tracks. Guess they're leadin' away our hosses."

Listening intently, the dull sounds which came to their ears told them without room for doubt that the two horses were being taken from the wood. There were then a few more calls out on the plain, and afterwards silence again settled down.

"S-s-s-h!" whispered Steve, as Jack attempted to move, for his limbs were a little cramped. "I'm thinkin' there's a bit of a trick bein' played. Lie still fer yer life, for I thought I heerd someone movin' not three yards away."

He whispered ever so gently in Jack's ear, and again his restraining hand fell upon our hero's shoulder. An instant later it was dragged forcibly away, for someone had gripped Jack by the arm, and with a sudden jerk he was hauled in the opposite direction. A man closed with him, grasping his hair with one hand, while the other held a knife poised in the air. And, luckily for Jack, his fingers closed upon the wrist ere a second had passed, while his free hand sought for and finally fell upon the man's neck. He gripped it as a terrier takes a rat between his teeth, and then made frantic efforts to upset his opponent, who lay above him. And all the while, as the two struggled desperately in the darkness of the undergrowth, there was silence; neither uttered so much as a sigh, and the only sound to be detected was the snap of breaking twigs and the hiss of their laboured breathing. For Jack was in the grip of one of the deadly Indians, and the struggle between them could end only with the last breath of one or other of them.

CHAPTER XII

A Tight Corner

"Jack, Jack. Aer yer there? aer yer there?"

The words came from Steve in an eager whisper, and, though repeated time and again, received no answer. Instead, the disabled hunter heard only the dull sound of blows, the hiss of sharply-indrawn breaths, and the snap of breaking twigs. He ground his teeth in his vexation and anxiety, but as he could not rise to his feet and walk, for his legs still refused to carry him, the gallant little fellow rolled on to his side and dragged himself towards the combatants. Very soon his eager fingers fell upon one of them.

"Injun!" he exclaimed, running his hand down the man's back and discovering the shoulders bare. "Then it are time I lent a hand."

Swiftly his fingers sought for his own hunting-knife, for Steve realized that the Indian was kneeling upon Jack, who lay beneath him, and argued from that fact that our hero was getting the worst of the conflict. Dragging his weapon from its sheath, he raised himself on one elbow, and made ready to strike. And to make sure that he had made no error, and that his blade was thrust in the right direction, he again groped for the shoulders he had felt a moment before. There they were, lean and muscular, and at once up went the knife, while Steve braced himself for the stroke. But he never delivered it; for of a sudden the straining muscles beneath his finger tips relaxed, the heaving, sinuous movements of the Indian's shoulders ceased, while the man seemed to become in one instant limp and helpless. He subsided on to his opponent, and then rolled heavily to the ground. The silence which followed was broken by the laboured breathing of one man only.

"Jack, Jack," whispered Steve again, his note more eager and anxious than before.

"Here," came the answer. "Here, safe and sound."

"Yer killed him?"

"Yes," gasped Jack.

"Gee! How?"

Jack sat beside his comrade for a minute and more before he ventured upon an answer. All the while he breathed deeply, in jerky spasms, as a man does who has been sorely tried, and who has striven to the last point of endurance. His whole frame was trembling with the intensity of the struggle, while his fingers were crooked and rigid with the strain of prolonged gripping. Then, getting his breath again, and the use of his fingers by gentle movements, he crept closer to Steve and whispered his answer.

"I had luck," he said. "He took me by surprise at first, and I wonder he didn't send his knife through me. But he missed his stroke, and before he could make another I had a grip of his wrist. At the same time my other hand got a hold on to his neck."

"Gee!" The scout gave vent to a low exclamation. "Yes?" he asked.

"I knew that was my only chance, so I hung on like a bull dog. He's dead, the life choked out of him."

"Sure? Sartin' he ain't foxin'. There never was any ter play possum like an Injun. Ye're dead sure he's done?"

Jack moved from the side of the hunter for one moment, and ran his hand over his late antagonist. There was not a doubt but that he was dead. The chest was motionless, and not a breath left the lips.

"He'll never fight again," he said sternly, creeping back to Steve. "Do you think they'll come to find him?"

There was a low growl from the hunter. "Think!" he whispered scornfully. "In course they will. But his absence'll make 'em mighty careful. I've told yer an Injun don't like to get beat. His game's always to kill, and go scot free himself. But they'll search this here group of trees till they find him, and then——"

He ended suddenly, and propped himself up to listen; for there was no need to explain what would happen. Even to Jack's inexperienced mind the ending was only too obvious. The horses had been found, and now themselves. Of that the Indians would have not the smallest doubt once their comrade failed to return, and failed also to answer their signals.

"Huh! There they go barkin' As ef any fool couldn't tell as it warn't a fox. That'll tell 'em right enough that something's happened," whispered Steve, "It ain't o' no use fer me to send 'em back the call, 'cos I can tell yer no white man can manage it proper. Them Injuns get practising when they're no higher than a dozen dollars piled one on t'other, and there ain't a one as tries it later on as kin git quite at the right sound. H-h-hish! Ain't that someone movin'?"

Intense silence fell upon them again, while Jack raised himself on his knees, so as to prepare for a second struggle. Yes, somewhere directly in front of him, and perhaps four yards away, a twig had stirred, while the gentle rustle of a leaf had reached him. He stooped, pressed Steve's hand to show him that he was ready, and then silently gripped a rifle which lay beside the hunter. To raise himself to his feet was the work of half a minute, for deathly silence was essential. But once upon them, he stood in a tense attitude, bending slightly, both hands gripping the barrel of his weapon, while the stock was raised above his head.

Click! The tip of a brier, or of one of the smaller branches of a bush, swished as it was released by some unseen hand. In that intense silence it sounded to our hero almost as loud as the report of a pistol. And it told him as clearly as possible that this new antagonist stealing up towards him was directly in front, and already somewhat nearer. He held his breath, and waited, his eyes staring into the darkness. Click! The sound was repeated.

And then, for one brief second, an uncanny sensation came over him. For something touched his boot, and that something ran nimbly up to his knees. Was it a forest mouse, scared by the intruder creeping towards Jack with murderous intent? Or was it the man himself?

Quick as a flash Jack decided the matter. A few weeks before he would have waited a little longer to make sure. But he had already had more than one lesson teaching him that indecision is often fatal. Besides, he knew now what he had never guessed before. He had already, this very evening, had an object lesson of the craft and stealth of the Indian, and realized that where a silent and unexpected attack was necessary their skill was phenomenal. Knowing that, Jack struck with all his strength. He struck blindly at the darkness, till the heavy butt of his rifle was stayed in its course by some unseen obstacle. Then he swung it up again, and sent it crashing through the air till once more its course was arrested.

"Gee! That are a blow. H-h-hist!"

It was Steve's voice, low and cautious, and with just the faintest trace of exultation in the note. For Steve was no craven, and even if he were powerless to defend himself, he could yet appreciate that power in others. And the hunter had been in so many engagements and had come successfully out of them, that now that the tables seemed turning a little in their favour, and the outlook did not appear quite so bad as it had done a little while ago, he could not help a feeling of exultation.

"Ef he ain't the boy, this here Carrots!" he murmured to himself, as he peered up in the direction in which he knew Jack stood. "Ef he ain't showing an old hand how these here things should be done. He jest cotched that feller an almighty whack on the head, and guess that's an end of him. Jack," he said a little louder.

"Well," came back the laconic answer.

"How'd yer come out of that 'ere business? Yer ketched him a whop? Eh?"

"Dead," said Jack curtly. "I felt his fingers on my leg. He didn't know exactly where I was till then. I struck out with the rifle, and——"

"Gee! Ef you ain't fine! But hist a moment. Them varmint'll be somewhares about."

It seemed indeed more than likely that the Indians who had entered the trees, and of whom three still remained, would endeavour to follow their comrades. Although Jack's rifle butt had slain the second man in absolute silence, his struggle with the first had produced sufficient noise to attract attention, and without a doubt the enemy were fully aware of the fact that the men they sought were amongst the trees. No doubt they were still uncertain of their exact position. But that was a difficulty which these crafty men would soon overcome.

"They'll send more of the young chaps in," whispered Steve, "and this time they'll hunt in couples. Jack, lad, ye've got ter do a bit more fightin' ef yer want ter keep yer haar."

"You think they will soon find us, now they know we are in the wood?" asked our hero suddenly, kneeling close to his comrade.

"Think!" At any other time Jack would have roared with laughing, for the little hunter's tones were full of indignation and contempt. "It don't want no thinkin'. A baby could tell yer that them critters would find us, and quick, too. That ain't what's worryin'. It's the fact that they'll come along in a bunch, and sence there's you alone to fight, why, in course, it don't leave us a dog's chance."

"And supposing they don't come along?" asked our hero. "Supposing they decide to leave the matter for a while."

"'Tain't likely. But ef they do, the end's jest the same. They'll set a close watch right round the place, and not one of them varmint'll close an eyelid till the light comes. Droppin' asleep when he's watchin' is a thing an Injun can't do. It's clean right up agin his nature."

"Then, that being the case, we'll not wait here either for them to attack us in a bunch or for them to find us in the morning."

Jack spoke quietly, and cautiously raised himself on to his feet. "I'm going to carry you to the edge of the trees, Steve," he whispered. "I tell you, if they're bound to find us in any case, so long as we stay where we are, why, I ain't going to stay to be butchered, and I ain't going to leave you, either. Just take a grip round my neck, and hold tight if we meet anything. That'll leave me with my hands free. Now."

Steve gaped at the words, and more at the tone of them than anything. Little by little as the moments had passed he had seen something in our hero which he had never detected before. He was wont to look upon Jack as a lad who, by accident perhaps, had been enabled to come between a band of train robbers and their victims. He did not deny that he had shown pluck. But that this young fellow was a fire eater, that he could on occasion become a stern, commanding man, and could coolly face a difficulty such as this one, had never occurred to him. More than that, Steve, with all his age and experience, had always been the one to lead and to guide, to give hints as to the manner of doing this, and timely warnings and advice as to the methods to be employed in some other sudden difficulty. Now, suddenly to find the position reversed, to know that Jack was giving orders, and was about to act as seemed best to himself, wholly regardless of his own inexperience, why, it took Steve's breath away.

"Gee! Ef he don't beat everything!" he murmured. "He jest treats me as ef I war a kid, and—and——"

"Hold fast, and don't worry if I have to drop you suddenly. I'll stand by you whatever happens. There! Up you come."

It was all done without hesitation, and in absolute silence. No one could have admonished Jack for lack of caution. His orders were whispered into Steve's ear, and every movement was slow and gradual. He stood, at length, to his full height, Steve gripping him round the neck, while with one arm he held the scout's useless legs suspended. The other hand gripped the haft of his formidable hunting-knife. Then he began a slow and stealthy progress towards the edge of the wood.

"Take yer time, take yer time," whispered Steve. "It would be fatal ter make so much as a sound."

Advancing inches only at a time, placing each foot cautiously in front of the other, and carefully avoiding branches which grew in the way, our hero at length reached the very edge of the trees. Once there he set down his burden for a few minutes, while he lay at full length, and placing his ear to the ground listened for sounds made by the enemy.

"Hist! Did yer hear that?" asked Steve, when some minutes had passed. "Them chaps is startin' in at the far side of the wood, and I should reckon as thar's a heap of 'em. Do yer hear 'em?"

Jack fancied he had heard some sounds, but was not at all certain. But to Steve there was not the smallest doubt.

"They're over yonder," he whispered, a note of conviction in his voice, "and I tell yer there's a good twenty of 'em, else there wouldn't be so much noise. It stands to reason that an Injun kin creep through a wood same as this silenter than a snake. But ef he's got a crowd of comrades with him, some of 'em's bound to be less careful. Yer kin take it from me, them critters has got it fixed in their minds that we're trying to make out over in that direction."

"Then all the better. Let 'em continue to think that," whispered Jack hoarsely. "We ain't going in that direction, but just clear out here in front of us, and if we meet one of their men, well——"

He came to an abrupt halt, leaving Steve to guess his meaning. But if ever determination were conveyed by the tones of a whisper, why, Jack's showed without a shadow of doubt that he was resolute. Indeed, those two death struggles in the wood had hardened him. A little while ago his thoughts had been entirely engaged with the task of escaping the enemy and rescuing his comrade. Now, however, added to that endeavour was a stubborn resolution to punish these men who had wantonly attacked him. He argued that if he with a number of friends had come upon a couple of harmless Indians, he would have shown them kindness, and would not have instantly sought their lives. Why, therefore, should these natives of the plain so diligently seek to kill him and Steve? What right had they to interfere with them? As they had dared to do so, why, they must be made to pay the penalty. In one brief hour, in fact, Jack, who hitherto had had no great dislike of the Indians, for the simple reason that he had never come across them, was possessed of an intense hatred for them, a burning animosity, a desire to come to hand grips with them, and a fierce determination to fight any who crossed his path. Nor in that was he different to the old hunters of the plains, men like Steve and Tom.

"I can see what they mean now," he thought, as he and Steve lay on the outskirts of the wood. "They've told me time and again how the people crossing over to California, to the diggin's, have scoffed at all fear of Indians, have imagined that they would become friendly with them without meeting with unusual difficulties. But those who have lived to reach the diggings have done so with a different understanding of the Indian. They know him by then to be a fierce and relentless enemy, a man who will butcher for the sake of butchering, and who will spare neither a sick white man nor a woman nor a child."

"Jest listen to 'em!" suddenly whispered Steve, interrupting Jack's thoughts. "Ef I ain't right I'll eat me boots. Them critters think we're makin' for the far side. They heard the ruction you had with them two varmint, and though they guess that something bad's happened to 'em, they aer wondering whether the noises ain't caused by us. Yer see, it's right up agin Injun nature and cunnin' ter make a sound. So, ef them noises wasn't caused by fightin', they was caused by us. Reckon a mouse couldn't get through on the far side."

"But a man can on this. Get a grip of my neck again," commanded Jack. "Now, I'm going to strike clear away into the open. If you hear or see anything, jest give my neck a squeeze. That'll stop me, and give me a warning."

It was lucky for our hero that he had such a crafty fellow as the little hunter with him, even if he happened to be helpless. But for Steve Jack would have blundered into one of the Indian sentries. As it was, Steve arrested him with a gentle squeeze of his arms within five minutes of their setting out.

"S-s-sh!" he whispered. "I seed something direct ahead, standin' up agin the white fringe of the clouds. It's an Injun, sure. He'll be shoutin' in a jiffy."

"Then we will turn and make along till we can pass him," suggested Jack.

"Yer might," came the cautious answer. "But I think as you'd be sartin to run up agin another of the varmint. Twenty yards is as much space as they'd dare allow between each man on a night same as this, and ef yer tried to pass between them it means you'd be within ten yards or so. That ain't enough. They'd be sartin ter spot yer. Let's lie down a spell. There ain't no sayin' what the critters aer doin'."

Jack took his advice promptly, for there was not a doubt but that the utmost caution was necessary. Steve might or might not have seen one of the Indian sentries, but it would be madness to attempt a forward movement till they were certain that the road was clear. So for a long quarter of an hour the two lay stretched side by side, the cunning little hunter with his ear glued to the ground, while Jack peered into the darkness ahead. Then, suddenly, a commotion was heard from the direction of the wood. A shrill call awoke the echoes, while instantly following it came that well-known signal, crisp and clearly, now from the centre of the wood, later from one end, and immediately afterwards from the far side.

"Them critters has lit upon the men as attacked you," said Steve hoarsely. "Reckon when the hull lot gets to know that two of their pals is dead there'll be a bit of a bother. It'll make 'em downright mad. But they ain't goin' ter take us, Jack. Somehow, after all that's happened, I feel as ef we was bound to come through, ef only to give me a chance of talkin' ter the boys. But it ain't goin' ter be done easy. Ye've got ter—hist!—That 'ere chap's movin'."

Keen and ever watchful, Steve detected a movement in front instantly, and in a moment he had gripped Jack by the arm, and was directing his attention in that direction.

"He's riding this way. See him? Gee! ef he ain't comin' right on top of us."

"Lie still. Leave him to me," said Jack, peering ahead of him. "Do you think he'll see us easy as we lie here?"

"Might—mightn't," came the curt answer. "Jest depends. Ef he's listenin' to them critters over thar in the wood, why, maybe his eyes'll not happen to spot us. But, as a gineral rule, there ain't no sayin' what an Injun won't see. A needle ain't much too small for the varmint. Ef he comes close, what'll you do?"

"S-s-sh! He's coming quick. Lie still."

Pressing the hunter down with one hand, Jack lay himself full length, his body squeezed as close to the ground as possible, and in that position he had no difficulty in detecting a figure riding towards him. The man was urging his horse on, for there came the dull sound of a moccasined heel applied to the side of the animal. And then followed the muffled thud of the footfalls. Yes, the Indian was riding in a line which would take him almost over the bodies of those he sought, and in that event, even if he himself failed to detect the two figures prone in the grass, the animal would not miss them. Jack braced himself on hands and knees, his feet drawn up beneath him as a panther gathers its limbs preparatory to a spring, and there, hardly daring to breathe, he waited, while the footfalls came nearer. A moment or two later the animal was almost over him. Then it suddenly drew to one side, shying so unexpectedly that the rider was almost thrown. But, gripping the saddle with his knees, the Indian retained his seat, and at the same moment pulled at his reins, for he as yet had seen nothing. It was an opportunity not to be missed, and promptly Jack launched himself at the man. With one bound he was beside him, then, quick as lightning, he gripped him by arm and leg, and, tearing him from his seat, threw him heavily to the ground.

CHAPTER XIII

Dodging the Enemy

There was an intense silence immediately after Jack had thrown the Indian, broken only by his own deep breathing.

"Dead?" asked Steve huskily, for the stress of the fighting and their difficulties were beginning to tell upon the little hunter. "Ye've killed him—eh? I never knew an Injun downed so easy."

"Stunned, I think," whispered Jack sternly. "He's still breathing a little."

"Foxin'? You're dead sartin he ain't foxin'? I've knowed one of the critters lie as if he was as dead as meat, and then get his knife into the man as thought he'd downed him. Aer yer sure? 'Cos if you ain't——"

"Certain," came Jack's emphatic answer. "He fell on his head with a terrible bang, and he'll not recover for a time. Jest take a grip round my neck. We're going to move."

They had spoken in low whispers only, for neither had forgotten that in all probability there were Indian sentries on either side of them. However, it did seem now that fortune was to be kind to them; for at this very moment the outcry which had broken out some few minutes earlier from the direction of the wood was again heard.

Shrill, angry calls came through the darkness, and were answered from a dozen different directions. Then, immediately to the right of them there came a muffled thump, followed by the dull sounds of a horse's footfalls.

"Warn't I right?" asked Steve. "Another of the critters thar, and a second 'way to the left. Now's your time, young 'un. Let's git as slippy as we can."

Jack needed no second invitation. He too had heard the sounds on the right and those calls from the wood; and, realizing that, though the distraction had come just at the critical moment, and would call off the attention of the circle of watchers from themselves, yet it indicated probably a full discovery of that struggle which had taken place amongst the trees, and with it a knowledge that the fugitives had fled, he gripped Steve firmly in his arms and swung him up on to the back of the Indian pony; for the well-trained beast had remained beside its fallen master. To sling his rifle and leap up behind the hunter was the work of a moment, and straightway he set the animal in motion. But almost instantly he was faced by another difficulty.

"Where away?" he asked, for the darkness confused him.

"Dead straight ahead fer a while," came the whispered answer; "then slick ter the right, whar our camp lies. Likely as not some of the boys is riding over ter meet us, for they'll have reckoned by this that things aer queer. Gently does it, Carrots. There ain't no use hurryin'."

At a gentle walk, therefore, they rode away from the small collection of trees which had proved their salvation, and at the same time had very nearly seen their ending. When the pony had covered a quarter of a mile, or thereabouts, Jack turned it to the right, and, setting the plucky little beast at a trot, went on into the night.

"They'll follow?" he asked, after a while; for the cries which they had heard for some time had ceased now for the past five minutes. "I suppose they found those two men and then had a palaver, as you call it?"

"Yer kin put it like that. Them critters has had a hard nut to crack, 'cos, don't yer see, the trees and the darkness bothered 'em. Yes, they found them two critters you downed in the wood, and, in course, they made sartin we was still there, in hidin', but shifted from the old quarters. So they sent their best men in ter ferret around, and in a while they found not a soul save their own comrades."

"That is when we heard their cries, I suppose?" said Jack.

"Right agin. That aer when they began ter shriek. That ain't much like Injuns, and jest shows that their dander's been properly up. They sets to, then, to have a palaver, and——Gee! That aer bad!"

Once more a chorus of shouts came from behind them, and told Jack and his comrades that something more had occurred to disturb the enemy and raise their anger.

"It aer as clear as daylight," said Steve shortly. "Them varmint was bothered when they found the wood empty, and set to to cast all round, and question the critters placed there to watch. They've jest dropped on the feller as you pulled off this here hoss, and—wall, even on a dark night an Injun'll follow a trail."

"How?" Jack was a practical fellow, and this night's adventure had made him critical. He failed to see how even the most astute tracker could follow a trail in the darkness. But Steve soon enlightened him.

"'Twont take 'em many minutes," he said, a note of conviction in his voice. "Yer see, it don't matter to them ef we get to know as they're follerin'. They has it fer sure that we're gettin' away on one of their ponies, and that he's got ter carry double weight. That tells 'em plain that they can easily catch us up once they're on the trail. So they ain't likely to make no bones about the matter. They'll strip the bark off some of them pines and make torches. That'll light the way, and show 'em what line we've took. Now, how aer we to get top side of 'em?"

The little hunter lapsed into silence, while Jack dug his heels into the pony and set him at a fast canter. But it was clear that the animal could not keep up the pace for long. He was not a big pony, indeed was hardly up to Jack's weight. With Steve added he was decidedly overweighted, and the next quarter of an hour proved that fact without the shadow of doubt. The Indian horse was blowing heavily by then, and going slower.

"It stands ter reason he can't last," cried Steve suddenly. "Now I'll tell yer what we'll do. This last ten minutes we've been riding down a slope, and there's a rise behind us which hides them Injuns. We can't say as they're on the trail yet, 'cos we can't see. Likely enough they've got their torches by now, and are skirmishing round fer the trail. If that's so, they'll be after us afore two minutes. But that 'ere rise hides us jest the same, and it'll give us one more chance. Jack, aer yer willing ter do what I suggest?"

"Perfectly. Anything but leave you. I've taken you in charge, and I don't leave you behind for anything."

There was a ring in Jack's voice, a manly, elated tone, which told the little hunter that his companion was anything but disheartened. There was a suspicion of raillery in the voice, and the tone tickled Steve immensely. He leaned back against our hero and laughed heartily, a laugh which shook him, but which, with all his native caution, was as silent as a gentle whisper.

"Yer do fetch the band!" he smiled. "Ef I ain't beat holler, and thet by a townsman. But 'tain't a time ter play, leastwise not yet. Them varmint ain't done with us by a long way. Now jest yer listen. A friend of mine, an old hunter, war once up agin a difficulty same almost as this. And he jest played a trick that cleared the Injuns. It aer our one chance, and we'll take it. The wind's in our faces, though I ain't so sartain that it'll stay thar. Ef it don't, the trap we set'll catch us instead of the Injuns. Jack, jest hop right down and get a bunch of that 'ere grass."

Quick as lightning Jack slipped to the ground, and did as Steve suggested.

"Now, set it afire, and slippy with it. When it's blazin' properly, jest run along with it and fire the grass in as many places as yer can. Don't wait a second longer than you're obleeged ter."

There was a note of tense excitement in the hunter's voice, and he watched eagerly as Jack struck a match and fired a bundle of grass. Then he chuckled as a spout of flame burst from each patch of the long prairie growth he touched.

"Ef anything'll save us, it's that," he said to himself; "save us or cook us. That 'ere fire ain't ten yards wide now, but you wait. In ten minutes it'll have spread to a mile if the wind holds. Get at it, Jack. Hop along as fer as yer like. The farther the better."

Long before this Jack had grasped Steve's meaning, and had realized that in proposing to fire the grass he hoped to stretch a curtain of flame between them and the Indians. But never in all his life had he been so utterly astounded at the result of his action. For it was at the end of the hot weather, and the long rank grass which just there covered the plains was as dry as tinder. Indeed, more than once lately they had observed prairie fires; but some irregularity of the ground, a river, or some hilly and broken ground had in every case limited the conflagration. But even those glimpses of fires had given our hero no idea of their tremendous spread, of the fearful rate at which the line of fire progressed, for distance had diminished everything. Now, however, the thing was at his elbow, and he was struck with awe. As if eager for the flames, the grass caught in every direction, and then surged away with a seething hissing sound, casting up but little smoke. It raced from him on every hand. Patches which he had ignited ten yards from one another were joined hand in hand before he could think, so that in an incredibly short space of time a wall of fire lay before him. He was terrified at his handiwork. But Steve was jubilant.

"Hop on, and let's git," he said easily, as Jack returned to him. "Ef the wind don't change there'll be a wall of fire round which them Injuns'll have to ride, and they won't fancy the business over much. 'Sides, they'll have to divide. There won't be any knowing whether we've gone dead straight on or have turned to one or other side. Gee! Ef this ain't a doin'."

"Supposing the wind does turn?" asked Jack, digging his heels into the horse and setting it at a slow canter.

"Yer won't have much longer need ter worry. This here trouble that you've got tucked out er sight at the back of yer mind'll be done with, 'cos there won't be no escapin'. This hoss couldn't do it, unless he had only one to carry, and I've got the idea as you ain't goin' ter quit with me till things aer quieted down a bit."

Jack heard the little scout chuckling as if it were a good joke, and then felt his bony, strong fingers suddenly fall upon his hand.

"I ain't pokin' fun at yer, lad," said Steve seriously, a little jerk in his voice. "But I aer fair amused ter think that a townsman aer done it, and aer been able to show Steve somethin'. It jest fetches the wind out o' my sails, as the mariners say. Yer see, bein' an old scout, I kinder took you by the hand ter show yer a thing or two. And kinder reckoned ef we got into a muss, as ain't so unlikely hereabouts, I'd be able to protect yer. But, gee! ef this ain't jist the opposite.

118

Reckon ye've saved my life ten times over, Jack. Ye've a right to feel proud of yerself, for ye've done it cold. Do yer foller?"

Jack did not, and intimated that fact.

"All the same, there's no need to say another word," he exclaimed grumpily, though his face was flushed with pleasure, and he was tingling from head to foot.

"But there aer. Every need. Yer ain't goin' ter bully me as ef I war a kid. Ye've ordered me about till I don't know as I'm right in me head. There are need ter say more. Yer did it cold. I mean out thar by the buffalo, when yer was warmed with the chase, yer played a right plucky game, and it took some grit, that did; but in thar between the trees, when we was waitin' and watchin' fer the enemy, it war cold shivery work, the kind of stuff that sets men's knees knockin' tergether and their teeth chatterin'. I ain't exaggeratin'. I've knowed brave men in sech a fix get shiverin' all over. It aer their nerves, I suppose, and it's a skeary feelin' that makes a brave man a coward. Now ye've got the hang of what I mean. Yer played that other game dead cold. I don't forget that I owe yer my life, and that it war downright pluck as did it. So thar!"

Having said his say, Steve, who had become quite garrulous when with Jack, lapsed into silence, and presently lay back against his young protector as if he were utterly worn out. And so for an hour the horse cantered on, bearing them in the direction of their friends. As for the fire, it quickly assumed gigantic proportions, and long before the hour had passed a broad line of fire extended on either hand rushing in the opposite direction. And instead of the wind changing round, it got up as the night advanced, and blew still harder, fanning those terrible flames.

Half an hour later, when their horse was almost exhausted, and his pace had descended to a walk, Steve suddenly sat up and shook himself as if he had but just awakened.

"I seed somethin' over thar!" he exclaimed, pointing to the right. "And I guess as it ain't Injuns. Likely enough it'll be Tom and the boys. Let's give 'em a halloo."

But, before he could call out, a sharp hail came through the darkness.

"Stand thar!" someone shouted. "Ef yer move we'll put lead into yer——Jest sing out and say whar yer come from, and what's yer business."

"It aer Tom sure enough," cried Steve. "Hi, Tom!" he called back at the top of his voice.

In less than a minute Tom and Jacob rode up, and at once dismounted.

"A fine scare ye've given us!" exclaimed Tom, striding to the side of the horse. "When it fell night and yer didn't turn up, we didn't make so much of it. 'Cos we'd heard shots, and thought ye'd most likely been gettin' meat. But when it got later and later, and there warn't a sound, why, me and Jacob saddled up and come back on the trail. What's kept yer?"

A few words sufficed to tell them.

"Yer can take it for sartin as we've got ter fight it out," said Steve in his cool voice. "Them critters has had a knock as they can't forgit, and won't forgive. Two of their young braves has been downed by this here Jack, and a third aer got a headache that'll last him past the mornin'. Wall, what'll yer do? Yer kin put me on one side. I kin lie up in the wagon, and I kin shoot. But I ain't no good fer riding."

It was obviously a case where conjunction of forces was necessary, and at once Tom took Steve up in front of his saddle, while Jack climbed up behind Jacob. Then, leaving the Indian horse, they spurred away across the plain, and within an hour had found the camp and their friends.

"They'll be here with the mornin' light, them critters," said Tom, addressing all hands. "And ef we've got an ounce of sense we'll be makin' ready fer 'em. Now it seems to me as we'd better carry on a runnin' fight. 'Cos ef we stay, and fix up a bit of a fort, them varmint'll sit down to starve us out, ef it takes 'em a month."

"That aer sense," agreed Jacob. "There never was a critter ter sit down and wait like an Injun. He's got the patience, yer see, and doin' nothin' kinder suits him. He aer an idle dog when he's not fightin' and takin' scalps. Wall, how's it ter be done, Tom?"

"Jest like this. I war in a muss same as this once before, though there warn't so many of the varmint. We fought 'em runnin', same as they do at sea when thar's a naval battle. Guess that wagon aer big enough to take the hull crowd, and, that being the case, we'll pile into it. Jacob here'll drive the hosses. Our mounts'll be tied up along by the wheelers, so as we kin get at 'em slippy ef we want. Then we'll make a kind of cover under the tilt, something that'll keep out their arrows and bullets, and the same forward and aft. Ef we can't make a handsome fight of it then, why we ain't fit ter get through. Let's have a light. David and Jacob here kin get to at the cover. Jest take some of them 'ere empty sacks and nail 'em to the bottom boards. Then string 'em up to the tilt hoops. When ye've kind of made a long sack yer can fill it with grass. Ef it's stuffed in well it'll stop a bullet, and the weight won't be anythin' ter speak of. Make it jest a nice height ter cover a kneeling man. Jack, you kin jist sit down along of Steve and get to at some food. Ye'll want it badly by this. I'll make back along the track a little and keep a watch, while ye other boys kin hitch the hosses in, get the guns ready, and lay out ammunition. Thar ain't no use in movin' yet. Better wait till daylight, ef them critters'll allow us."

There was calmness and order and method about these experienced scouts, and at once each man occupied himself with the task allotted by Tom. As for Jack, he was ravenous, and at once began to forage for food for himself and Steve.

"You kin jist give my back another rub when we've filled up inside," said Steve, as Jack laid him down at the tail of the wagon. "I kin move a hull foot now, and bend the knee a little. That shows the works is gettin' in gear again. But they've had a mighty shakin', they have, and seems to me it war near bein' a bad business altogether."

Four hours later, when the dawn began to break, the little band of scouts was marching slowly and steadily across the plain, Jacob plying the whip from the front of the wagon, where a breastwork of boxes had been built to protect him. On either hand rode Tom and Seth and the others, their eyes searching the plain for a sight of the enemy. But for a while nothing was seen of them. Away behind them a black pall of smoke covered the countryside as far as the eye could see, and beyond, no eye could penetrate.

"But they're there, the skunks!" exclaimed Tom, as he rode knee to knee with Jack. "Steve's had a sight more experience on the plains than any man of us, and he allows as thar ain't a chance but that they'll follow. As fer me, I feel sure as they won't dare to sit down and take their lickin' humble. Yer see, it's a case of what their people'll say when they returns home. Ef they come with a tale of defeat they'll never hear the end of it, and the squaws will jeer at them. They're dead bound to go on with the chase, and they won't give it up till they've got our scalps, or till we've given 'em a proper hidin'. Say, Carrots, Steve aer talkin' a heap. Aer it all true what he says? I know he ain't the one to make a thing bigger than it aer, but he's had a bad shake, and maybe he's a bit wandering. Aer it true as you stood beside him through thick and thin?"

Jack modestly acknowledged that he had refused to desert his comrade, and for a while he had to listen to the praise of the man who had first befriended him. Then, too, the other hunters rode their horses up—for Steve had called them one by one to the wagon, where he lay at full length—and eagerly shook Jack's hand.

"Yer ain't no longer a tenderfoot," said one of them. "I allow as a youngster can do a brave thing once, and save an old hunter's life. But it ain't often a youngster from the towns gets his teeth into it, so to speak, and when there's a chance of skipping from a hull heap of Injuns, refuses point-blank, but sticks to his partner. And Steve says as you got quite uppish. Treated him like a kid, and

121

that ef you hadn't done so both of you'd have gone under. Shake, Jack, I'm glad I am along with the party."

It may be imagined that our hero was covered with confusion; for there was no conceit about Jack, and he had no desire to receive thanks or praise from anyone. Still, all the same, his senses tingled, and it was a happy young fellow who rode beside Tom. For Jack felt within himself that he had acted as a man should. He felt now, more than ever, that he could hold his head up and scoff at those who had accused him of that crime for which he would have been convicted had he stayed at Hopeville. More than that, so helpful are kind words from those who surround us, he began to look to the future hopefully. He felt as if the tide of misfortune had turned, and that somewhere, sooner or later, he would be successful in his search for that miscreant who had gone off like a craven, and had left no word, not even a wish, to clear the young fellow accused of the crime which he himself had committed.

"Thar they aer, ridin' strong!" cried Tom, suddenly pointing across to the left. "They've rid round the edge of the fire, and by the way their cattle is goin' they've had a longish way to come. Boys, it aer time to get into the wagon. Jest get yer barrels filled, and then lay doggo. There'll be time and enough to fire. What we want is to coax them critters ter come within easy distance, and then we'll give 'em pepper. 'Tain't no use to play with 'em. We've got ter handle them roughish, and, when they starts in shootin', jest remember we've got ter give 'em pepper."

CHAPTER XIV

An Attack in Force

The light was strong, and the pink tinge in the sky away to the east was already giving place to a golden hue, the forerunner of a scorching sun, as the Indians came in sight. Turning in his saddle, Jack could see them riding in a cluster, and coming at a sharp canter.

"Likely as not they've seed us ten minutes ago," said Tom, taking a close view of the pursuers. "They're right up agin that cloud of smoke, so that it aer not so easy fer us to see them. But we're clear out on the plain, and anyone could spot the tilt of the wagon miles away. Wall, youngster, aer yer skeared?"

Jack laughed. Somehow, for no reason at all, so far as he was aware, the thought of the coming conflict gave him not so much as a qualm. Had the same thing been about to occur three days ago he would perhaps not have been so cheerful; for it is uncertainties which try men, doubt as to the future, and, where blows are to be expected, a vague wondering as to how they will bear themselves. But Jack had met danger already, and met it manfully. In his heart he knew well that he had earned the esteem of these hardened scouts, and at the thought he threw up his head and laughed again.

"Jest like that, aer it?" smiled Tom. "Wall, I knows how yer feel, and I ain't surprised. Yer ain't got no call to fear any ruction in the future, 'cos ye've had an innings, and that teaches a chap a heap. But it aer time to climb into the wagon."

By now all the friends were gathered close beside the huge vehicle save Jacob, who gripped the reins, and Steve, who lay on the boards within. Not one of the men appeared anything but absolutely cool. Indeed they displayed a certain amount of cheerfulness which would have helped to keep up the courage of any weakling, had there been one amongst them. Slipping from their saddles, they unbuckled girths and carried the saddles to the back of the wagon, where one of their number built them into a breastwork. The others at the same time made the bridles fast to the headstall of the wheelers drawing the wagon. Then, at a call from Tom, they came clambering into the wagon.

"And jest you watch them legs of mine," sang out Steve cheerily. "This here Jack's saved 'em fer me with a bit of trouble, and it aer cost them varmint back thar a hull heap, not ter speak of a bad headache that one of 'em's got. Wall, jest keep yer big boots off me. I don't want ter discourage a youngster, and I jest want ter show Jack thar that them legs is goin' ter get useful yet."

They placed the smiling little scout at the forward end of the wagon, and at his urgent request piled a heap of ammunition at his head. A biscuit box propped up one elbow, while the sacking, with its thick padding of grass, was pulled down a few inches.

"So that I kin see ter shoot over," growled Steve, "I ain't fergot as them varmint aer had a bit of fun outer me. Wall, I never did like owin'. I'm agoin' ter pay back prompt, and I'll give 'em full measure ef I can work it."

By now the enemy were within three hundred yards of the wagon, and, looking out, Jack saw that they were riding slowly, while a number were bunched close together, and were carrying on a heated conversation. Behind them rode the younger men, and it was clear from the manner in which they broke from the throng ever and again, and reluctantly rejoined it, that they were eager to begin the attack.

"In course they'll divide," said Tom coolly. "And some of their best men'll be told off to ride in and shoot the hosses, or hamstring 'em if they kin get close enough. Wall, Steve and me'll see to that, and two of the others kin help. Jacob'll shake up the hosses every time the critters make a rush, so as to give 'em harder work ter do. You others'll get in a shot whenever yer kin. It don't need tellin' that yer might jest as well not shoot as miss. Ye've got ter kill every time, or damage a man so bad as he can't move."

"They're dividing," sang out Jack a moment later.

"And by the look of 'em they're goin' ter play some new kind of game. Keep yer eyes skinned, boys, and whatever happens don't let the critters get too near to the hosses. The guns they has ain't much good over a hundred yards. Jest keep 'em that far off, and we shan't come to any hurt."

Five minutes later it was apparent that this body of Indians was led by a crafty individual; for, having divided, instead of dashing forward and attacking the wagon on either side, the two bands, some thirty strong in each case, cantered past the wagon till they were well ahead. Then, to Jack's amazement, they spread themselves out on either side of the track which the wagon would take if it continued the course it was then following.

"They've set their mark on the hosses, boys," sang out Tom at once. "Their game are as clear as daylight. They're jest waitin' fer us to trail on between them, when every man'll let fly with his popgun. Ef they bring down the hosses we're stranded, and they kin then set to work to tackle the wagon. Say, Jacob, bring yer team up smart towards 'em, and, when yer judges you're jest outer shot, wheel 'em sharp to the left, and again to the right when you've run a couple of hundred yards. That'll put all the varmint on one side. Not a shot, boys, till I shout. Them critters ain't got no notion what sort of guns we've got. We want to coax 'em nearer, so as we kin give 'em pepper."

With the huge odds against them it was obvious that it would be to the advantage of the little party of hunters to inflict a severe lesson on the Indians at the very onset of the conflict. And all realized that Tom's scheme was best calculated to bring that about. Kneeling behind the breastwork formed all round the wagon, the scouts peered out from beneath the tilt, their weapons ready to their hands. Jacob, sitting high on the box, wielded the reins with a master hand. Leaning forward so as to give his whip arm free play, he sent the long lash cracking and swishing over the team. Then, having brought them to a canter, he steered them direct for the open space left between the two lines of Indian horsemen. There was a howl of rage as he swung the team to the left, and a great galloping to and fro as he swung to the right again, so placing the wagon to the left of the Indians, but just out of gunshot.

"Them fellers is jest cryin' with rage," laughed Steve as he peered out. "Guess they'll give up all thought of the hosses in a little. It's clear agin Injun nature ter trouble with hossflesh when there's white folks about and scalps to be taken. But jest watch it, Tom. Some of 'em will try a rush in, so as to put a bullet into the team."

Indeed, in less than a minute one of the young braves accompanying the enemy suddenly started from their ranks and galloped madly towards the wagon. His reins lay on the horse's neck, while already his gun was at his shoulder. Tom instantly threw his own weapon into position, paused for a moment, and then drew the trigger.

"Jest the right height, I reckon," cried Steve. "Yer hit him plumb, Tom, and it aer a lesson. But watch it. There'll be more of 'em axing ter be killed."

It was not likely that an old Indian fighter like Steve would be mistaken, and indeed the next few minutes proved that, for other braves dashed from the ranks, singly or in twos and threes. And on each occasion Tom and his comrades defeated their object. None of their bullets went astray. The men who were firing were no hotheads, no untrained recruits. They aimed steadily and coolly, and never missed.

"That aer checked them fer a little," said Tom, as the Indians drew away and rode on a level with the wagon, but some three hundred yards to the right. "They'll get to and have a palaver fer a bit, and then they'll try a rush. That aer what we've got ter fear. Thar's a good fifty of the critters left, and ef they can get all round us, why, some of 'em'll do fer the team while we're busy with the others. Then there won't be no stoppin' them. Yer know the game to play, Jacob?"

The big hunter, perched high on his box, looked round and grinned at Tom.

"Yer bet," he answered. "It's ter be a circus. Yer kin calkilate on me ter do the right thing at the right moment. I'll give the team an easy time till them critters gets frisky agin."

For more than half an hour the little party proceeded on their way, the team walking, while the Indians rode their horses still at the same distance from the wagon. For a while they had stopped, and there had been a palaver. Then they had followed at a trot, and as soon as they were level with the wagon had begun to walk their animals.

"Yer kin see their new game," cried Tom after a while. "Thar's roughish ground ahead. Yer kin see rocks rising in the grass, and they calkilates ter charge when we're fixed up amongst the boulders. Thar wouldn't be the same chance of manœuvring then, and things wouldn't be so favourable by a heap. What do yer think, Steve?"

"It don't want no thinkin'. Ef we push on into that ere rough ground, we're doin' jest what them Injun varmint aer axin' us ter do. That ain't reasonable, and ain't the way of men sich as we aer. We're in fer a muss with them critters, either here or down among the rocks. Wall, do it want decidin' what we aer ter do?"

"Pull the team round, Jacob," sang out Tom promptly, "and get yer irons ready, boys. Thar'll be a bit of shouting. Gee! It fair makes me grin to think how them critters'll be swearin'."

Once more Jacob's whip cracked over the team and set them in rapid motion, a pace which the enemy rapidly adopted. Indeed, it seemed as if the party at whose capture or death they aimed was actually hastening to its own destruction. But the Indians had as crafty a set of men to deal with as themselves. A howl presently escaped them as Jacob swung his team in a complete circle, and sent them heading back over the wheelmarks they had just made.

"Jest watch it, boys," sang out Tom. "Human natur can't stand that 'ere sort of thing, and Injun natur in partic'ler. They've jest been bamboozled, and ef there aer a thing that's sartin ter raise the dander of them varmint, it aer bein' bamboozled. Jest keep yer eyes skinned, and start in with the shootin' as soon as they aer within easy range. Yer kin keep yer shooters till they're up ter the wagon."

For five minutes perhaps the Indians rode beside the wagon, keeping pace with it—for the team had again dropped to a walk—and maintaining the same distance from it. Then Steve suddenly drew the attention of his comrades to a remarkable fact.

"Ain't they cute!" he cried. "They're givin' the idea that they're jest ridin' along at the same distance. But ef yer watch carefully, them critters is edgin' in all the while. In a bit they'll be near enough to make a rush. Jest sit tight, boys, while I put in a sorter warnin' shot."

He leaned well over his sights and squinted along the barrel, aiming at an Indian who, by his gestures, and the manner in which the others followed him, was undoubtedly the leader. Then the interior of the wagon was filled with blinding smoke, while a thundering detonation deafened the little party of white men. Instantly the Indian chief threw up his arms, fell back on the quarters of his horse, and slid to the ground. And at once there arose such a babel of shouts and shrill yells of anger that anyone might well have been alarmed. For it was contrary to Indian habit to give way so openly to wrath. It seemed, indeed, as if the conflict they had entered upon with these whites had tried the temper of the enemy more than usual, and if Jack had only known it his own unexpected success against them, the manner in which he had slain two of their most cunning young braves, had maddened the others. They felt as if their reputation, even their bravery, had received a sore check. Now, on top of that, this solitary wagon was being manœuvred in a manner which outgeneralled all their schemes, for the parties of diggers making across the plains upon whom the Indians were wont to make attacks fell too easy victims to their craft and cunning as a general rule.

"That aer the end of it," said Tom, turning to see that all was ready. "Flesh and blood can't stand no more of sich knocks, and them critters'll be coming."

The words had hardly left his lips when the whole band of Indians swept their horses round to face the wagon, and, digging their heels into the flanks of the animals, spurred them forward at a mad gallop. What a picture they made too! In more or less close formation, their feathered headdress flying in the breeze, and the trimmings of their overalls and moccasins fluttering, they raced towards the wagon with eyes staring and arms brandished over their heads. A perfect tumult of noise proceeded from their ranks, while they had hardly covered ten yards before their guns spoke out, sending bullets hissing across the space which divided them from the white men.

127

"THE INDIAN CHIEF THREW UP HIS ARMS"

"Shake 'em up, Jacob!" cried Tom at the pitch of his voice.

But the big, cool man handling the reins needed no instructions. Already he was bending forward, while the crack of his long lash broke the silence before the Indian guns spoke. He called to the horses as only a practised teamster could do, and at once the wagon swayed and rocked and jerked. Then it gathered momentum, and long ere the enemy had approached within a hundred and fifty yards the big, lumbering contrivance was well under way, dashing over the prairie at a pace which caused the Indians at once to swing their horses forward and gallop harder so as to come within reach In fact, it was this sudden movement which proved the safeguard of the little party of hunters. For otherwise, had they been stationary, they would have had fifty or more of the enemy about them at the same moment, and so quickly, too, that there would have been little time for the rifles to make an impression. As it was, they had some breathing space, and much use did they make of it.

"Leaders always, mates!" sang out Tom. "It aer always the best. It throws the others into a fix and delays 'em."

Short, sharp, and precise the shots rang out from the wagon, while the interior was presently filled with thick, sulphurous smoke. But that made no difference to the defenders, for the pace at which they were moving constantly cleared the atmosphere. It was Steve who first opened the duel. His weapon cracked sharply, and at once one of the leading Indian horses fell with a crash, throwing his rider. The animal following managed to leap over his fallen comrade, but a second tripped, and after him a third came to grief, leaving a pile of struggling men and lashing hoofs on the grass. But such an incident could not stop such large numbers. Spreading a little, they came racing in towards the wagon, while the heavy thuds outside told that bullets were flying. But missiles were also passing in the opposite direction, true to their mark, for each one of the scouts was a master hand with a rifle. Even Jack made good use of his weapon, and brought more than one of the enemy rolling, while the negro who accompanied the party, to tend to the team and cook, helped gallantly in the defence.

"Shooters!" shouted Tom at length, when the enemy were within ten yards. "Me and Seth'll see that they don't get nigh to the hosses. Ye other boys make time with 'em at the sides, and jest see that the critters don't climb in behind. Jack, post yerself thar, and give 'em fits ef they try it."

Dropping their empty weapons, each one of the defenders gripped his revolver, and in some instances they had two. As for Jack, he crawled to the back of the wagon, and, leaning over the saddles, waited for the time for action. And it was not long in coming. With a heave and a roll the wagon swung sharply to the left, for Jacob was a cunning hand. And the sudden change of direction threw the aim of the enemy out. A moment or two before several had been within easy reach of the wheelers of the team and had drawn their tomahawks; but the swerve left them behind, while in the case of one man on the far side, the wagon bumped into him with terrific force, and threw him and his mount to the ground. With a shout the others galloped up behind, and in a second there was a sea of faces, of bobbing heads, and of tossing manes presented to our hero.

"Take 'em cool!" shouted Tom, who seemed to have an eye for everything and everyone.

Jack levelled his weapon steadily, aimed at the foremost man, and sent a bullet crashing into his head. At the same instant he was almost blinded by a spurt of flame, while something hissed past his head, and, passing through the length of the wagon, buried itself in the box on which Jacob sat.

"Bully fer ye, Jack!" shouted Seth, springing to our hero's side. "Yer bagged him fine, and he near plugged yer. Get in at 'em."

It was short, sharp work at the back of the wagon on that occasion, and when it was ended Jack remembered nothing beyond that first shot, the fall of the Indian, and the ball which had hissed past his own cheek. Yet, there he was, standing beside the breastwork of saddles, holding an empty and smoking revolver in his hand, while directly in rear was a bunch of fallen men, with their patient horses standing beside them. And all the while he had a dim perception that shots were echoing all round him. From either side of the wagon a stream of bullets had hurtled, and even now men were being added to that bunch upon which his eye was fixed.

"Yer kin take it slow and cool," sang out Tom at last, his voice startling our hero. "Them critters has had their pepper, and ef they're wise they'll sheer clear off. Anyone the wuss?"

"Wuss. Yer don't call that wuss, do yer?" asked Seth indignantly, displaying a wrist from which a stream of red ran. "That ain't nothin'. Jest a pip what happened to come my way, and kinder seemed ter like me. Boys, I aer been in many a muss, and gee! I ain't the one as likes to come out without somethin' to remind me of it. That aer a pinprick."

He coolly rammed cartridges into his empty revolver, reloaded his gun, and then with the help of a fine set of teeth and a neckerchief quickly bound up the wound.

Meanwhile Jack had looked carefully about him, for the smoke had again cleared from the interior of the wagon. One thing struck him with amazement. The white tilt of the wagon, which had been rolled up so that the defenders could see from beneath it, was no longer the neat, nicely hung thing it had been. The curtain was punctured in numerous places, while there was more than one long slit.

"Jest ter remind us!" laughed Steve, seeing Jack's attention was attracted to the rents. "Them critters came close, and would ha' got to the hosses ef it hadn't been that Jacob had the ribbons. But yer can see how close they war. Reckon this here padding aer saved some of us."

It was clear, indeed, that but for the timely preparations of the scouts they would have fared badly, for the enemy had actually battered the outside of the wagon with their tomahawks, and had their weapons been loaded when they arrived at such close quarters no doubt they would have poured bullets into the interior. But they had expended their shots on the way, trusting to their terrible tomahawks for close hand-to-hand work, an opportunity for which had never been allowed them.

"It aer been a lesson," said Tom, after a while. "These here bits of padding ha' saved our lives no end, while the game of a runnin' fight aer bothered them critters more than anything. Boys, the time aer come to give 'em more pepper. It don't stand to reason that we should sit in here and see 'em palaverin', and makin' ready for more devilry. So I'm fer advising that Jacob swings the beauties round agin, and takes us in amongst them varmint. Ef we goes on, we shows we aer afraid. Ef we turns in amongst them, we lets 'em see we're axin' fer more. Get yer irons loaded."

For a few moments only the ring of ramrods was to be heard, and the click of revolver locks.

"Guess we're ready," said Seth shortly, a wide grin on his face. "Ef thar's a one here as don't fancy the business, he'd best get down now. Thar aer room out thar on the prairie."

A chorus of laughter greeted this sally, but was silenced by Tom.

"Ef Seth thar, Tricky Seth as we calls him, ain't specially careful," he sang out, "we'll hang him out in front as a scarecrow fer them varmint ter shoot at. Jack, jest you come forward. It does a young 'un like yer good to have a bit of experience. Jest come along with me and keep a watch on the hosses. Now, Jacob, boy, you kin fetch 'em round and give 'em their heads; and don't ferget to swing them ef the muss gets too thick. That last turn of yours jest bamboozled the critters more than anythin'."

Swinging the team round, Jacob set them towards the Indians at a smart pace, while a shout came from the scouts.

"Jest to tell 'em we're perky," smiled Tom. "Gee! They're goin' ter stand up to it, so it'll be a fight. Boys, you kin get in with the shootin' when ye're ready."

A short, sharp and extremely savage conflict followed, during which the Indians crowded round the wagon, while Jacob manœuvred his team in such a manner that they could never actually obtain a grip of the huge conveyance. And all the while Tom and his comrades emptied their weapons into the enemy, knocking numbers out of their saddles. Indeed, never before, in all probability, had this particular tribe been so severely handled, and, unable to face the punishment, they turned swiftly and fled, leaving many of their comrades dotting the plain, while no fewer than seventeen horses stood cropping the grass.

"Which shows that the varmint aer properly scared," said Tom exultingly, when the enemy had broken and fled. "An Injun likes to get away with his dead and wounded ef he kin. Ef he kin't, and leaves, it's a sure sign he's been mauled. Boys, thar are hosses out thar that'll pay to keep. Let's get into our saddles."

Jacob pulled in his team with a jerk, while the hunters leaped from the wagon. Saddles were swiftly thrown on the backs of the horses they had secured to their own wheelers, and in a trice they were riding away. It took but ten minutes to round up the Indian ponies, which were secured together by passing the reins of one through those of another, and so on, till all were secured.

"We can move along now," sang out Tom at length. "Them critters is away over thar watchin', and they'll be back to tend to their men as soon as we're gone. We ain't got nothin' more to fear from 'em. We've give 'em real pepper."

CHAPTER XV

Giving 'em Pepper

It was a jovial party which sat round the camp fire on the evening following the defeat of the Indians, for even the old and tried hunters could not help a feeling of elation.

"It makes yer feel jest like a kid," said Steve, as he blinked in the firelight, and looked across at Jack, who was tending the buffalo steaks hissing over the embers. "It ain't so many hours ago as me and Carrots was, as yer might say, fair up agin it. I didn't look to come out clear. And yet, here we aer, and I'm watchin' thim steaks pretty close, which seems to show as thar ain't nothing much wrong."

"And the back, mate?" asked Tom, striding across towards him, and looking particularly big.

"Jest as well as ever," came the hearty answer. "I'm that young and skittish, seems I could kick the carrots off Jack's head. Hand over one of them steaks, young 'un. A man same as me don't oughter be kept waitin'."

"We was talkin' of pepper," began Jacob, one of the hunters, when the meal was ended, and all were smoking their pipes. "That 'ere word minds me of a time when we give them red devils pepper same as we did to-day, only 'twarn't in these here parts, and we wasn't fer makin' gold in Californy."

"You kin get to at the yarn," sang out Seth promptly. "Thar ain't one of us as feels he aer got any use for a blanket yet awhile, and seem' it's fine and pleasant, why jest wet yer throat, and then let's have it from the beginnin'."

He leaned across to the hunter and handed him a brimming pannikin, which he had just replenished from the keg of spirit the party carried, and from the water bag in which the precious fluid was stored. Jacob let his head fall back promptly, raised the pannikin, and for the moment the silence which had fallen on the camp was broken by the gurgle of the fluid.

"Thanks, mate," gasped Jacob, getting his breath. "We was talkin' of pepper."

"We war," admitted Steve, edging a trifle closer to the fire.

"And we aer fair greedy fer the story," smiled Tom. "You ain't got no call ter look up ter the sky. The yarn ain't thar. Ye've got it stowed in yer head. Give it a shake and out with it. Ef not, I'll send Carrots here ter see whether a little hammerin' won't help you any."

There was a hearty laugh as Tom spoke, but the words made not the smallest difference to Jacob. He sat back on his elbows staring up at the sky, as if endeavouring to collect memories of past times. Jack took a look at the big hunter, wondered whether he himself would ever present such a decidedly manly appearance, and then fell to admiring the heavens too. For they were on the verge of California, and overhead hung a cloudless vault, speckled with such bright, twinkling stars that even the moon rays were paled.

"It war a night same as this," began Jacob at length, "jest fer all the world same as this. The stars and moon that bright and clear yer could see to read easy. Wall, I ain't here ter tell of the stars and sichlike. I'm mindin' the time when I was workin' the cattle fer a boss a goodish way south of this, in a country that's even now more Injun than anythin'. He was rough, war that 'ere boss, and we ended a long day amongst the beasts with sharp and bitter words. I 'low as a man as hires me has a right ter git the value of his dollars outer me. But I don't cotton to no bossin'. I don't see that 'cos a man employs a hand he has a right ter bully him, ter shout names at him, and rile him every hour of the day. That ain't in reason."

He looked round the assembled scouts, as if to gather their views on the matter.

"Git on with it," shouted Steve shortly.

"Them's my views in a nutshell," cried Tom. "No man ain't goin' ter be bullied."

"So I thought," continued Jacob. "And though it war evenin', and dark to be expected precious soon, I jest give the boss back some of the lip he'd been throwin' at me, and at the same time told him I war quittin'. We squared up the wages right off, and then I climbed into my saddle and rid away from the farm. I war mighty angry and hot."

"And likely as not didn't take no partic'lar direction," sang out one of the listeners.

"Ye've got it right and early. I was that mad with the boss I jest kicked the flanks of my hoss and rid right off like a whirlwind. But a man finds a gallop across the grass kinder clears his brain, and takes the anger out of him. I soon got to rememberin' that I hadn't touched a crust sense breakfast, and that war early with the sun risin'.

"Ye're a fool, Jacob," I says to myself. "Ye've rid off hot and hasty, like a child, and now ye've got ter suffer. Whar's best to go?"

"The hoss could tell yer," cried Tom.

"Right agin!" agreed Jacob. "That hoss knew better than me whar I was likely to find food. I've seed the same thing many a time out on the plains. Ef a man's lost, and don't know from Adam whar he aer, it's better to give a free rein and leave it to the mount. Suppose he scents somethin'. Anyway he generally knows whar he's likely to get a feed for himself and a drop of water. I jest give my critter his head, and somewhar's about eleven that night we come to a shanty with a wooden stockade right round it."

"Same as settlers has in an Injun country," remarked Steve.

"The very same, and seems they need them 'ere stockades. Wall, thar the shanty was, outlined clear in the light, lookin' that peaceful yer wouldn't ha' thought a fly could ha' come to harm. But I hadn't got within seventy yards when thar was a flash from the house, high up under the roof, and then a loud report."

"Injuns in already," ventured one of Jacob's companions.

"Wrong, fer sure," growled Steve. "Ef Injuns had been thar, they'd have burned the place within a few minutes. A white's house aer pison to an Injun. It makes him fair mad. He can't keep his hands off it, nor fire away from the roofin'."

"That comes of havin' Injun experience," said Jacob, resuming, and sending a nod in Steve's direction. "It warn't Injuns. All the same, when thar's bullets flyin', reckon one don't sit still thinkin'. I was off my hoss in a jiffy, gettin' cover under the stockade. Then I put my hands to my mouth and sent the folks in the house, whoever they might be, the shout we was used to give in them parts. Heard it?"

He did not wait for an answer, but put his hands at once to his lips, and sent forth a halloo which awoke the echoes.

"Thar ain't no mistake about a call like that," said Jacob, decision in his tones, "and the folks in that shanty couldn't help but know that it was a white man outside, one as was friendly."

"And so the shootin' stopped," suggested Tom.

"Wrong. A bit of a bullet kicked a stone at my feet and sent me howlin'. Reckon a flint can hurt most same as a bullet. Anyway, that 'ere stone give me a blow that staggered me. And after it half a dozen shots rang out from the shanty."

"What in thunder did it all mean?" asked one of the men.

"And then there was a shout, an answerin' shout."

"Yes," said Steve, edging a trifle closer, "an answerin' shout."

"A woman's shout. A shrill sort of a scream. A thing you couldn't call a shout, but there ain't no other name as I knows of."

Jacob looked round at his audience questioningly, while each one of the party wore a different expression on his face.

"Reckon you was wishin' you hadn't row'd with the boss," grinned Tom.

"P'raps you had fallen asleep on your hoss," cried Seth, "and was sorter dreamin'."

135

Jacob snorted with indignation. "As ef that war likely," he cried. "Didn't I say as I howled with pain when the flint struck me? No. You're guessin'. The shanty war there, standin' black in the moonlight, and them shouts were real. They were shrill, and come from a woman. They kind of scared me fer a minute."

"Yer bolted again?" asked Steve.

"I jest hooked the reins over the corner of a post standin' outside the stockade, and clambered over."

"More bullets," suggested one of the men.

"Shots, yes, but not in my direction. Thar was shoutin', a man's and a woman's, and then shootin'. Then the door of the shanty war opened and I ran in."

Jacob stopped for a moment at the most critical point in his narrative, causing all his comrades to sit up expectantly.

"Wall?" demanded Tom irritably, stuffing his pipe with his finger.

"It was Injuns," asserted one of the men. "Yer was taken by a bit of foolin'."

"It warn't," answered Jacob shortly and curtly. "It war a madman."

"A madman! A madman!" The words were bandied from one to another. The listeners looked askance at one another, for madness out on the plains was in those days exceptional, and in nearly every case ended in a terrible tragedy.

"Man or woman?" asked Seth. "Seems either's likely."

"It war the man," said Jacob slowly. "It war the man, a white man, same as you and me. Seems he'd gone suddenly crazy at sight of me, and set to at shootin'. It war his wife's voice I'd heard, her's and her two boys. When I got in to the sorter parlour place in the centre of the shanty, thar she war, with the two young 'uns, holdin' on to the man fer their lives."

"Gee, that war strange!" muttered Steve. "P'raps something outer the ordinary had scared him."

"Or he'd been thinkin' so long about Injuns, and likely attacks, that the thing had kind of got on his mind and unhinged it. I've heard tell of a similar thing afore. A man gets fidgety, specially ef he ain't used to Injuns and the plains, and ain't been brought up to the life. His nerves git shook up, and one fine day, when there ain't no real danger, he takes his own shadow for an enemy, and blazes off with his gun. Often enough it's someone he's most fond of that he shoots."

Tom delivered himself of the statement calmly and slowly. Then he carefully refilled his pipe, while his comrades looked round at one another. Jacob, the slow, ponderous Jacob, who so seldom launched into a tale, had provided the camp with a subject, a riddle, and all struggled to come to a solution.

"It war that, or near it," agreed Tricky Seth.

"Or he'd been ill, and was jumpin' mad in his delirium," suggested another.

"I dunno as you're right or wrong," came slowly from Jacob. "Reckon he war ill, ill with grief and anxiety, and reckon his nerves was fair shook up. He war mad, stark, starin' crazy without a doubt, and we had to make him fast so as he shouldn't do anyone a mischief."

"Yer ain't told us why," cried one of the men. "What had come along to upset this here man so? Somethin' outer the ordinary."

"Yer kin guess so. It war somethin' outer the ordinary, and sense I started this here yarn by sayin' that I knew of a time when we'd given the critters real pepper, you can 'low as it war Injuns as war the cause. Injuns had come along and upset this man till he was worried clean off his head. Now I'll tell yer how it happened. Allen Rivers war a new settler out in them parts, a brave man fer all his madness. He'd been warned time and agin to beware of the Injuns, specially of Hawk Eye, a critter that was chief of a tribe huntin' in that neighbourhood. And yer must understand that although trouble with the redskins war as a general thing to be expected, yet thar war times when powder and lead and sichlike articles was runnin' short in the wigwams, and the critters had need to come in to the white man's settlements and be friendly. Allen Rivers had set up a sorter store. He'd had visits from the Injuns, and he'd done smart business with Hawk Eye. The chief had been that smilin' that Allen had taken him into the stockade, and once into the house, and the Injun had been able to get a good look round. Wall, Allen had two boys—the youngsters that met me on the doorstep—twelve and fourteen years of age, and proper plucked 'uns too; thar war his wife, as brave a woman as you could meet in a week's march, and besides them three, a baby, a gal. Wall, now——"

Jacob coughed. He was one of those slow men who take a deal of rousing, and who seldom indulge in a yarn, but, when once induced to speak, do so at their own pace and leisure. The burly scout was exasperatingly slow in his utterance.

"Ye've got to the pith of it," sang out Steve. "Thar war a baby."

"Thar war. A baby gal, and Injuns has a strange sorter likin' fer baby gals as is the children of white people. They thinks they bring 'em good luck; and it seemed as Hawk Eye's own wife hadn't got no children. No doubt the chief got to tellin' her of Allen Rivers's shanty, of his wife and kids, and set her wishin' fer the gal. Anyway, Hawk Eye had done trade with Allen jest two days before I come there, and seemed to have ridden back to his own place. But that very mornin' the child was taken, taken from its bark crib, which Mrs. Allen had jest set down outside the door of the shanty. And though every one of 'em searched fer all he could, and though Allen climbed on to his horse and rid round and round, thar warn't a trace of the kid, not a trace. But one of the boys picked up a feather, and then they knew as it war Hawk Eye and his people that had done it."

"I've knowed a similar thing," said Steve, interrupting. "Them critters looks upon a white kid as likely to bring 'em victory in their fightin', and fortune in their huntin'. You aer made no error. Push on with it, Jacob."

"Allen guessed that ef they'd taken the kid they might be up to more mischief, and, bein' a nervous, jerky sort of feller, blest ef he didn't go off his head. That's whar we get to when I arrived. Allen warn't no more good. He war, instead, a worry. Thar war me and the two boys and Mrs. Rivers."

"With Injuns round about?"

"With the critters on the far side of the stockade," agreed Jacob. "Seems I had missed 'em by a chance. I was jest a quarter of an hour too early for 'em. But I hadn't been in the shanty more'n a few minutes, and had made Allen fast, when I seed a figure clamberin' over the gate of the stockade. Remember, it war a bright night, same as this, and dead agin the Injun's chances. But they reckoned to take the place easy, and wasn't over cautious."

"Yer give that feller pepper?" asked Seth.

Jacob nodded. "I dropped him same as a bird, and that set 'em howlin'. The shot took 'em all by surprise. They looked to have the gate of the stockade open and to be in the shanty afore Allen and his wife war properly awake. The critters set up a howl that was enough to scare one, and then three of 'em came clamberin' after the man I'd shot.

"'Jest get to them other windows, boys,' I sang out; fer there were loopholes in the corners of the shutters on all four sides of the shanty. 'Shoot down any man as yer kin see, and ef ye're bothered, jest sing out. I'll be with yer in a jiffy.'

"Countin' Mrs. Rivers thar was just four of us, and for ten minutes we was kept precious busy. But them lads could shoot, and their mother like 'em, so that, presently, the critters crept off from the stockade, leavin' seven of their braves chewin' the grass inside. Yer see, they'd stood out clear and easy as they climbed, and, the range bein' a short one, thar warn't no missin'.

"'Gone?' asks Mrs. Rivers, when there wasn't no more of 'em to be seen.

"'Don't yer believe it, ma'am,' I answered. 'Thim critters has got their eyes on the goods in this store, and fer that reason they ain't likely to give up the business. And now there's those braves down thar. We've killed seven of 'em, and the others won't dare to go back to their wigwams with sich a tale, and with nary a scalp to show. They're bound to come agin, and we've got to look precious lively. Thar ain't no sayin' whar they'll come, but come they will, yer kin take my davy. Ef I wasn't sure that the critters was outside, I'd suggest that one of the youngsters tried to leg it away from the shanty so as to fetch help.

But they're outside, the skunks, and on a night same as this the lad wouldn't stand a ghostly.'

"Wall, mates, we got back to our loopholes, and kept a pretty close watch fer a couple of hours without seein' a sight of them Injuns. But they was thar, close outside. I heard 'em callin' to one another. Then suddenly I cottoned to what the artful critters was doin'. The moon was sinkin', but as bright as ever, and them Injuns reckoned that one of the walls of the stockade was castin' a biggish shadow on the yard inside. They war busy diggin' their way in under it."

There was a murmur from the hunters assembled round the fire.

"Jest like the critters," growled Steve. "I've knowed 'em do the same in similar cases. And the wust of the business aer this: yer kin feel sure as that aer their game, and sense the shadow's deepest in one partic'lar spot, yer kin reckon to a foot or two whar they're diggin'. But yer can't stop the varmint. Ef yer put an eyelid over the stockade, there's a man ready with an arrow, and ef you think to blaze at 'em through the woodwork, why, it aer like loosin' off a gun into the air. Even ef you hit a man, the others jest lie quiet, so yer don't know what's happened. But maybe one of the critters gets to the hole ye've made in the stockade, and then it's your turn to look out fer bullets."

"Jest so. That's how we war situated," agreed Jacob. "It war one of them tarnation bothers that tries a man's nerves. I'd been in more than one ruction with the redskins afore that day, and I knew somethin' about the critters. It war as clear as daylight that when they war ready they'd let the earth on our side fall in, and then the varmint would come rushin' fer the shanty. It war an almighty fix. It jest made me give up thinkin'. I got lookin' fer the first of them critters to come clamberin' in, and listenin' all the while to Mrs. Rivers prayin'. Then one of them bright lads come out with a suggestion."

"Ah! That's like Carrots," ventured Tom. "'Tain't always the old hand that kin manage a fix of that sort. What war his partic'lar idea? Blest ef I ain't mighty bothered."

"I'll tell yer. It war a case with him of kill or cure, as you'll agree as I get on with the story. And he didn't come straight to me to ask what I thought of the business. Joe war his name, and a kid chuck-full of larnin'. Wall, seems he got rummagin' in the place whar his father stored the stuff he traded with the Injuns, and then slips outer the door.

"'Joe's gone out ter see what he kin do with 'em,' says Hal, his brother, comin' across the shanty to where I was watchin'. 'Jest see you don't shoot him.'

"Yer kin guess I was mighty surprised. 'Gone outside!' I cried. 'Why, they'll shoot him quicker than ever I shall. What for? What's he doin'?'"

"Hal hadn't a notion, and so, seein' as something precious bad might come of it, I slipped out of the shanty to join him. And when I came to the edge of the stockade whar we reckoned the Injuns was diggin', there warn't a doubt that they was there, on the far side of the woodwork, precious near ready to break through and finish the matter. Joe war there, lyin' on his face, and sense I knew they'd hear me ef I even whispered, I laid down beside him and learned what he was doin'. He was diggin' fast with his fingers, tearin' the turf and soil away bit by bit, and makin' not so much as a sound to give the enemy a warnin'. Within four feet of him, perhaps, there was Injuns workin' at the same game, cuttin' the earth away with their knives and tomahawks, and ef I was asked to guess their true position, I should say as they were closer even than that, and in a little while would be carving their way into the hole which Joe war making.

"Two foot ahead of Joe there war a dark object, and when I crept across to feel around it, and see what it was, you kin guess I jest started. It war a powder keg, same as we carry, already opened, and ready for firin'."

There was excitement now on the faces of the men gathered round the camp fire. Excitement and some curiosity. For difficulty and danger were everyday affairs to these scouts, and a tale which demonstrated the cunning of the Indians, and the bravery and resource of those who were opposed to this deadly enemy, was always sure of an attentive hearing. Tom drew in a deep breath, while Steve grunted.

"Powder," he said, as if he were thinking deeply. "That war a kill-or-cure remedy sure! Seems to me that ef you could be sartin of gettin' the hull crowd of the Injuns close together, yer might kill a heap and scare the rest so badly as to make 'em ride away. But ef yer failed, why, it stands to reason yer would blow a hole through your stockade big enough to allow a hull tribe of the critters to pass, and might jest as well be askin' fer a funeral. Get along, Jacob. Yer make a man want to be tellin' the story hisself, instead of waitin' fer you."

"It war a case of kill or cure," agreed the burly scout, ignoring Steve's remarks, "but Joe warn't the boy to spoil his plan for a bit of waitin'. He finished that hole while I lay thar, and popped in his keg extry careful. Then he rammed the earth round it with his fists, laid his fuse, and sat listenin'.

"'We'll wait till one of them strikes the keg with his knife,' he whispered, fer the Injuns happened to be making a tidy heap of noise, and so there warn't no fear of their hearin'. 'That'll be the time ter fire it.'

"And jest yer remember to lie as flat as yer kin when yer put down the match,' I answered. 'The explosion of that powder will smash the stockade to pieces, and I ain't so sure as it won't wreck the shanty.'

"Wall, to come to the end of it, Joe waited there listenin' like a terrier till there war the sharp click of a knife falling on the keg, and a grunt from one of the Indians. That war enough for us. Joe and I crept away from the place as quickly as we could, yer may guess, and lay down agin at the far end of the trail, which was jest outside the shanty. Then Joe lifted his pistol, laid the muzzle along the train, and drew his trigger as steady as if he warn't shootin' nothin' in partic'lar. Them critters was smashed to pieces. That is, eight or nine of them was killed by the explosion."

A chorus of exclamations came from the assembled hunters. There was a sparkle about their eyes which showed that they had listened to the narrative with more than usual attention.

"Gee! That war a brave kid!" cried Seth. "A right down plucked 'un! What happened? The hull stockade war blown to matchwood, one would guess, and perhaps the shanty with it? Git on! Fer a slow 'un ye're as bad as any I've ever met."

Jacob grinned. He was slow, and he knew it. At the same time he was far too cool and burly an individual to be intimidated.

"I never was a hustler," he said, "and I'm too old now to begin. Ef Seth, thar, Tricky Seth, as he's ginerally known, aer in a hurry, why, I'll quit talkin', and he kin take the field. I'm always game to listen."

"Get in at it, Jacob, man!" shouted Tom, shaking his fist at the hunter. "That 'ere kid fired the trail with his pistol, and the keg of powder blew the Injun varmint to pieces. Wall—"

"Wall, someone's asked about the stockade. It war broke into tiny pieces. Joe and me was hoisted pretty nigh on to the roof of the shanty, while the door of the place was shook clear off its hinges. Old man Rivers, as was as mad as any hatter a minute before, was blowed back to his proper senses. Leastwise, all I knows is that he was crazy afore the explosion, and afterwards, when me and young Joe had picked ourselves up, and had kinder cleared the dust and dirt away—fer we was properly covered—Allen war smilin' all over, and talkin' to his wife as ef he hadn't never been mad. And warn't he proud of that ere kid!"

"What about the Injuns?" demanded one of the listeners eagerly; for, after all, the whole point in the narrative depended upon them. Scouts, one and all, could appreciate a gallant if desperate action, fer they were brave men themselves; but their interest, once the tale of daring and courage on the part of their own race was told, was centred in the common enemy, the Red Indian warrior, the fierce man of the plains who had waged such ceaseless warfare with the white invaders of his hunting-grounds, who had caused them such cruel losses, and who, because of his terrible cruelty—because he killed not men alone, but women and children—was detested by hunters and prospectors throughout the country. It was the attackers Seth and his comrades longed to hear about.

"They was blowed to pieces," said Steve. "Wall, what become of the rest? There was more than eight or nine of the varmint."

"There was fifty, as we reckoned," said Jacob solemnly, "and they was scared pretty nigh outer their lives. Hawk Eye, him that had caused the whole ruction, rid off as ef there was powder kegs exploding under his horse's heels all the way; and reckon they got back to the wigwams fewer than when they left, and with a yarn to give that would make the squaws howl at 'em. They was beat, mates, badly beat, and a slip of a boy did it. Old man Rivers had come back to his senses properly, and guess he set to at once to rig up his stockade again, and make all ready against another attack. And ef he was a wise man—and I heard tell as his madness didn't ever occur agin—he never afterwards made the mistake of lettin' a red-skinned varmint look into his store. Them critters is never to be trusted. Ef they find ye're rich, ye've kinder asked them to come in the first time thar's an opportunity, and take yer scalp and everything that's yours. Keep the varmint at arm's length is my motto; or, better still, keep 'em always well ahead of your gun, and see as ye've powder and ball handy."

The burly hunter subsided into silence, reached for the pannikin, and poured himself out a helping of spirit. He filled up with water, tossed his head back into characteristic position, and again the gurgle of fluid was heard. For scouts were rough men; their manners were not of the nicest.

As for his listeners, they began a very animated discussion as to the merits of the yarn just narrated, and the incident of which Jacob had been a witness recalled many another incident, totally unlike that recorded by him, but nevertheless showing the courage and resource of the white man and the determination of the common enemy. Then Steve imposed silence upon the group by stirring the fire vigorously with his boot and causing the sparks to fly upwards.

"Mates," he said in his dry-as-dust style, "mates, this here Jacob ha' given us a yarn that kinder stirs a man, and we aer glad to hear as he had a hand in beatin' them varmint. He was caught in a muss, so to say, and, seein' he had rowed with his boss, and got lost on the plains, why, seems he had hisself to blame. Still, ef he hadn't arrived at old man Rivers's shanty, them critters would ha' broke in, fer Jacob shot down the first as climbed the stockade. He came out of the muss nicely, and now that he ha' told us, he has gone silent agin, same as he is generally. But he ain't finished, not by a bit."

All looked across at the burly hunter. Jacob was filling his pipe in a dogged sort of manner, and scowled at Steve as he finished speaking.

"Thar ain't no more," he growled; "leastwise, none that I'm goin' ter tell. Besides, it's husky work talkin'. I've finished. Reckon it's time we took to our blankets."

"Yer ain't said never a word about that 'ere kid that Hawk Eye stole from the Rivers's," accused Steve, pointing a finger at Jacob.

"And I ain't goin' ter," came the short, sturdy answer. "I've done talkin' fer the night. Time we was turnin' in."

There was a scowl on his face, and something more. The big scout, usually so stolid and so transparently straightforward, looked confused and almost ashamed of himself. He made a grimace at Steve, and commenced to rise from his seat. But Tom put a heavy hand on his shoulder.

"Steve aer the lad fer spottin' things," he laughed. "Let's have the rest of the yarn."

"I ain't goin' ter talk no more," came the surly answer.

"Then I'll give the yarn, mates."

It was Bill Huskins who spoke, "Black Bill", as he was known, because of his dark complexion. He was short and wiry, like Steve, a merry enough fellow, but given to taciturnity and silence, as was customary with scouts. He grinned across at Jacob, ignored his threatening gestures, and then put himself into a position of ease, as if determined to tell his tale, whatever happened.

"I war along with that 'ere boss as had the words with Jacob," he announced, "and seein' as Jacob thar', ain't able ter speak, why, I'll get in with the yarn. Thar's more to tell. A hull heap more. That 'ere kid was took right off to Hawk Eye's wigwams, and it stands to reason white folks wasn't goin' ter sit down and put up with sich a thing. 'Sides, Mrs. Rivers swore as she'd ride there all alone herself, ef there wasn't a man ter do it. So in course we went, and here's what happened."

CHAPTER XVI

The Bashful Jacob

It was useless for the burly Jacob to frown and scowl, and shake a threatening fist at Black Bill. The latter took not the slightest notice, save that the reflection from the camp fire, falling upon his dusky features, showed a certain twinkling of the eye which was somewhat unusual.

"You, Bill Huskins, yer ain't no friend of mine ef yer get to talkin'," growled Jacob at last, seeing that grimaces made no difference, and had no effect upon his comrade. "I gives yer fair warnin' that that tale ain't to be repeated. These here mates of ours ain't got no interest in it. 'Sides, it's time we war in our blankets."

"I dunno," exclaimed Tom warmly, holding his fingers to the blaze. "I dunno so much about that, Jacob. There's men here as would be glad to listen. It might come to you or ter me ter marry one of these here days, and then ef a kid of ours was snatched by the red-skinned varmint, we'd get to and remember a yarn, and maybe find something in it to help us. Jest you sit still and chew a plug of 'bacca. Bill, fire away. It aer only Jacob's 'tarnal bashfulness."

"My, you should ha' seen him when he rid up with young Joe Rivers beside him," said Bill, nothing loath to tell the story, and grinning widely at the irate Jacob. "Jest put yerselves in his place fer a few seconds. Here was Jacob, not so old as he aer now by a goodish bit, riding back to join an outfit he'd left jest a few hours afore, and left too with words hot and fiery agin the boss. There's only two ways of lookin' at a thing like that. It aer right down cheek, or it aer murder that brings a man back. I've seen men as was fired from an outfit, and went away peaceful. But they got to thinkin' that they war injured. They sat broodin' over the matter, till their danders was properly up, and then they rode back to face that 'ere boss and have it out with him. Guess it looked as ef Jacob thar had rid back fer a ruction, and old man Staples as was our boss must have thought the same. Any way, he sees Jacob comin', and then gets his hand down close to his shooter. I war ridin' in from the opposite direction, and when I caught a sight of Jacob, I slipped outer my saddle and got round the end of the shanty. Bullets gets flyin' on sich an occasion, and a man ain't no use when he gets in their way. He can't easily stop 'em. They has a way of layin' him out."

There was a chorus of approval from the assembled hunters, and even Jacob gave a nod. Indeed, his growling and his grimaces had all been a part of his dissembling. To the looker-on it seemed that there must be something about this part of the yarn with which he disagreed, something perhaps likely to lead to his own embarrassment. But he could enjoy the recollection of his action with regard to the boss with whom he had exchanged heated words.

"It war cheek," he agreed. "Gee! Now that I comes to think of it, he'd have been in the right ef he had shot me down without a word and without waitin'."

"He wasn't sich a bad feller," continued Bill. "Old man Staples had a softish heart under as rough a skin as ever I saw. He dropped his hand to the butt of his gun, as I've said already, and kinder worked his way along till he stood behind one of the big corner posts of the stockade. Then he took a close look at Jacob and at the boy. Yer should ha' seen our mate over thar. He climbs outer his saddle extry slow. Guess he was wonderin' how he was to get to at the matter. Then he walked straight up to Staples.

"'Yer ain't got no cause to fear me, boss,' he says. 'I ain't here to quarrel. As man to man I tell you that you're over rough with your tongue, and that there's few but blacks that could stand it. I'm here to ask fer help.'

"That took Staples' breath away. 'Help!' he calls out, as ef he was puzzled. 'A few hours ago you rid away as hot as anything, and then I was the last man, according to your own words, that you'd come to for anything in the way of help. What's it mean?'

"'It isn't fer me I want it,' says Jacob. 'It's fer the kid's mother and father.'

"Wall, when the matter were put before old man Staples and the boys, yer may reckon there wasn't much jawin'."

Bill looked round the circle, and there came an emphatic nod from each of the men.

"I'll give 'em all due credit," admitted Jacob warmly. "Old man Staples and every one of the outfit was hot to get to at Hawk Eye. Yer don't have to ask hunters and cattlemen twice when thar's a rescue to be tried, specially when it's a kid that's been taken, and the Injun critters has something ter do with the matter. Reckon the chance of a fight with them varmint would draw any man from the ranches."

"'Yer kin count on every man jack of us,' sings out Staples; 'and, Jacob, you and I'll agree to be friends fer the time being. Shake hands,'" continued Bill. "'Thar's seventeen of us here, and we'll call in at Romney's ranch on the way across to Rivers's shanty, and pick up his crowd. He's sure to have some twenty to thirty, so we'll be nearly fifty when we're ready. Now, boys, get to and pack grub and ammunition. We'll be off in ten minutes.'"

"It war quick work, mates," said Bill, looking round for the approval of his fellows. "But men of an outfit same as that aer pretty nigh always ready fer something. Thar was enough dried flesh in the camp to feed fifty men fer more than a week, and of course we had heaps of powder and lead. Men don't take to ranching in an Indian country onless they have good guns, and plenty of the proper stuff to put in 'em. And so, within a quarter of an hour we war ridin' away, nineteen of us in all, counting Jacob and Joe, and with our mate thar and the boss he'd rowed with so lately riding ahead, chattin' as ef thar'd never been a word between them. That's how chaps of our sort act when thar's trouble in the air, and someone is askin' fer help."

The dark-featured scout looked into the fire for a while, and took a breathing spell, while his mates nodded their approval. They knew thoroughly well the truth of Bill's statement. Out on the wide plains of America men quarrelled just as they did in the cities. Indeed their quarrels were rather more frequent than amongst men working under different surroundings, and often enough resulted in severe wounding, or in the death of one of the contestants. But they could and did sink the most pressing personal quarrels when duty called, and to these rough men, inured to every sort of hardship, there was no duty that appealed so forcibly as one where the rescue of a fellow white was concerned. A woman sought for their help. That in itself was sufficient. That call was so strong that there was not a man in the plains who could ignore it, and not one, who, if he were coward enough to be deaf to such a call, could continue to live in friendship with the hunters and cattlemen. He would be branded as a craven, and forced to ride from the country. Remember, in considering this, that these hunters of whom we write were the descendants of men who had fought for and won America, and that their sons to-day form a part of that nation which is the wonder and envy of the world.

"At Romneys we was extry lucky," said Bill. "It happened that he'd fitted out a big outfit, and there war thirty-three men, counting Romney himself and one son. At Rivers's shanty we picked up the other boy, leaving Allen hisself to ride back ter Romney's with his wife, for it warn't safe for them to remain behind in a ruined stockade. Then we set to ter follow Hawk Eye, and Jacob thar warn't long in lickin' up the trace. My, this talkin' do tell on a feller. Just get to at it fer a bit, Jacob boy. Yer ain't no need ter fear. I'll take on agin when ye've got right into the business."

It was a clever manœuvre on Bill's part. As he was telling his yarn he had kept an eye on the burly scout, and noticed, with a grin of delight, that Jacob could not restrain his own interest. Indeed it was only natural that the narration of deeds which he had himself helped to carry out should rouse any hunter, nor was it wonderful that Jacob, forgetting his former behaviour, and surliness, should at once comply with Bill's request.

"He's put it right, yer may take it, mates," he said in his slow manner. "It warn't long afore we dropped on Hawk Eye's traces, and then we set out to follow slowly. In a general sorter way we knew that the varmint had his camp thirty miles west of Rivers's shanty, but, in course, he war often moving. An Injun don't stay long in one country. As soon as beasts begin to get few he moves, onless thar's other attractions."

"Sich as scalps," interrupted Steve.

"Or men and women to be murdered without a chance of gettin' hurt yourself," added Jacob bitterly. "That's what makes us chaps hate them critters wuss than pisen. Ef they fought us alone, and with all their cunning, we shouldn't want ter grumble, 'cos all's square and fair in this sorter warfare; but when they gits to killing women and children, then it makes a man's blood boil. I reckon it aer bound to be warfare between white and red man to the bitter end, till the red varmint aer cleared outer existence. Wall, I was sayin', we picked up Hawk Eye's trace, and rid after him easy. Fer we knew he'd have moved. It stood to reason that he would expect ter be followed, fer wheniver thim critters has stolen a child before, us hunters and scouts has never rested. It ain't likely neither."

"It ain't, yer bet," came emphatically from Tom. "The bosses on the ranches has a hard time ter get men when thar's sich a case. A chap kin camp out on the plains with his mates, and spend not a dollar. He don't need ter work fer a time, and kin shoot all his food. So, when them Injuns has done a thing same as this, the boys give up work. They settle down to life in the open, and they turn to huntin' the critters till they're wiped out. Git on with it."

Jacob glared at Tom. He realized that he was slow, but here was an excuse. Tom had deliberately interrupted him.

"He warn't thar when we came to his camp," he said deliberately. "And his ashes was stone cold, showing that the squaws had stamped them out the instant he arrived back. They may have left at once, thar warn't no sayin', sence the ashes war cold. But me and old man Staples put our heads together, and come to the conclusion that they hadn't hustled. Yer see, Hawk Eye had rid thirty miles hard, and his hosses must have been done. Then it takes a time to pack up an Injun village. Them critters don't leave their squaws and children behind, same as we would ef we was fightin' against white people. They know that their own red brothers would slaughter the lot ef the fighting happened to be against them. And they ain't never given us whites a chance to show what we're made of. They can't believe that we would leave women and children alone, and even feed them ef need be. Howsomever, he warn't there, so the next business was to find out whar he'd gone to."

"Yer may put it down fer sure it's the mountains," said Staples, who'd seen a heap of Injun fightin'. "Thar's other red tribes up thar in the gullies, and ef Hawk Eye can set up a friendship with them, or make 'em believe that we're comin' to attack the hull lot, then in course we have got a precious lot of work before us. What do you say?"

"I said I was with him. But we couldn't afford ter make a mistake, and so we divided, thirty of us ridin' slow towards the mountains, while twelve followed Hawk Eye's trail across the prairie. It ran clear from the village away from the mountains."

"It did," interrupted Bill, agreeing emphatically. "I war one of them twelve, and I'll tell yer what happened to us. We rid fifteen miles straight off over the plain till we came ter a river. It war jest a bit of a thing, twenty feet wide, and pretty shallow. On the far side yer could see whar the Injuns had climbed out of the water, fer the grass was all beaten down. Guess they war travelling with all their horses, and the wigwam poles war slung in their usual way, trailing behind. Wall, there war the marks of the poles on the ground. They ran on for a mile, then stopped altogether."

There was a chuckle from more than one of the scouts. The trick played by the Indians was so simple that none of them could possibly have been taken in. Each one knew that it was an old Indian custom, when travelling, to sling the wigwam poles to the horses, letting the ends trail on the ground behind, and loading their belongings, including their women and children, on the poles, converting them, in fact, into a species of wheelless cart.

"They jest hooked up the poles, turned, and came back to the river in course," said Tom with a significant look.

"They did that. The hull crowd of the critters rid their horses fer five miles up the stream. Then they took to the grass again, and their trail cut clear up fer the mountains. We didn't need to follow too closely. We knew that Jacob and his crowd would hit upon the tracks higher up, and, sure enough, when we come up with 'em that evenin' they was camped beside the trace. Next day we rid on up a gully, still followin' the tracks, and that second evenin' hit upon the spot Hawk Eye had chosen. He war an artful cuss. Ef ever thar war one, it war him. He warn't cornered, don't yer think it. But he war thar, almost within shoutin' distance. Now, Jacob, yer kin come in agin."

"Yer kin guess whar they was," said the latter shortly. "Hawk Eye and his women and children had taken to a cliff that was as steep as a wall, and higher than any yer ever saw. He knew, in course, that we would follow, though, accordin' to his nature, he'd played every sort of cunning trick to throw us off the trace. And when we got thar, he sat up on the face of his cliff grinnin' at us. Guess he thought he war dead safe. Along with him he had his women and children—the hull tribe, in fact. Yer could jest see the tips of their wigwams laid out back of a flat place near the top of the cliff. Above them thar was jest red rock, with a broken edge at the top. But don't get thinkin' we could come at them from that direction. There was a hull crowd of the critters on the sky line, letting us take a square look, jest to kind of remind us that they war ready in case we war inclined ter do a bit of climbing ourselves."

"It war a tarnation tough job, it war," admitted Jacob, scrubbing his bristly chin with the back of a hand which was huge, to say the least of it, and burned, by the sun and exposure, to a dirty-brown colour.

"Yer was beat fer the moment, so to say," suggested Steve, stirring himself and stretching his legs. "But yer wasn't fer givin' in."

"We warn't," came stolidly from Jacob. "It stands to reason we wasn't goin' back to the ranches with the kid still in the Hawk Eye's wigwams. We'd kinder sworn to get done with the job, and in course we war fer stayin'. But there warn't a single sarcumstance as seemed likely to help us. Yer could look round that 'ere gully, and thar you was same as before. Jest the plains runnin' away from under your feet right out into the open, a bit of a rocky hill to the right standin' all alone, and then the cliff, the face of a mighty big mountain. Yer might say as we could ha' ridden round, mounted from the far side, and then come along ter the Injun camp. But Hawk Eye knew what he was doin'.

"Thar ain't no use thinkin' of the far side,' said old man Staples when we asked him. 'It's too rough fer hosses, and if we was to go afoot we should be dropped upon by other tribes of the varmint. That 'ere Hawk Eye climbed up that cliff. That's what we've got to do, so the sooner we sets to work to find the path he followed the nearer we aer ter rescuing the kid.'

"Wall, it war a teaser, and no mistake. Yer couldn't get near enough to Hawk Eye's post to take a clear look but yer was fired at by his critters, and, sence they had guns in plenty, it war precious warm work, so warm that old man Staples called us off.

"'Best form a camp and get to watchin' the varmint,' he said. 'My idea is that we take up a post on this here hill. It'll show Hawk Eye that we ain't fer leavin', and I've a sorter notion that when we git higher we shall have a chance of seein' more, and perhaps of gettin' a sight of the path used by the Indians.'

"It war sound advice, and in course we followed it. We rid our hosses to the hill that stood all alone by itself, within five hundred yards of the cliff, and then me and Bill thar was sent ahead to locate a path easy fer the hosses. We found it after a goodish bit, and went up. It was steep, in course, too steep fer hosses as a general rule. But them critters we rode out on the ranches was as clever as cats, and hills didn't frighten 'em. This one war a goodish deal higher than ye'd have thought, lookin' at it from below; and when we war on top thar was Hawk Eye's camp as plain as possible. Thar was grass, too, fer our hosses, and a spring throwing water into a hollow, from which it trickled down the side of the hill.

"'Jest the likeliest place that ever was,' says Bill thar. 'I'll go down and call up the others.'

"It war nigh sundown before we was all located in the camp, and in course we warn't able to eat and smoke and sleep as ef we war in a friendly country. There ain't never no knowing what an Injun'll be up to, and so old man Staples war right when he posted ten of us as a lookout, with ten more to relieve in two hours' time, and so on, through the night. As to Hawk Eye, he and his critters didn't seem to take no notice of our movements. They let their fires die down soon after sunset, and then thar warn't a sound from 'em. But they wasn't sleepin'."

"Yer bet!" came sharply from Tom. "I've lived in this here country, man and boy, and most times thar's been Injuns around. Wall, it aer pretty near always war to the knife between them and whites. It ain't that we don't want ter live peaceful with them. We do. But they can't kinder see a white man anywhar but they want to take his scalp. Seems we're nateral enemies. Anyway, I guess that that 'ere Hawk Eye and his braves wasn't fer bein' so quiet and harmless as they seemed. We ain't forgot that Joe, with Jacob to help him, had blowed some ten of them to pieces. Yer ain't goin' ter kid me that Injuns could forgit or forgive that."

There was an exclamation from most of the scouts. It was an obvious point to them, one and all. Their close acquaintance with Indians and their methods told them, without shadow of doubt, that Hawk Eye would neither forgive nor forget the injury he had suffered, but would strive to the utmost of his power to retaliate.

"They was jest laughin' in their sleeves," proceeded Jacob. "Seems that they was hopin' we would camp somewhars near at hand, 'cos Hawk Eye and his braves had been pretty busy. Back away over the top of the mountain thar was a hollow which was big enough ter shelter a hull nation of Injuns, and, ef only we could ha' seen the critters, it war thar that Hawk Eye and his braves was on the night we climbed ter the top of our hill. Thar was a mighty palaver, it seems, and when we woke in the mornin', and the light allowed us to look out, thar was the result of all their talkin'. Thar was three hundred red varmint skirmishin' about round the hill, and Hawk Eye and his men scrambling down their cliff, whilst their womenfolk was dancing a kinder war dance on the top. It war a fair surprise. It jest took our breath away."

"Gee! That war serious," interjected Steve. "Hawk Eye had patched up his quarrels with the other tribes, I suppose, and had persuaded them to come in to wipe the hull party of whites out. Wall, seein' as you and Bill aer here, yer wasn't wiped out. Yer managed to slip between the fingers of the critters. But it war a tight fix. Injuns aer that cunnin', and they never want sleep when thar's a scalp to be taken. Yer was flummoxed, Jacob."

"We war. We got extry silent eatin' breakfast, and jest waited ter see what they would be doin'. But we wasn't going ter be taken easy. Old man Staples war a fine fellow, though I say it, and he soon fixed us up with boulders and tree stumps, so that we had a stockade all round us. Then we set to work to hunt fer likely places where a man could climb, and filled 'em with the biggest boulders we could find.

"'That ain't enough,' said Staples, when we'd done. 'An Injun could crawl over them, and most likely he'd have his knife into one of our boys before he knew it. We'll lay a trap for them.'"

"A trap! A kind of ambush?" asked Seth.

"Ef yer likes ter call it that, yes. Reckon Staples had got the idea from young Joe, and thought he'd give Hawk Eye and his critters a second turn of powder ef they was fools enough ter come and take it. So he sets us ter work jest as dusk war fallin', and right behind each one of the barriers we'd formed on the paths up the side of our hill we dug a hole with our knives, or formed it with rocks. Then we put in a goodish charge of powder—perhaps four handfuls in each hole—for Romney's men had brought along a spare keg. Thar was canes growing on that hill of ours, and it war Bill's idea about the train. We let one of the canes down into the centre of the hole with its charge of powder, and filled in rocks all round, stamping them down. Then it warn't difficult to fill the centre of the canes with powder, and take a train from thar, under cover of leaves, to where it was wanted. Last of all, we fixed a shooter at each place, tied firm ter pegs driven into the ground, and rigged twine across whar the critters was likely to come, fixin' the ends to the triggers of the shooters. It war a proper idea.

"Gee! It war," admitted Steve, his praise unstinted. "I'm jest burnin' to hear what happened. That old man Staples were shrewd."

"He war," admitted Jacob warmly, a fact to be commented on, considering the fact that the two had had a bitter quarrel. "That dodge of his saved us a heap of worryin', 'cos, though we set guards, in course, they hadn't need to be extry careful, for them mines we'd laid was pretty sure to keep out the Injuns."

"They attacked that night?" asked Tom.

"Wrong! They set to and had another palaver. Them critters always makes me think of the time I war a boy, and war sent to the settlement for some eddication. In course I was often rowin' with other boys, same as most lads do. Wall, ef my memory ain't serving me a bad trick, we didn't so often get to with our fists right away at the commencement of the ruction. Thar was ginerally a deal of jawin'. 'Touch-me-agin-and-I'll-knock-yer-down' sort of thing. Then, when our blood was hot enough, we'd set to at one another, and, gee! warn't them scuffles warm!"

Jacob sat back at the recollection, opened an enormous mouth, and laughed—a laugh which was a bellow, and which exposed a set of big strong teeth, blackened by much smoking. A kick from Bill brought him to his senses.

"We ain't talkin' of schools," he reminded Jacob. "Git in at the business. Them critters had a palaver. Gee! Ef you ain't slow enough fer a funeral. It's enough ter make the boys swear."

There was indignation on Jacob's face for the moment. Then his mouth broadened out into another smile. "Yer do git impatient," he said in his sleepy way; "but I ain't fer tantalizing anyone. Them critters had another palaver. Reckon they smoked the pipe of peace between themselves, arranged what was to be done with the scalps they war going to take, and then dug up the hatchet. They was round us as thick as bees on the following morning, and we could see them climbing down from Hawk Eye's camp on the cliff ledge. Then, since it's dead clean up agin Injun nature to begin an attack of that sort without a bit of talking, they sent Hawk Eye and three other chiefs to parley with us.

"'You kin clear out, safe and sound, and without us touchin' a haar of yer heads,' he says, 'so long as yer leave the one as fired that train down at the shanty. We don't want no struggling, so you'll hand over all guns and knives too.'"

There was a giggle from the circle of scouts, and a derisive laugh from Seth.

"My!" he cried gaily, "them varmint do take the white man fer a fool! Yer agreed to them terms, in course?"

"We warn't wantin' to have our scalps raised jest then," came Jacob's slow and satirical reply. "An Injun aer that ontrustworthy that it wouldn't ha' done to take Hawk Eye's word at all. 'Sides, there war Mrs. Rivers. Ef we left the camp and returned to our ranches without the boy, and without the gal as Hawk Eye had stolen, thar was the mother to face; and, I give you my word, thar warn't one of us in that crowd as wouldn't have been dead ashamed ter do so. In course we refused. Old man Staples, as knew the Injuns like a book, answered Hawk Eye with the same sorter blarney.

"'You git right back to yer camp,' he says, 'and bring along the kid. Then, ef she ain't been harmed, and ef all them braves of yours down below has gone off quietly to their wigwams, we'll git back to our homes without hurtin' yer; but, ef thar's been damage done, and ef yer ain't slippy about quittin', we'll make yer feel sorry all your lives that yer was ever born.'

"That war Staples's style of talkin', and it fair tickled the Injuns. It war the sort of thing they'd have said theirselves, and so they could relish it. But it didn't bring them no nearer to our scalps, and, sence sittin' down below wouldn't help neither, they made up their minds to have a turn at the job that very night. Wall, reckon forty of the critters came creepin' up somewhares about half-past two in the early mornin', and you kin guess what happened. One of the parties found our barrier before the others reached the boulders blocking the path they was following. Them strings worked as ef they was part of a machine, and, I tell yer, the sparks flew. The explosion didn't give Hawk Eye and his chiefs any chance of larnin' what had happened, 'cos the critters that came up agin the mine wasn't left to be axed any questions.

"In course it made 'em even more careful, and when another of the mines had exploded, and cleared out a second party, the braves was called back, and them chiefs got to at another palaver. And next mornin' the terms they offered us was a little easier. We could go, so long as we left only our shooters and knives. They'd dropped wantin' the boy, yer see; fer in course it war Joe who had fired the train down at his father's shanty. But Staples let 'em see that we was even more determined than before. 'You kin get back to yer friends,' he says, 'and tell 'em this: We want the gal you stole, and we want a brave and a squaw from each tribe. We'll take good care of them; but they'll be like hostages. Ye'll have 'em back, safe and sound, once we've reached the ranches.'

"That fairly roused the Injuns, mates, and within an hour of Hawk Eye leaving us after the palaver the best part of three hundred of the critters galloped up to the hill, and started climbing it as fast as they was able. And this time the daylight helped them, fer they knew we'd laid mines, and was on the lookout for the strings. Still, one or two of 'em was careless, and got blowed sky high. The rest came on with a rush, and for a time it war warmish. We was bunched together behind our barricades, and, as I said right away at the beginnin' of the yarn, we give them proper pepper. But they was too many, and it soon come to hand-to-hand fightin'. Wall, we beat the critters, and, jest to finish the yarn without more talkin', we got that kid, and took her safe back to the mother. Blow'd if I ain't sleepy. Time we was turned in. Good night, mates, I'm goin'."

The ponderous Jacob showed astonishing celerity. It was the first time that any had seen him rise so quickly under similar circumstances, though, to be sure, the burly fellow could move quickly enough when needed, as he had already proved that day.

"Hold hard, sonny!" cried Tom, detaining him with a firm hand. "That's too short an ending. Yer was surrounded. That's whar we got to. Let's have the rest quietly, and not thrown in all in a hurry."

"I ain't goin' ter say no more. I'm off ter my blanket," came the stolid answer.

"And that's jest whar I come in," cried Bill suddenly. "Yer remember Jacob lad was fer moving earlier on. That's when I began to help him. This time he's clean shut up, so I'll have to take the yarn to the very end. Jacob thar says it war hand-to-hand fightin'. In course, when the business was over, and we had time to take a look round, there was a goodish few of us as had been wounded. Two of our chaps was killed, while I guess we'd laid out thirty of the Injuns. But that ain't all. It war gettin' dusk when them critters was driven off, and you kin guess as it took a while to decide how many of our mates had been hurt, and to tend to those that needed it. It warn't fer half an hour, perhaps, that old man Staples sings out fer Jacob.

"'Whar is the man!' he asks, kind of anxious, fer he seemed to have taken a sudden and violent fancy to him. 'Whar is he?'

"And when we come to search high and low there wasn't a sign of the critter. He war clean gone."

"Gone!" exclaimed one of the men. "Whar? What fer?"

"Ha! That's what I'm a-comin' to," grinned Bill. "It aer that part of the yarn as wild hosses couldn't drag from Jacob. But he has got to hear it. Jest sit right down on him, Tom, and hold him. Gee! Ef his bashfulness don't beat me altogether."

CHAPTER XVII

Black Bill to the Rescue

"You kin fire away as soon as yer like. We've got a hold of him, and ef he kicks we'll show who's strongest."

Tom shouted the words, and at the same time sat himself down heavily beside Jacob, while Seth placed himself on the other side. The manœuvre, coupled with the frowns and grimaces of the stolid hunter, caused a roar of laughter from those assembled round the fire. Black Bill grinned, a grin of huge enjoyment, while Steve increased the hilarity of the proceedings by beckoning to Jack.

"Jest draw yer shooter" he said with a dry smile. "He knows as yer ain't over practised, and ef he sees you fingerin' the trigger pretty close to his head he'll lay quiet, same as he's ordered. Now, the party's ready; yer kin git in at it, mate."

Thus bidden, Bill at once proceeded with his yarn.

"Old Jacob war clean gone," he said, "and no amount of hunting would find him. So we guessed that some of them Injun varmint had collared him and dragged him off in the scrimmage. 'All the same, mates,' said old man Staples, 'we'll be extry careful when we're shootin' to-night. Ef Jacob aer been hauled away he may be able to give 'em the slip before they kin kill him.'

"It war lucky he gave that warning. Somewhares about midnight Jacob thar crawls back into the camp, and precious nigh gets a bullet in him. In course the hull crowd of us was anxious to know why he'd gone, and how he come to be able to git back. But ye've seen fer yerselves what a critter he is fer keepin' his mouth shut when he's axed questions, and blessed ef he'd say a word about his doin's. 'I want a man,' he says, squatting down beside the fire, 'a man as ain't too fond of this life. Who'll come?' Wall, I happened to be right next to him," explained Bill, looking round at the circle of friends apologetically, as if he were mentioning something he had need to be ashamed of. "In course I said I war his man. I warn't over tired of life, and not now, neither, but I kinder wanted to see what he was up to. It war sheer curiosity."

There was a murmur from the scouts, and a general shaking of heads. All knew very well that the words were prompted by Bill's modesty.

"You was like the rest," said Tom deliberately, in a manner there was no correcting. "Every one of them boys was game to go. Yer knew the business was likely ter be warmish, fer Jacob had as good as said so. It warn't curiosity—it war duty. Git on."

Bill would have gladly remonstrated with him. The words were actually on his lips. Then he changed his mind. It was obvious to him that his comrades had already formed their own conclusions.

"Wall, curiosity or not, I war next him, and the fust ter get a chance of speaking. It aer curious; though there war some fifty boys in the crowd, and all had heard Jacob sing out fer a man who wasn't too fond of his life, every man jack of the crowd found he war in that position. They shouted to be his man. They was too late, as I've told yer; fer, sense I war the first ter offer, in course I was the one ter go.

"'We'll take knives and shooters, and enough grub ter last us a couple of days,' says Jacob, when the shouting was done with; 'and then we'll wait for them critters ter come along. They'll be here agin by two in the mornin', and when we've let 'em see that we're lively, and askin' for a ruction, why, they'll clear back ter their wigwams. That'll be our time, Bill. We'll move away with them. You, mates, can look to see us back most at any time. All depends on sarcumstances.'

"That was all we could get outer him that night," went on Bill. "He jest sat silent, eatin' his supper, and thinking. Then he turns into his blanket and sleeps. But at two in the mornin' he war up and lively like the rest, and seems he was right about the Injuns. They came creeping like snakes up the hill, and it warn't till one of our mines went off, and gave the alarm, that we guessed that they were near. Then we took to shooting, and precious soon sent them critters down to the plain agin.

"'Now's our time,' says Jacob. 'Aer yer ready, Bill?'

"'You bet,' I says. 'What thin?'

"'Got yer grub and thet shooter?'

"I jest nodded.

"'Then slip these over yer boots, or, better still, take 'em off and put on these moccasins,' says Jacob, handin' over a pair he'd likely enough taken from one of the Injuns we'd wiped out 'Now. Ready?'

"Wall, thar ain't over much talkin' from Jacob thar, as ye've seen fer yerselves," went on Bill. "But blessed ef I didn't feel inclined ter shake him before very long. Did he talk to our mates afore we left the hill? Not much! Did he open that 'ere huge mouth of his once we was off? Nary a word could I git from him, till I began ter get savage. 'Look ye here, Jacob lad,' I says; 'you and I are pards on this here excursion, and seems to me as things ain't equal. I'm your man, whatever happens, but thar's maybe sarcumstances as I should understand. Yer might get wiped out, and then whar should I be?'

"I could kinder hear the critter grinnin' to hisself in the darkness, some hundred yards from our camp," said Bill, looking round at his audience; "and, I tell yer, I felt jest like kickin' him. But Jacob aer a trifle too big fer me. 'Sides, he owned up as I war in the right.

"'I'll tell yer, curious!' he said, grinnin' still. 'We're off to Hawk Eye's camp, to that ledge whar his wigwams aer pitched, and in course yer don't want to ask fer what we're goin'. Thar's that kid ter be rescued. I axed fer a man as was kinder done with his life, 'cos I didn't see much chance of gettin' outer the business. Still, I've been thar, and got back. Two may do the same.'

"'You?' I asked, under my breath, fer yer must remember we had to be specially quiet. 'You've been up thar on the ledge?'

"Wall, the critter allowed as he had. He'd followed them Injuns out of our stockade after their first attack, had kinder mixed hisself up with them, and had coolly climbed with the varmint up to the ledge. Then he'd laid doggo in some hole he'd come across, had seen all there was ter be seen, and had heard 'em plotting the attack which had jest taken place.

"'What we're up to now,' he says, 'is to climb up thar agin, and wait fer a second business same as to-night. That'll be our time to snatch the kid and come away. In course ye'll be wonderin' why I didn't manage that whilst I war thar. But thar's a critter on guard at the top of the track, and a second down below. I knew I shouldn't have no chance ter get away with the kid with them thar; fer I was bound ter raise a ruction in their camp when I went fer the kid, and by the time I got ter the track those two Injun varmint would have others ter help 'em. So I says to myself that I would git back to our camp, call fer a man as was a man, and then return to the ledge. Even with two the job'll be a skeary one. It ain't likely to be all milk and cream.'"

Bill looked round his listening circle reflectively for a few moments. No doubt he was passing in review those incidents which had occurred now some years ago, and, if the truth were only known, was recalling his own impressions, his own feelings as the risk of the undertaking became plainly apparent to him. His audience regarded him closely with interest, and perhaps a little impatience. Then Tom broke the silence, and gave him encouragement.

"Gee! It war a teaser," he said. "Thar's some men as I've met who would ha' backed out. Jacob thar was kinder asking yer to a funeral."

Bill laughed. "It war ticklish," he admitted. "As ter the funeral a man don't think of them 'ere things when he's warmed up. I was dead keen on gettin' the kid. There warn't no more ter be said, so Jacob led the way fer the cliff. In course there was Injuns about, but it was dark, as I've said, and, 'sides, we'd come away with our blankets, the same sort of thing as used by the Injuns. With them over our heads, and the moccasins on our feet, there wasn't much chance of being spotted. In addition, it began ter rain, and when it rains even an Injun critter likes ter have a covering. So guess they made tracks fer their wigwams, and tried ter sleep off the licking we had given them. Jacob and me found the cliff path, and scrambled up it. It war steep, steeper than a wall in parts, whar they had fixed poles and cross pieces ter help them, sorter ladders, which leaned right out, making yer climb like a fly. But we didn't mind the steepness so long as the enemy wasn't anywhar's about. And after a bit we reached the top. Even thar thar wasn't a critter, fer I guess the rain had driven him in.

"'Them's the wigwams,' says Jacob, pointin' to somethin' that might have been one, or may have been a piece of rock. Anyway, I took his word for it. 'We're right on the edge of the ledge,' he whispers, 'and the hole I located is dead straight back, as dead straight as yer kin go. Jest remember that, ef you have ter make a run for it. Now let's get under cover.'

"It was an old bear hole he'd found," explained Bill, "a deep cleft in the rocks, twistin' and turnin' as it went, and runnin' into the cliff for perhaps fifty feet. Leastwise that's what I guessed by creepin' round and feelin' with my fingers. Jacob jest went in as far as he was able, and then rolled himself in his blanket.

"'Reckon a man don't want to set a watch,' he said. 'Thar's never an Injun as will dare to come in here. Most likely they think it's haunted by a spirit, and, ef not, then thar'll be a bear, though that ain't likely. Take a sleep, Bill, and ter-morrer we'll be fresh and lively.'

"It war a queer place ter rest in, and I don't mind admitting ter you mates here as I was skeared. I couldn't make up my mind ter sleep fer quite a bit, but kept creeping to the opening ter look out. And most times thar was nothing to see. Not a star even, not a sight of the critters as would have torn us bit by bit ter pieces ef they only could ha' known that we was thar. But near to morning the clouds were swept aside, and then one could see the outline of the wigwams, not forty feet from us, with the dead ashes of the fires they had been cookin' at the evening before jest in front of their skin shanties. While not so far away, seeming quite close in that 'ere sorter light, was our camp, on top of the hill, whar our pals lay. Precious little use they could ha' been ter us ef there had been a call. It war skeary work!"

Bill passed his hand across his forehead, as if even the recollection of his daring made him hot, while Steve and his comrades drew in a succession of deep breaths.

"It war the riskiest thing as ever I heard of," said the former slowly and seriously. "I 'low now that any man called upon fer sich a job had a right ter back out. It were downright the darndest bit of foolery as ever I come across. Yer was kinder puttin' yer heads into the open mouth of a hungry lion, and I'm fair surprised to see yer here. It don't seem possible that them critters could ha' missed yer, and yet—wall, I've knowed pretty nigh as wonderful cases," he admitted after a few moments' thought. "Them critters is queer folk. They're superstitious, ef that's the right word fer it, and I've known 'em back away from bear holes, not because they was afeard of the beast, but because they thought they would be meddlin' with some spirit. Gee! I 'low as this here fix war a teaser."

"It war," came from many quarters.

"But this here big lump of a Jacob didn't seem to think nothink of it," proceeded Bill, pointing a condemning finger at the huge scout, whereat the burly fellow flushed a dusky red and fidgeted as if he had cause to feel ashamed. "I war jest jumpin' with nerves when the morning came, and them braves began ter sneak out from their wigwams. It war warm and fine, and there they stood, jest without a move, staring down at our camp on the hill, while their women bustled ter find dry wood, ter light the fires, and ter cook the grub for their masters.

"'It makes yer hungry,' says Jacob thar. 'Jest fetch out that 'ere dried meat of ours, and we'll have a square meal. Them critters ain't fer talkin' till they have had their fill.'

"We sat in that 'ere cave all day long, outer sight of any of the braves, staring at them through a chink that opened on their camp. And it gave me a better idea, so to speak, of their ways of livin' and eatin' and speakin' than ever I had had before, or sence, fer the matter of that. And we warn't long in seeing that they was fairly mad with our pals. They sat thar on the ledge, fifty of the chiefs of the various tribes, chewin' the ends of their pipes, and fairly glarin' sparks at our camp. And one by one the chiefs got up on their hind legs and palavered. One wanted ter get ter work right away, another advised an attack in force that night, a sudden retreat as ef they was scared, and then a return to the business. Hawk Eye war cautious. Yer see, he'd been having a fair gruelling, and he warn't so keen ter be hit harder. 'The white man is strong,' he says, when he gets to his feet, jest as ef we hadn't proved that already, 'but he can be beaten by craft together with force. And when he are beaten, there are his farms, his wives, and his children, all fer our taking.'

"Yer see," commented Bill, "Hawk Eye war an artful critter. He could see as he had let the other tribes into a hot business, and so he told 'em first of all of the things they would gain, not forgetting the scalps. And in course, jest like all Injuns, the very talk of scalps made 'em forget most everything else. Them critters has sich hate fer white men that the mention of one aer like a red rag to 'em. Anyway, they said they were ready to follow him, and he warn't long in coming out with his plan.

"'We are many,' he says, 'and they are few. Yet they are so strongly posted that my brothers are likely to suffer heavily if we attack again. Let us lure them into the open. Consider; what are they here for? To rescue an infant whom we have taken, and whom the squaw, who is my wife, will cling to as if it were her own. They sit yonder on the hill waiting, knowing that the child is here. Let us move from this post. Let us leave a sufficient guard to hold the path to this ledge, and then, as to-morrow morning breaks, we will muster on the plain, with men dressed to appear as squaws, or boys will serve that purpose, with wigwam poles slung, and appearing in every way as if we were leaving this spot for another. Consider now, my brothers, what will happen. It is the child these white men seek. They will follow us, thinking the infant is with us. We will appear to ride away, as if in fear. But once they are far enough from the hill yonder we will turn, and then——'

"I give yer my word," said Bill impressively, "it fairly made a man's blood curdle to hear the grunts them critters give and the way their eyes flashed. In course they was fer Hawk Eye's scheme right away, and for the next few hours they sat talkin' it over, sharpenin' their tomahawks, or simply looking down at our camp, doin' nothing, not movin' so much as an eyelid, same as only Injuns kin do.

"'It aer a case of ter-night or never,' says Jacob, as evening came along. 'That wigwam thar,' and he pointed to the nearest, 'aer Hawk Eye's, and though we ain't never seen the kid, yet it stands ter reason she's thar. We aer got to snatch it once it's really dark, and then one of us has got ter get through. Bill, ye'll take the kid, I'll follow close with my shooter. We may have the luck ter get clear of the ledge without being discovered and afore they've found that the kid's gone. Ef we do, then all depends on her. She may howl. That would be enough ter finish us.'

"Believe it or not, mates, jest before it got too dark ter see, when the light from the fires was beginning to get helpful, a squaw come out of the wigwam that was Hawk Eye's, carryin' a kid. It war the white gal. We was sure then that she was thar. Then the squaw walks up and down a bit, and at last goes back to the wigwam. But she didn't stay in long. In five minutes she war outside, tending the fire burning on the edge of the ledge.

"'It aer the time,' says Jacob. 'Jest sit right here and wait. Ef I'm seen, and thar ain't a chance fer me to get away, I'll chuck the kid ter you; yer can make a run fer it.'

"He war gone afore I knew it, and I seed him creeping along beside the rock. Reckon he reached the wigwam without a soul being the wiser, and after that, jest when I was expecting to hear a hullabaloo, he turns up at my elbow.

"'Here's the kid,' he says. 'Let's be gittin'. Take it, Bill.'

"It warn't the time fer talkin'. Me and Jacob thar gets our blankets over our heads and moves out, the kid kinder tucked under one of my arms. And outside that cleft it war plaguey light. I knew right off that an Injun could see jest then as well almost as he would in broad day, so it wasn't altogether a question of whether the kid made a noise or not. And, in any case, we wasn't long afore we come bang up agin trouble. Thar was a critter standing guard at the top of the path leading down from the ledge."

A series of sounds, almost of groans, came from the scouts. Their sympathy was deeply centred in the fortunes of the two comrades seated with them, and in that of the comrades who were helping them to rescue a child and help a distracted mother.

"There was a critter thar, war there?" growled Tom, kicking the ground. "Yer didn't 'low——"

"I ain't never seed the varmint as could stop me ef I was minded ter move on," declared Bill sturdily, a flush on his dark skin. "I give that 'ere critter what for. He turned as we come up ter him, looked at us close, and then whipped out his tomahawk. Afore he could shout I give him one with my fist full in the face."

"Ah!" There came an exclamation of relief from his mates.

"He didn't stop fallin', I reckon, till he got to the bottom of the cliff, and when he reached ground agin, guess he warn't no more use to Hawk Eye. But he jest made the critters down below extry lively."

"Thar was more down thar then?" asked Steve.

"Thar was a round dozen. They heard us comin', in course, but couldn't rightly say who we was or what had happened. Yer see, their mate might have come by an accident, and fallen from the ledge in the darkness. They wouldn't never have known till we dropped amongst 'em ef it hadn't been fer the kid. She yowled."

Again there came a chorus of growls from the hunters. They realized thoroughly what that meant. If the rescued child called out, the cry would awaken every Indian within hearing, while the chance of Bill and Jacob reaching their friends again was almost destroyed.

"She yowled," repeated Bill solemnly, "while someone up above us on the ledge set to shoutin'. It war a woman's voice, and we knew, in course, that it must be Hawk Eye's squaw. Wall, within the minute the hull lot of the critters was dancing, and we could hear 'em coming down the path above.

"'Git behind me,' says Jacob thar, as ef he war boss of the business. 'When we're a few steps lower, jest feel about with yer feet. Thar's a branch in the road bearin' to the left and leadin' out on to smooth grass. Yer make along it. I'll go by the other, and give yer a start. There it aer. Move.'

"He aer a plaguey feller, he's that short-winded," grumbled Bill. "He jest pushed me and the kid on ter the second path and then went straight on; fer we was near to the bottom of the cliff thar, and the road was nearly level. And then what do yer think he did?"

"Set to at them varmint," suggested Seth fiercely.

"Run back and broke up them that was following," came from another.

"I aer seed his game. Yer git on with it, lad," said Steve. "It war a brave thing. No, Jacob, lad, you ain't got no call ter shake yer fist, and look as ef you'd like ter kill me. It war a brave thing. Ye'd have done it fer nothing, though, ef the kid had given tongue again."

"He would," came warmly from Bill. "Ye've hit it fust time, Steve. Jacob goes down the path, makin' as much clatter with his feet as he war able, and every second or so calling out in a squeaky voice, same as ef he war the kid. And in course it drawed every one of the critters in them parts on ter him. I heard his shooter going in less than a minute. It war warm work while it lasted, and I tell yer it aer luck that he come through alive."

"Luck!" shouted Jacob, suddenly rousing himself and turning upon Bill like a tiger. Indeed it seemed as if he were eager to draw the attention of his comrades from himself to the dark-skinned scout who had been yarning. "It warn't luck," he shouted, pointing at Bill. "It war him—Bill, Black Bill, him as had the kid. Do yer think he did as I told him? He war always a stubborn, stiff-necked sorter feller. He didn't run. He risked the child that we'd waited and watched fer, slings her somehow over his shoulder in his blanket, and comes right back to help me. It warn't luck that made me get off from them critters. It war Bill."

RUNNING A RISK

Had the listeners not been so full of the yarn they would have shouted with laughter; for the two scouts, Bill and Jacob, glared at one another for some few seconds as if they were mortal enemies. Then Bill grinned, kicked the fire vigorously, sending a column of sparks flying into the air, and lay back with an air of resignation.

"Gee, how he do talk!" he cried. "Ter hear Jacob, yer would think as he war telling the yarn. Ef yer don't mind, mate, I'll get through with it. It war luck as saved him. I 'low as I went back to help him, 'cos no partner could slink off and leave a mate ter them red varmint. Thar warn't nothing in it but common duty, same as every man owes ter his mate. With Jacob thar it warn't the same. He'd no call ter take all the risks on his own shoulders. But, howsomever, we was both in the thick of it, them critters coming at us all the while, and me and Jacob hopping from rock to rock, keeping our faces to the braves, and setting our shooters barking at them. Thar was a dozen of the Injuns down thar, and precious soon we thinned their numbers. Then Jacob shouted out fer me ter run with him, and sence it warn't no longer a case of leaving a pal, why, in course I runned."

"Yer got back ter the camp without more fighting?" asked Steve.

"None worth talkin' about," came the short answer. "Thar was critters here and thar, doing their best ter cut us off. But the darkness helped us, and what with that and our shooters we came through ter the bottom of the hill. And thar was Staples, with some of the boys, ter help us. My! You should ha' seen that old man shaking Jacob's hands! Them enemies! Gee! I'd like to see the man as would ha' dared to mention it. They was like brothers."

"And the Indians?" asked one of the hunters. "They tried their little game in the morning? They did their best to draw yer out into the plains?"

"Not they," came quickly from Bill. "They was flummoxed by the loss of the kid. It seemed to have turned their luck. They waited, I reckon, fer the next day."

"And then?"

"We wasn't thar ter help 'em," grinned Bill. "Old man Staples was worth a better trick. We kept our fires going precious late that night, and when everything in and about the Injun camp war quiet, we slipped down the hill and out on ter the plain. It warn't till two hours after dawn as they twigged what had happened, and then every man of them rushed fer the hosses."

"Wall?" asked Steve.

"They wasn't so nigh and handy as Hawk Eye and his men imagined. Jacob aer an artful feller. He and a dozen of the others had rid round the end of the gully where we reckoned the critters kept their ponies. They was so sure that we was kept in our camp on top of the hill that they hadn't put more than ten of the braves to guard them. Reckon Jacob and his mates went in with their shooters, and before you could wink they had them ponies runnin'."

"Then you got back to the ranches?" asked Tom, with something like a sigh of relief.

164

"You may put it like that. Gee, how it did make Jacob thar blush when Mrs. Rivers kissed him fer handing back the kid! Mate, you ain't got no call ter look thunder and wuss at me. This yarn aer true. You was axing, Tom, ef there was more business with thim Injun critters. There war. Hawk Eye and his men war that mad at the trick we'd played 'em that they followed in full strength, and fer a time it war nearly a case with us. Thar was seventy whites in all; fer we had called up the other ranches, while Hawk Eye rode with four hundred Injuns. But some of thim had had a maulin', and we didn't sit down and let 'em forget it. We sent 'em to the rightabout, and though I was four years longer in thim parts, thar was never any further trouble from the varmint."

"In fact, you gave them a thumping," suggested Steve.

"It war pepper," answered Bill, smiling. "Wuss almost than we give the Injuns to-day. Pepper aer the only word fer it."

Sleepy after their day's exciting adventure, it was not long before silence reigned round the camp fire where Jacob and Bill had been yarning. On the following day they pursued their way unmolested, and presently climbed the mountain slopes of the Nevada range. Thence they descended into California and reached at last the goal for which they had been making. By then Seth's wound was healed, while Steve was as active as ever.

"And here we begins ter think about minin'," he said. "Thar ain't no more Injuns to disturb us, so it's gold from this very instant. See here, Jack, I'll teach yer how ter look and keep yer eyes skinned, so as ter light on likely places."

CHAPTER XVIII

The Gold Rush

The gold rush to California was no new thing when Jack and his friends crossed the craggy heights of Nevada, and reached the green valleys to the west. Indeed it was already some years since the first of that long stream of eager individuals had pushed across the plains with the object of discovering gold. Some had made huge fortunes, many had made simply a living, while not a few had failed miserably.

"And a tidy sight of the poor things has left their bones out on them plains," said Tom, when discussing the matter. "I mind the time when America went mad about this here gold rush. Everyone was fer throwin' up a good and steady job, and ample wages, ter get over to Californy and try his luck. And in the minin' camps yer could meet the hard-working navvy, the store clerk, the doctor, the lawyer, and a host of others. There war men who had lost their all way back east, and fer whom the finding of gold meant everything. Mostly they was disappointed, 'cos gold diggin' aer a gamble, and gamblin' aer a game that ain't never safe ter play unless yer kin afford ter lose. Even then it ain't good. A man was meant ter take up a settled job, and put his back into it. Gamblers hope ter make a pile and live easy on it fer a time without troublin' to work. Wall, that ain't right. Men like that ain't much good ter their country."

"Hear, hear!" called out Steve.

"Yer see," went on Tom, "me and Steve was hunters first, and huntin' ain't a steady job, as it war. It includes makin' money as best we could, and it so happened that him and me was Californy way at the very right moment. We struck up pals, and went into partnership, and thar yer are. Wall, as I was sayin', yer could meet most any sort of man at the diggin's. The cut-throat and robber, as wasn't much good ter no one. The foreigner, the English gentleman, sailors and soldiers. Some came across the plains. A tidy few crossed Panama, and took ship ter 'Frisco. And thar they war, diggin' fer their lives, lookin' cross-eyed at their neighbours, lest they should strike a pile fust. This here Californy's chock-full of minin' camps that's been abandoned and worked out. All them diggers settled on the easiest and most likely spots, and yer may take it that they've cleared the gold most everywhar whar it war easy ter get at. It ain't no longer any use comin' along and stakin' claims and workin' 'em. Ye've got ter prospect a heap, and then set up a plant bigger than any of them first diggers had."

"And ye've got ter settle down ter hard work," burst in Jacob.

"Ye have that," agreed Tom. "What do yer boys thar think of doin'? Me and Steve and Jack thar aer partners, as yer all know. We've lumped in a goodish sight of money, and we've got sufficient plant ter tackle any job. But we shall be wantin' labour."

"And six men ain't too many," said Steve quickly, lookin' across at Jacob.

Tom and Steve and Jack had talked the matter over on the previous day, and it had been agreed amongst them that they should invite the six scouts who had accompanied them across the plains to become their partners.

"Yer see," said Steve, when broaching the matter to Tom and our hero, "'tain't like takin' on men as we don't know. Jacob and the other boys has proved themselves real pals, and we kin trust 'em. It would pay us all ter go on as we aer."

"Look here, boys," cried Tom, facing the six men, "me and my mates has been having a jaw, and we decided we'd get to and ax yer ter come in along with us. We want help, willing help, and guess yer want work. Wall, now, there's seventeen Indian hosses, and away here in Californy horse flesh is mighty scarce jest now, and hard ter get. Ef we sold 'em we should make a fine lot of dollars, 'specially ef we didn't do a deal in too great a hurry. I mean, we could sell one here, another thar, and so on, gettin' good prices all the time. Then, once we've located a spot as seems likely, we kin get to and sell some of the team. Our saddle hosses kin pull the cart later on, if it aer needed ter get moved. Yer share of them seventeen hosses would give yer a little bit to put into the partnership. We'd pay yer so much wages ef yer didn't like that arrangement. But seems to me yer could each buy an interest. Then we all work fer the common good. Ef it pans out rich, we share according to the interest each man has. Ef we strike a bad egg, wall——"

"Yer try and try again," laughed Jacob. "Now, look ye here, Tom, and you, Steve, and that 'ere Carrots. We've took to yer proper. There ain't been a sore word among us these past months. Wall, nat'ral like, we've been wonderin' what we'd do once we struck Californy. We aer here fer diggin', and sence ye're the same, why, we kinder estimated as ye'd be axin' us this question. We aer ready ter come in on these terms, and we think the offer handsome. Rightly, sence this here outfit aer yourn, them hosses we took from the Injuns aer yourn also. But sence you'll divide square, why, that aer a good sign that we'll get on friendly in this new venture. Me and my mates'll stand in ter win or lose. Seems ter me, seein' as we have some dollars ter work on, and needn't therefore rush at the job, as we stand an uncommon good chance."

It took but a little time to complete the arrangements, and accordingly the little party halted outside the first town they came to, where a lawyer drew up the proper agreements. Meanwhile a purchaser had been found for the Indian horses, which fetched a good price, and the share that Jacob and his five friends obtained allowed of their buying quite a respectable interest in the firm, though they would not, of course, have such a large interest as was held by Tom and Steve and Jack. A couple of days later they shook the dust of the town from their feet, and, with their cart replenished with sugar, flour, and other simple necessaries, took to the road again.

"There aer a gulch as me and Tom spotted last time we was over here," said Steve that evening. "We allowed as we'd make fer it when we came here agin, fer it promises somethin'. It aer been clean worked out in the flats by diggers."

"But that don't say as there ain't gold left," added Tom. "You, mates, haven't no experience of diggin', it seems, and so I'll tell yer a bit about it. Reckon gold aer been washin' outer the rocks of the mountains hereabouts fer centuries. It has got floated along in the streams, and where they run swift it hasn't settled. But as soon as ever it has reached a spot where the ground is flat, them 'ere specks of gold has come down to the bottom. In course of ages, what with dirt and gravel and sichlike, the bed of the river aer got filled bung up, and the water aer made a different course. Diggers has staked claims whar thar's been some old river bed, and have dug the gold from the gravel. They've took pretty well every ounce by now from sich sort of places; but they ain't by a long chalk got all the dust thar is in this country. Steve and me struck a gulch that seemed likely, and we're goin' thar to prospect."

It took the party another three weeks to find and reach the gulch of which Steve had spoken, and, once arrived, they set about prospecting in earnest for gold.

"Yer can see whar the old diggers came and dug their claims," explained Steve to Jack. "Everywhar down in the flats thar's holes and heaps of dirt. But none of them seed what Tom and me did. This gulch is narrow and flat; the sides come in suddenly, and rise to somewheres about four hundred feet. And up thar there's a big kind of tableland that runs back fer miles. Wall, now, the stream that come into the gulch back in them early times aer moved, else the miners wouldn't have been able ter stake their claims. Yer can't see it now, but ef yer ride ten miles up the gulch ye'll find it pouring over a cliff and crashin' down ter the bottom. Do yer see what I'm drivin' at?"

Jack thought he did. "I suppose your idea is to find the old stream, or the place where it once entered the gulch. I should say that if the land up there is flat, and the river shifted years and years ago to some other place, it must be because the bed up there got filled with gravel and stuff, and so deflected the course of the water."

"Right! That aer the thing that happened, I guess. Wall, now, we've got ter find the spot whar that 'ere stream tumbled over the cliff, and ter do that we don't need ter ride clear up the gulch and search all along. Them old miners are done that. Their diggin's don't go more than three miles up from here, and, as ye've seen fer yerself, there ain't any down lower. So I reckon that stream came over the cliff somewhars along these three miles. It may have been down here, or mebbe it war up thar. Thar ain't no sayin', and it ain't of no use ter go by the fall of the land. Thar's been earthquakes and queer ructions here in past days, and the land aer altered."

It took a week's patient and careful scrutiny of the gulch to discover the point where the stream must have flowed into the gulch in past ages, and when the place was found, to the amazement of all it was almost precisely where they had made their temporary camp.

"Which aer a good omen," observed Jacob.

"Thet water must have been comin' over fer a sight of years," said Tom, as he clambered with Jack up the steep face of the cliff. "A chap might hunt and hunt, and never have no notion that it war here it come over. But a spade helps a deal in these matters, and here we have a solid stretch of gravel, sixty yards across, roughly, wedged in between a couple of rocky walls. Do yer foller what happened?"

"I think I see clearly," said Jack. "There must have been a deep slit in the rocks years ago, and the water flowed along it and emptied into this gulch. I suppose the water drained from mountains right over there?"

"That aer so," agreed Tom. "Thar's a big watershed back away at the top of the cliff, and thar must have been a flood coming along this channel."

"Slowly, I think," said Jack, "else the channel would have been continually washed clean. But it has filled and filled, till, in the course of ages, the whole thing has become blocked and the water has found a new channel for itself."

"And aer left us here a pile of gravel, which may or may not hold gold. Reckon, seein' that thim diggin's down thar is extensive and deep dug, that the miners in this camp made something of it. So thar's every chance that gold did come down. Ef it did, thar's a sight of it in this gravel. Not here, perhaps, for the stream would quicken a bit, just whar it was goin' ter fall; but a few yards back. Anyway, we'll set to and test it."

That afternoon picks and spades were hard at work on the wedge of gravel between its rocky walls. A cradle made of sheet iron was filled and taken down to the stream which passed the camp down below, and water was allowed to flow into it while Steve and Tom rocked it. Thar were anxious faces peering into the depths of the cradle, when at length the contents had been sufficiently washed. The water was allowed to drain away, big pieces of rock and stone were carefully removed, and finally a layer of sand was come upon. It glistened in the sun.

"Hooroo!" shouted Tom. "That aer gold. Not a heap of it, but gold; and tidy rich, I should say, seein' it comes from the face of the gravel. Now we'll take another sample."

They worked till night fell, and again on the following day. Choosing the very centre of the wedge of gravel, they burrowed some three yards into it, testing samples from time to time, and finding a richer deposit of gold dust in the cradle the deeper they went. Then, with a shout of satisfaction, Jacob unearthed a nugget the size of a bean.

"There ain't no need ter go farther," said Tom, when the night had fallen, and they were seated round the camp fire. "Thar aer work here fer the crowd of us ter take us a hull year. Now we has to engineer the business properly, fer it stands ter reason nine men, nor ninety, can't dig all that stuff away. It would take years. We have ter make some other sorter arrangement, and fer that we've the apparatus in the cart. What we'll do is this. We'll tap the river 'way up thar. Me and Steve measured it up yesterday: it aer jest twenty-eight yards from the edge, and out of line of the old stream. Perhaps it was formed only lately; but it carries heaps of water and will give us all we want. We'll lead it down through a wooden sluice, take the water ter an iron nozzle, and wash the dirt out into a wooden trough below. Now, mates, we want wood first of all, and some of us'll have ter get off ter the nearest sawmill ter buy and fetch it. T'others can fix the camp while they're gone, and get ter work diggin' the new channel up thar."

The whole plan of operations was quickly agreed upon, and promptly, on the following morning, Jacob and three of his mates unloaded the wagon, and went off with a full team to the sawmill, some twenty miles away. The others clambered to the top of the cliff, and for three days laboured at digging a trench three feet wide and as many deep. They brought it from the bank of the stream mentioned by Tom which ran across the height above within reach of the edge, to the point where one of the rocky walls that had once enclosed the stream cropped into the open. Then they searched for a bed of clay, and finding some, puddled it with water till it was thin enough for their purpose, when they smeared it over the sides and bottom of the channel they had dug.

"It'll dry hard by to-morrow," said Tom; "then we'll give it another coat. It'll keep the water from washin' stones down into the nozzle and blockin' it. Jack, reckon the time's come fer yer anvil."

For the week following Jack found his hands filled. Up at cockcrow in the morning, he donned his leathern apron, and set his fire going. Then his hammer fell and clinked musically as he forged stout iron bands, which were to support the wooden framing his friends were constructing. It cost a great deal of hard labour to bring all their arrangements to a satisfactory completion; but when the task was finished they had a channel completed above, with a sluice by means of which they could allow water to enter at will. Another blocked the stream which they were tapping, just below their channel, thus giving them an ample head of water. The other end of the channel, where it ended at the edge of the cliff, was completely boxed in with boards, held together with heavy forgings, and from this point the water poured down a long, square wooden pipe, strengthened in the same manner. At the very end the stream was led into a huge iron pipe, which got smaller and smaller, till it eventually presented a six-inch orifice, while the last six feet were capable of some amount of movement, whereby the course of the jet could be deflected.

"A man couldn't stand before it," said Tom, surveying the jet when all was ready. "The force of water'll be sich that ef we was ter close the jet it'd bust the wooden pipe above. As it is, thar'll be a stream comin' from that 'ere nozzle that'll eat into the gravel quicker than the hull lot of us, and it'll wash piles of dirt down into the catches we have made. Ter-morrer we start in right away at the real business."

It had been no easy matter to arrange their catches below the point where the water was to play upon the cliff and gravel. But Steve was a knowing fellow, and had insisted that the jet should be brought as low as possible.

"So as ter undermine the rest of the stuff," he explained. "Then it'll fall in easy."

A wooden channel was erected below the spot where the jet was to play, the width of which, great at first narrowed steadily, while the channel itself descended at a sharp angle. Every ten feet along it bulkheads were erected across, in wedge-shape pattern, the apex of the wedge being presented upward. Finally the channel ended in a basin, with an overflow to take the water off.

"It's down below we shall get the dust," said Tom, surveying the whole plant with no little pride. "Them iron washing troughs will soon collect it for us, and with much less diggin' than we should ha' had to do. Up here, whar the channel's steeper, and nearer the jet, we aer likely ter get nuggets. Reckon it'll pay us ter go steady. We'll play the jet first thing in the morning, till the channel and the partitions in it aer pretty full. Then we'll shut off the water, and get to at washing. There's a trough fer each of us, and one man can do a heap, considerin' the arrangements we have made."

The whole plant was, in fact, splendidly engineered. In order to save labour, they had not only pressed the water from the stream above into their service, with the idea of making it dig by its force, and bring the gravel away from between its rocky walls; but they had so contrived matters that they could open a sluice at the bottom of the huge wooden pipe which fed the water to the jet, and could pass the contents down a narrow channel, running beside the one constructed, to catch the dirt. Suspended in this, one opposite each bulkhead, was a long wooden trough, either end faced with a plate of iron, in which Jack had bored numerous holes, small at the bottom, and getting bigger towards the top.

"They're jest like the washing troughs used by diggers," explained Tom, "and me and Steve's rocked 'em day in and day out. Yer see, the stuff one shovels into them gets broken up by the rocking, while the water carries the grit away. One pitches the big stuff out with one's hands, while the sand and the gold settles. Gee, ef after all this here preparation, we don't make a pile, why, bust me, I'll take ter scoutin' agin!"

Let the reader imagine the excitement amongst this little party on the following morning. Tom lit his pipe to show his coolness and his utter disregard of results, and clambered to the top of the cliff. But it was not the same cool Tom who had commanded the movements of the band when attacked by Indians. His hand was trembling as he manœuvred the sluice gate above, while his anxiety to see the water shoot from the jet was that of a little boy.

"Gee-whiz! Did you ever!" he exclaimed as the water spurted from the jet, and, hitting the face of the gravel, began to dig a path into it. "Ef that ain't better than diggin'! Though it has cost a sight of labour ter get it all ready. Look how the dirt comes down. Reckon it won't be long afore we have ter pipe farther along, so as ter follow the grit."

That afternoon, when the bulkheads and the channel in which they were placed were crammed with fallen gravel, the sluice at the bottom of the wooden pipe was opened, and the spurt of water from the jet ceased. Then the various individuals of the party set to work with their shovels, and, each selecting one of the troughs, threw the stuff which had been washed down into it, and rocked vigorously, while the stream played through the holes at the head of the trough, washed the dirt, and trickled out at the farther end. The most exciting time of all had arrived. Each one of the party wondered if, when he had laboured for a while, and had at length cleared away the débris, he would find the bottom of his trough filled with common sand, or whether amidst the yellow particles there would be others, gleaming bright in the sunshine, the gold for which he laboured and on which he had set his heart.

CHAPTER XIX

Tom makes a Find

"Gee! Come here, boys!"

It was a shout from Tom that broke the trying silence that had fallen upon Jack and his comrades at their several troughs, and at the sound they flung down their spades, or ceased rocking the cradles, and hastened to the side of the hunter. Tom's face was flushed a brick red, which extended under his sunburn down over neck and chest and arms. The pipe gripped between his teeth was wabbling and trembling strangely, while this habitually cool man was actually shivering with excitement.

"Boys," he said in a thin voice, as if he were dazed, "didn't we come here fer gold, ter find somethin' to pay us fer all them weeks of travel, fer fightin' with the Injuns, and fer all the labour we've put in here? Say, ain't thet it?"

"Guess so," answered Steve laconically, while the others nodded, some briskly, with a smile of expectation, others with a grin; for Tom's obvious excitement was catching, while others again jerked their heads in a curiously spasmodic manner, and stood looking at the scout awkwardly, as if ashamed to show too much interest, and yet disclosing by the brightness of their eyes the undoubted fact that they were eager for his news.

"Wall!" asked Jacob. "You've struck it, eh? I ain't had time ter look into my little lot, but others may have done."

"And I ain't had time to get searchin' in amongst all the stuff that's left in my cradle," cried Tom, blurting the words out rapidly. "But yer kin see whar I am. Top of the lot of yer, jest whar all the heavy stuff is sure ter lie. Yer see, the fall is thet sharp that light stuff and grit gets washed over the catch jest here. Only big stones and sichlike gets caught. Wall, aer that a stone?"

His face was all wrinkled with smiles, as Tom flung out the hand which up till that moment he had held behind him. In the open palm a dirty, discoloured object of irregular shape was lying, and at a rough guess it was nearly as large as a cricket ball. The scout turned it over, and then moved his hand in a half-circle, bringing the object beneath the eyes of each one of his partners in turn. Then Steve stepped forward, and, taking the mass, as if it were actually only a common stone, threw it up some few inches into the air, and repeated the process. Passing it to his mouth he then tried his teeth on the surface, and

174

finally, with a quick stride, stepping to the side of the little stream which delivered water to the washing troughs, he dipped the object in it, rinsed it thoroughly, and then brought it into the strong sunlight again. And now it had changed its character. The mass was no longer soiled and discoloured. It was of a dull, golden colour, deeply scored here and there where the shape was most irregular, and displaying a perfectly smooth, rounded surface in other parts. In the very centre of this rounded part, emerging half an inch from the golden mass was a splinter of flint, firmly embedded in the metal.

"Boys," said Steve coolly, though the little scout's eyes were strangely bright, "I 'low as this aer the evenin' when we kin have a picnic in the camp. We ha' worked hard, and travelled far, and it aer gold we've come fer. Wall, thar it is. Thar's a nugget, ef ever I saw one, and it's tidy sartin it ain't the only one as we shall drop upon. Ef thet's the case, me and you, mates, will have somethin' ter take back with us ter repay us fer all the labour. Thet bein' so, it aer clear thet it aer Jacob's duty ter bring out thet bottle of spirits ter-night. Abe, too, might get to pretty soon and cook us a meal that'll lick anythin' we've touched this many a month."

There was a roar of applause as the little scout finished, and then all crowded round to examine the nugget which Tom had discovered.

"It war the fust thing my fingers hit upon when I got to search in the trough," said Tom, "and I wouldn't be surprised ef I found more. Mates, supposin' we gets back ter the business. That 'ere nugget ain't enough in itself ter pay us back fer all the outlay we've put into the plant, sayin' nothin' of the labour."

It was with a feeling of eager expectation that all went back to their troughs, and recommenced throwing dirt into them and rocking. At the end of three hours, when they ceased work for the night, it was found that Tom's bulkhead had indeed caught the richest harvest. There were a dozen nuggets to be seen, though not of the same size as that which he had first discovered. Three more, about the size of a bean, were unearthed from the next two troughs, while the washings of the troughs below were without nuggets. But the harvest of gold dust was plentiful, so good, indeed, that it became obvious at once that if only such fortune could continue for a week, the party would pay all outgoings, the expenses of their return to New York, if need be, and still leave a sum in reserve which, when divided, would give each member of the firm a handsome sum to bank.

"But we ain't goin' ter leave in a week," said Tom with a grin of exultation, as he sat hugging the camp fire that night and nursing a pannikin of spirits. "There's dirt enough between them cliffs ter keep us going fer a year, and I looks at it this way: Ef it's rich out here, at the end of the stream, so to speak, it'll be richer still the farther in we goes; 'cos the stream will have been more sluggish. That will have allowed the gold ter settle, and whar thar's been big rocks and boulders, with holes and pockets in 'em, the chances aer we shall hit upon more nuggets. Of course we shan't get all the gold thar is, by a heap. Some'll be washed through the troughs, and the catch tank we've made won't hold it all. But, ef it's thar, as I ain't a doubt, why, we'll get enough and ter spare of it."

As the days went on it became evident that the little party had become possessed of a veritable gold mine, for their takings at the end of each day were greater than those on the first occasion. But they were not all the while engaged in rocking the cradles. There was much hard work to be accomplished, and in this Jack took a fair share. Indeed, he worked for hours at his anvil, forging new iron bands to bind extensions of their wooden waterway, or making various fittings for other parts of the plant. There were spades and picks to be repaired now and again, though not so often as would have been the case had they not pressed water into their service.

When he had a few idle moments, nothing delighted him more than to clamber towards the point where the gigantic nozzle was secured in its wooden cradle, to watch the jet of water surging from it, and to see the stream splay out as it leaped into the open, and then dash itself into thousands and thousands of the minutest drops as it struck the trembling gravel. There was something wonderfully fascinating about the iridescent colours which played to and fro in the spray, as the sun's rays flickered and poured upon it. There was a note which was almost musical coming from the very lip of the nozzle, while without cessation there was the slither of loosened stones and dirt, the thud of heavier pieces and of boulders, and, on occasion, when the jet had undermined the gravel to some great extent, a mighty, awe-inspiring commotion, as tons upon tons of material came thundering down.

If he tired of the neighbourhood of the jet, of that fascinating gush and gurgle of water, and of the rainbow colours which played about the spray so long as the sun's rays fell, he had merely to step down a few paces, and there was more to interest him. For, from the point where the water played, a surging stream tumbled and roared downhill in the huge channel prepared for it—a yellow, dirty flood, as if the water came from a river after heavy falls of rain. Who would have thought to look at that yellow stream that it contained riches, riches long hidden in the gravel, scoured from the rocks of past ages, and lying for many a century undisturbed in the river bed? Riches, too, which man's industry and courage and astuteness were now bringing to light, and separating from its grosser surroundings.

"Though I don't know as it aer always fer the best," soliloquized Steve one day, as he stood watching the scene with Jack beside him. "This here hunt fer gold don't always lead ter goodness. Thar's a sight of bad blood made over it, either here, at the diggin's, or way back in the settlements. In the first place, it seems ter me that the scum of the earth collects whar the men aer at work, lookin' ter make their fortunes—thieves, and gamblers, and sichlike—hangin' about like a set of jackals, ter take the stuff from the men who find it. Thar's murders been committed, Jack."

"I know, to my cost," answered our hero after a while; for up till now he had never ventured to tell his comrades that his own father had lost his life at the diggings. "A—a relative of mine was shot in one of the saloons out in California. He was murdered."

There was silence between them for a while, and then Steve spoke.

"Ah!" he said, as if he had been thinking deeply and looking back into the distance; "them murders was frequent some ten years ago. Out here in Californy thar was the biggest set of blackguards round the camps that was ever ter be met with. They ran saloons, and robbed the men as went thar, robbed 'em not only by providin' spirits that were so bad that they pisoned a fellow, while the price was that big it frightened yer, but robbed them at cards and games of chance. Then thar was bands that held up the gold trains makin' fer Sacramento and other cities, to bank the riches thar. And thar was scoundrels that looked like ordinary miners, and acted the part, but all the while they was ready fer murder, so long as they could steal the gold which others had made. I could tell yer a yarn about one of that sort, only jest now it wouldn't kinder suit this here place, it's that peaceful; and when I get to think of that 'ere ruffian, and tell of his treachery, why, it brings a bad taste inter the mouth, and one seems ter see quite different. One of these days I'll tell yer about him, and, ef yer like, yer can give me your yarn."

The very mention of such a matter sent Jack's thoughts back to the time when he was but a little fellow. He could remember his mother's grief when his father left for the diggings, and the great hope which he and his wife had that the trip he was about to make would prove successful and help them out of their troubles. He could cast his mind back, too, to that fatal day when the news came that Tom Kingsley had been killed in a brawl with his partner; that he had, in fact, been murdered. But he was too young at the time to feel the loss so greatly, though the tale had never escaped his memory. And then his thoughts wandered to his own troubles.

"They seem as far off almost as Father's death," he said to himself. "I never thought, when I stood in the prisoner's dock at Hopeville, that I should ever be happy again. Yet I have had a thoroughly jolly time, and I feel somehow as if the future would be clear, as if I should get to the bottom of the matter."

To look at our hero no one would for a moment have thought him capable of any criminal act. A tall, stout, sunburned young fellow he looked, and as he stood beside the stream there, his sleeves rolled to his elbow, his wide-brimmed hat tilted back till his red hair shone in the sun, one could not but admit that he looked happy, that he carried himself as every young fellow should, with that appearance of self-assurance and happiness which is common to youth, and with a steady look in his blue eyes and a fine poise of his head which spoke of resolution, of a conscience clear of all guilt. When he took himself to his anvil, and made the sparks fly, why, even Tom would come along and watch him.

"Gee!" he had exclaimed more than once. "He's as mild-lookin' as milk. Who would ha' thought as that 'ere young chap could ha' took Steve in hand! But Steve says himself as he felt like a chicken, and had ter do as he war bid. That jest goes ter show that it ain't always wise to judge by appearances. I mind a young chap, with stoopy shoulders and a bit of fluff on his lips, as looked as ef he couldn't do more than say 'boo!' to a goose. But when one of the rough chaps we has now and agin out on the plains set in ter play larks with him, why, that 'ere young fellow kinder shook off his soft looks and went in and hammered the chap as was playin' larks. Jack's one of them sort, only he don't never look soft. And, gee! he can work, kin thet young feller."

Our hero did indeed earn a fair share of the reward the party was gaining, and, being a jovial fellow, ready to listen to all the yarns that were going, and not anxious to pose as being better than his comrades, it followed that he was immensely popular, particularly when Steve, a well-known scout, had spoken so warmly as to his grit and courage.

"There's jest one thing that ain't right about that 'ere young Carrots," he had observed more than once in his hard, dry-as-dust manner. "Jack aer got something up agin him, and it has made a heap of play on his mind. Reckon he got into a muss 'way back in the settlements, and couldn't clear hisself. But he will. That chap sticks to things he takes up, and ef he wants ter clear hisself of that muss, why, guess he'll do it. Tom, jest pass along that 'ere keg of 'bacca. Yer ain't the only one as smokes."

Good friends they all were, though not often given to much conversation. They worked at the cradles or at repairing their plant from sunrise in the morning, and only broke off at evening, save for a few moments which were devoted to meals. It was when they had eaten their supper, and pipes were going, that the natural silence and taciturnity of the scout was broken before the warmth of the camp fire. Then, as the darkness got deeper, first Tom perhaps, then Steve, or

Jacob, or Abe, or one of the others, would tell some tale of their experiences—experiences which dealt for the most part with Indians, with thieves, or with some hunting expedition.

"Boys," said Tom one evening, having puffed clouds of smoke from his lips, "we ha' been at this here place jest a couple of months, and me and Steve has been thinkin'. It aer time we weighed up that 'ere gold, and sent it down to the town. Yer see, one never knows when thieves won't come along, and, though they ain't likely ter touch sich a strong party as we aer, still they might get the stuff by a bit of cheek and daring. What say, Jacob?"

"I'm with you, Tom. The bank's the best place fer the gold, and the sooner we send it thar the better. Supposin' we weigh out now."

It required a full hour to weigh carefully their gains, and when the work was completed Jack understood, to his amazement, that a sum was due to him which would enable him to live in comfort for a dozen years. The share of Jacob and the other hunters was less: but it was by no means an inconsiderable sum, for the mine had proved most rich.

"Now we have another proposition," said Tom, grinning at the circle around him. "Thar's heaps of gold fer us all in this here place. I believe that we ain't yet a while struck the richest spot, so thar's likely enough more ter come. Now me and Steve and Carrots thar ha' had another jaw. We aer prepared ter let you six chaps buy up even shares with us. Jack'll have to pay something, fer he ain't got quite an equal share with us, and in course yer will have ter pay a heap more. But ye've the stuff here, and when ye've paid thar'll be still a goodish pile fer each man to bank. How do yer look at the proposition?"

It required no discussion to induce the six scouts to do as Tom had proposed. Indeed, the proposition was extremely handsome. And when the terms were finally fixed, Jack found himself with still more to his credit.

"Now we'll fix about taking the stuff," said Tom. "Steve here'll boss the party; and, sence we ain't got no need fer an anvil jest now, why, Carrots had best go with him. Reckon two more had better volunteer, and that'll be sufficient."

The following day the gold was divided up and placed in sacks, which were lashed across the backs of two of the horses. Then the party set out from the camp, and turned their faces towards the nearest town.

"Now we've got ter fix up some sort of arrangement as ter watchin'," said Steve, once the mine was left behind. "Thar's me, and Jack, and Abe, and old Tom ter do the work; and though I don't fear that anyone'll attempt ter take this stuff from us, still they ain't all gentlemen in these here parts, and it aer jest as well ter be careful. See?"

"You bet!" exclaimed Abe. "When I was down in the settlements last week, buying pork and flour and sichlike, thar war a tale that a band of light-fingered gentry was out and had held up more'n one convoy with gold. That was up Sacramento way. But them thieves shift their ground when things get warm, and always when they hear that a party aer gettin' gold."

"Which they ain't done in our case," asserted Steve. "Thar's not a one of us as has blabbed about the gold; and though men has come along and watched us fer a time, they aer gone away again every time thinkin' us fools fer our pains most likely. Still, there ain't never no sayin'. Someone may have been watchin' and spyin'."

Had the little band of friends but known it, this was a method employed by a party of rascals who had infested the goldfields for some little while. Separating, and each dressed as a miner, the members of this band had kept watch at the various diggings; and whenever information had reached one that a convoy of gold was to leave the particular place he was observing, a message brought together all his comrades, and in many cases a seizure of the gold resulted. One such individual had for the past week lain at the top of the cliff, keeping watch on Tom and his comrades; and though he had never been sure that they were gathering gold from the dirt washed out of the cliff, still their obvious cheerfulness, their untiring industry and labour, more than half convinced him. And at length the preparations for Steve's departure carried conviction to his mind.

"That's gold, sure, in them sacks they're putting on the hosses," he said to himself. "Time I was movin'."

He retreated from the cliff stealthily, gained a spot some two miles away, where he had secured his horse beneath a tree, and, mounting rapidly, galloped off to take the news to his comrades.

"You kin never be sure," repeated Steve; "and, thet bein' the case, we'll march as ef we was in the enemy's country, as ef Injun varmint was skirmishin' round us. Jack and Tom'll ride beside the hosses, while me and Abe'll scout about."

"While I suggest something likely to help," cried Jack. "We've got three horses with us, two of which carry the gold, while the third has our grub and blankets strapped to his back. Now, if we change the loads, and make the grub and blankets look as if they were the gold, then, in case of a surprise, we might still manage to beat any who happened to attack us."

"Gee! That aer a bright idea!" cried Steve. "Carrots, fer all yer quietness, you ha' got somethin' in yer. In course we can swap the things around, and sence it don't make no odds ef gold dust aer put in bags or in blankets, supposin' we pack it in the blankets and fill the bags that aer got the gold now with grub and other things."

The precaution was one which might be useful in case of an attack, and in consequence a halt was made and the change effected. Then they pressed on, Jack and Tom riding beside the loaded animals, while the horse which from outward appearance carried their swags—by which term miners generally understood their personal belongings and food was meant—bore in fact the wealth of gold gathered from the mine. Nor was it long before Jack and his friends had cause to congratulate themselves on their foresight; for they were to meet with trouble before they completed their journey.

CHAPTER XX

An Ambuscade

Four days had elapsed since Jack and his comrades had left the mine before anything happened to disturb the even course of the journey. They had marched at a footpace all the way, Steve and Abe riding well ahead, as a rule, though at times they scouted out on the flanks. Jack and Tom, one of the scouts who had joined them at the very first, rode beside the horses, their rifles loaded and held in readiness. Then suddenly, on the fourth day, just as the light was getting a little uncertain, and the shades of evening were drawing in, Steve came galloping back to the little convoy, and Abe after him.

"What's amiss?" asked Jack, for it was a most unusual movement on the part of the scout.

"That's jest what I'm axin' myself," came the curt answer. "I happened to be ridin' way up thar on the spur of that 'ere hill, when I seed somethin' down in the valley whar this road leads. The sun war jest right bang in my eyes, so I couldn't make head nor tail of it; but out here it's as well ter be careful, and ef ye've gold travellin' along a road, and see something that aer strange, why, a chap hops back ter the convoy quick. Do yer see anything, Abe?"

"Nary a thing. Thar's a spur that hides the road. Thar ain't no need to be scared, even if thar's a party comin' along; but I 'low as it aer wise ter be careful. Ef folks want ter disturb us, they'll see as we're ready, and thet goes a long way when thar's villains about."

A quarter of an hour later the little convoy rounded the spur of the hill which shut out the view of the road ahead of them. By now they were riding in close order, Abe and Steve watching the hills on either side with lynx-like eyes, for the road ran through a somewhat narrow defile, and if an enemy were hidden amongst the rocks he would be so near that his bullets would reach the convoy while a rush would have been possible.

"Jest one of them ugly places," growled Steve, casting his eyes restlessly from side to side. "Jest the sort of plant that'd be fixed on by a set of ruffians ef they wanted ter hold up a convoy. Now, I tell yer all, ef thar's a shot fired, don't wait to reply ter it. Jest put yer spurs in hard, and ride. Waitin'll jest play into the hands of the varmint. Mind, I don't suggest as thar's ter be trouble, but somehow or other I've got a kinder feelin' as we're up agin somethin'. Why, ef thar ain't a cart 'way ahead!"

The road in advance was now visible, and some four hundred yards ahead a solitary cart was to be seen, a four-wheeled affair, which, from the cant it had to one side, had evidently met with some disaster. Beside it lounged a figure, above whose head hung a blue cloud of smoke, indicating that he was taking his ease, and was puffing at his pipe.

"And nary a hoss in sight," exclaimed Steve. "Wall, that aer ter be explained by the fact that his chums has gone ahead ter fetch help. Boys, I 'low as thar ain't anythin' here ter scare us; but jest you bear in mind what I've said already. Thar ain't never no trusting no one when ye've gold about. Ef ye're axed the question, jest answer that we're bound fer the settlements ter fill up with pork and flour and sichlike. Wall, stranger, what's amiss?" he asked bluntly, as the cavalcade came level with the stranded cart. "I see as ye've smashed a wheel."

"That's so. And a big nuisance it aer," came the answer, while the figure they had seen lounging beside the wagon rose nonchalantly to his feet, pulled the pipe from his mouth, and strolled towards them. The man was tall, wiry, and sunburned to the last degree. A ragged and unkempt beard almost entirely hid his features, while his clothing was far from new, and seemed to indicate that he had been travelling for a considerable period.

"Jest a big nuisance," he repeated, placing his pipe back between his lips so as to indulge in another draw. "And I don't mind tellin' yer why," he went on, glancing first at Steve, then at Abe, and afterwards at Jack and Tom in turn. Indeed, a pair of sharp eyes, almost hidden beneath bushy brows, seemed to take in particulars of the party within a second, while Jack caught the stranger's glances directed upon the horses and their loads. "I'll tell yer why," he proceeded, "and I see as thar ain't no harm in doin' so. It ain't every sort of man travellin' in this country that a chap can give his confidence to; but with you, gentlemen, one kin see as things aer safe. That 'ere cart aer stuffed nigh full with gold. Yer wouldn't think it, now, would yer? 'Cos, as a gineral rule, gold aer sent on hossback, same as ye're doin'. This lot is piled into the cart so as to blind any of them light-fingered gents as sometimes takes to the road. Cartin' aer my business, and I don't object to sich a valuable cargo so long as I ain't delayed; but I 'low that this here broken wheel has made me a trifle fidgety. My mates has taken the hosses on to the nearest settlement to buy up a new wheel, and, ef it ain't axin too much, I'd be obleeged if yer could stand by me till they come back agin. It aer too late fer you to ride on far, for the light aer nearly gone. And this here spot aer pretty pleasant."

Jack stared hard at the man, and, though his mind was full of suspicions, considering Steve's warnings, he was bound to admit that the tale was a plausible one; that, despite the roughness of this stranger's appearance, he seemed honest, perfectly frank, and at his ease. Then, too, the admission he had made that his cart contained gold was sufficient of itself to disarm all thought of treachery. The man was in a quandary, and in those rough days in California, despite the scoundrels to be found in every part, there were still, amongst the hundred-thousand and more of miners, huge numbers who showed the utmost kindness to one another. Indeed, the rough, blunt-spoken miner was always ready to dip his hand into his pocket when a subscription was required for a sick comrade, for a widow, or for some other urgent cause. Jack was therefore not surprised when Steve slipped from his saddle and gripped the stranger's hand.

"Ef that's the case, why, in course, we'll help," he sang out cheerily. "It ain't hard ter see as ye're in a fix, and sence it aer always a case out here of one man helpin' another, why, here we stay till your pards return. But I 'low as it ain't the sort of camp I should ha' chosen. Them hills is too near fer my likin'. How long is it sence your chums left fer the settlement?"

"Six or seven hours, I reckon. As thar ain't nothin' ter detain them, they ought to be back right here in another four; but thar ain't never no sayin'. Them boys ain't seen a settlement fer the last three months, and it stands to reason that they'll be tempted ter put in a time in one or more of the saloons. But they won't forget. Thar's this here gold ter remind 'em. Reckon they'll fetch back here somewhere about the early mornin'. Got much dust yerself?"

The ragged individual jerked his head towards the horses which Tom and Jack were unloading at that moment. Remembering Steve's caution, they took the swags from the one horse and tossed them carelessly into a heap, as if the blankets contained nothing of value, while the bags which had hitherto contained gold, and which were now crammed with food, with spare shirts and socks, and other articles, were taken from the horses with great care and stacked in a heap aside. Nor did the stranger fail to notice the removal.

"Got much over thar?" he asked casually.

"A tidy bit. Nothin' onusual," answered Steve warily, for this experienced little scout was always cautious. Jack had learned long since that it took time to break through the ice with which Steve surrounded himself, and that, for some reason or other, it was a long while before he gave his confidences to anybody.

"A tidy bit," he repeated in a confidential whisper.

"Jack," he sang out, "jest pile them bags a little closer together, so as we kin see 'em. We should be in a proper hole ef we was to lose that stuff. And what sort of a load have yer got, mate?" he asked in his turn, facing the stranger just as casually as the latter had done, and commencing to fill his pipe.

"Jest about double that lot. Look thar."

The tall, ungainly figure of the man was elevated from the boulder on which he had been seated, and, strolling towards the cart, he pulled the back boards down, disclosing a pile of bags within.

"Ef you and me and your pals here was ter divide, reckon we wouldn't want ter work after this," he said with a grin. "But duty aer duty. That 'ere stuff aer in my charge, and I see as you aer gentlemen."

"You kin put it like that," smiled Steve. "Now, seems to me, as your pals is due almost any time, it ain't no use fer us to unpack the swags. Perhaps you've got a bit of food ter spare, and a glass and a bottle?"

The cautious Steve wished to avoid unpacking his own store, for the very obvious reason that the food was packed within the bags which appeared to contain gold. And, for the very same reason, Jack and Tom, once they had removed their belongings from the horses, had made no effort to disturb them.

"Why, sure," came the hearty answer, "I'm jest obleeged to you fer standin' by me, and it so happens as I've a fine store, and good things with it."

There was a bustle in the little camp for the next hour, for the stranger threw wood on the fire and soon had it blazing merrily, while within a short while a savoury steam arising from the kettle suspended over it tickled the palates of the travellers. Then reared up on a couple of low boulders placed directly against the flames were a couple of ramrods, and on these sizzled two enormous buffalo steaks, toasting nicely in the heat, and now and again sending the flames leaping skyward as they dripped grease into the fire.

"It does a man good ter smell that," cried Steve, glancing towards the fire, "and in ten minutes or less reckon things'll be ready. Say, stranger, whar do yer fetch the water from? I jest think I'll take a wash afore I sit down."

"Over thar." The man pointed to a spot some forty yards away, now almost hidden in the darkness.

"Then, ef you're comin', Jack, why come along."

Steve strolled off into the gloom, followed by our hero, for he seemed to gather from some subtle note in Steve's voice that the hunter desired him to do so. They walked side by side to the stream, Steve whistling loudly and cheerily. Then the little man kneeled and splashed water over his face.

"Kin yer see the fire?" he asked in a low voice. "And that 'ere scaramouch beside it?"

Jack, answered again in the affirmative.

"Wall, now, jest you listen ter me. Jack, this thing ain't as right as it seems. Reckon thar's something queer about that feller down thar, and I've more than a notion that ef we was ter ax him ter 'low us ter look into his bags, it's not gold they aer holding. Savvy?"

To be perfectly frank, Jack was astonished. To his unsuspicious mind everything about the stranger down below seemed to be open and above-board. His nonchalance and apparent frankness had impressed our hero, while the open display of the gold bags, the broken wheel, and the whole tale seemed so very likely and real that he could find no room for doubt. But Jack was as yet, with all his harsh misfortune with regard to the robbery, but a child in experience, while Steve was a man who had been in every part of America, who had doubtless encountered many a rogue, and whose outlook on life was broader by a great deal, and far more acute than was our hero's.

"Yer don't. You've took that man fer a white man, one as is in distress," grinned Steve, laughing almost inaudibly. "Wall, when I was about your age I'd have done the same, and taken my davy as he war honest. And mind yer, I don't say now right off that he's a scamp. I ain't dead sartin, but I'm sure enough ter jest give you the wink, and to tell you ter pass it on to the others, though I expect as Abe ha' got hold of the same notion as me."

"But why? What is wrong?" asked Jack, somewhat bewildered, for even now he could distinguish nothing wrong, no false line in the tale told by the stranger.

"Why! Wall, look you here. It wouldn't do ter ax him to 'low us to see his gold, 'cos then, ef he's square and above-board, he'd get ter suspecting us. And ef he ain't, as seems nearly sartin, why, it stands to reason that he wants ter take us by surprise when his mates comes along. That bein' so, we wants to have a surprise fer them tucked up our sleeves. How do I see anythin' wrong? Wall, look at the springs of that 'ere wagon. They ain't down by near as much as they would be ef them bags was filled with gold. They're chuck-full, thar ain't a doubt, but the stuff in 'em ain't gold, or else the weight would be so big it would sink the springs, and bring the frame of the cart down on to the axles. Then, look at the broken wheel. Thar ain't a rut hereabouts ter break it. Thar ain't weight in the cart sufficient ter account fer a smash, so one has ter take it that it was done of purpose. Savvy?"

Jack did. Now that the matter was put so concisely and clearly before him he could see that there was a bad smudge across the story told by this stranger. His coolness and apparent honesty would have passed his tale with the ordinary miner, for often enough he came from the settlements. But with a scout it was a different matter. Steve had not lived his life for nothing. The habit of close inspection, of constant care to guard against danger and the ambushes of the enemy, had made him discover a flaw in what appeared to be a straightforward matter.

"Then you think we are to be attacked?" asked Jack, his heart beating a little faster.

"I'm nigh dead sartin. That's why I brought you off here. Ye've got ter act up to that man. Pretend yer ain't smelt a rat, and let him think ye're as soft as may be. But keep yer eyes open, and yer fist mighty near yer shooter. Tell Tom the same, and be ready."

A few minutes later they sauntered back to the camp, where the stranger announced that supper was ready.

"Hot soup and a cut from them steaks won't do none of us any harm!" he cried pleasantly. "By the time we've had a smoke it'll be time ter turn in. Reckon my mates aer likely ter stay a bit, and ought ter be here about mornin'."

They seated themselves about the fire, and were soon engaged in eating as good a meal as Jack had seen for many a long day; for at the mine they were, as a rule, too busy to leave the place to seek for fresh meat. They subsisted for the most part on corned beef and on salted food. Then pipes were produced, and for an hour the party chatted.

"My name's Ted," announced the stranger, "and I 'low as you have treated me handsome. Now, sence I've had a rest here, and ye've been on the road all day, I'm willin' ter take the watch to-night, fer, in course, someone must see that things aer right. Ef you don't like that suggestion, why we'll draw lots."

"Wall, I'm about dead beat," sang out Steve promptly, beginning to yawn loudly. "Fact is, me and my mates here has been hard at it at the mines for a long while, and then we've been coming along steadily. Ef ye're willing ter take the watch first, I'll turn in, and yer kin be relieved after midnight. Then I'll come on, and Abe here'll take it till the light comes."

The firelight flickering on the face of the stranger showed no sign there of annoyance. It was the same to him whether he took the night or the morning watch; and for the life of him Jack could not help but think that Steve was mistaken in his suspicions.

"The man seems absolutely honest," he said to himself, "but still there is something in what Steve says. If that cart were really loaded with bags of gold, the springs would certainly be down. As it is, the load might consist of feathers. Yes, it will be as well to keep a sharp eye open."

Borrowing the blankets of the men who, Ted, the stranger, said, had left with the horses to obtain a spare wheel, Steve and his friends threw themselves down on the ground near their own belongings. Near at hand their horses were picketed to pegs driven deeply into the earth, while their own heads reclined on the blankets which contained their store of gold. The bags full of their other belongings lay at a little distance, and the firelight playing upon them showed that they were secure. But it did not show the eyes of the stranger, nor the fact that that individual had fixed them upon the bags greedily.

"Listen here, mates," whispered Steve, as he lay down, having first heard the man Ted stroll a little from the camp. "Jack aer probably told yer that things don't look square. Wall, I'll take a sleep now, and Jack kin watch. Tom'll follow with a spell, then Abe, and finally I'll take a turn. That'll bring us ter the mornin'. It's then that the trouble'll come. And, boys, ef thar's a rush, yer kin leave our loads to theirselves. This chap Ted has had his eyes on the bags, and don't cotton that there's been a bit of a change. Them bags of ours aer heavy enough to mislead 'em, and ef they rush, why, they're welcome to the swags. Good night!"

He rolled over on his side, tucked the blanket well around him, and was fast asleep in less than five minutes. Long habit had inured the scout to thoughts of danger. He could sleep as well and as soundly, knowing that blows would be struck on the morrow, as he could when no danger was to be apprehended, provided always that he was sure that he had friends to aid him, who would remain watchful whilst he slept. And by now Steve was assured of that. The long trip over the plains had proved the reliability of Abe and Tom and Jack.

Then the deep breathing of Abe and Tom told that they too had fallen into a peaceful slumber, leaving Jack to guard them. Our hero lay with his face on his hand, his head propped up a little, and his eyes only half-opened, for the reflection of the fire might have been seen in them had Ted happened to look his way. He heard the steps of the solitary sentry now and again, and watched him as he strolled round the stranded cart. Occasionally he approached the fire, and, lifting a smouldering stick, lit his pipe with it. It was two hours later before he ventured farther. Listening intently, he slid across the ground which intervened between the cart and Jack and his friends, bent over them for some few seconds, and then walked to the heap of sacks. Jack watched him stealthily as he inspected the piled-up bags, and then turned his head to follow his further movements as he retreated once more to the cart. Then Ted did a curious thing. Jack saw him fumbling with something for the space of a few seconds, he stepped towards the smouldering embers, and the flickering light showed that his arm was suspended over the heat. It seemed as if he were warming his fingers. But no. An instant later a tongue of brilliant flame shot up into the darkness, and as suddenly melted into smoke.

"A signal, without doubt," thought Jack. "Ah!"

From somewhere in the distance a faint echo came to his ear—a faint, eerie whistle. The signal had been answered. There was no longer room for doubt that this Ted was acting a part, that the broken-down cart was merely an adjunct to a plot destined, if he and his friends were not very careful, to wipe them out of existence, and take from them all their hardly won gold.

"Gee," exclaimed Jack to himself, "if that isn't something! Time I woke Steve and the others. Time we made some sort of an arrangement to meet the danger."

CHAPTER XXI

The Outwitting of Tusker

"Lie low, whatever yer do! Now let's have the yarn," whispered Steve as Jack awoke him with a gentle dig in the ribs. "What aer it all about? Yer seem a bit excited."

Our hero was, indeed, somewhat disturbed by what had so recently happened, but not frightened. To do him but justice, Jack had passed through such dangers already that his nerves were hardened, and his courage had been tried. However the thought of what was before them, the cunning of this man Ted, served to thrill him more than was usual, to stir his pulses. So it was in a quiet and steady whisper that he imparted his news to the hunter.

"Jest as I thought," answered Steve when he had finished. "I kinder reckoned we'd got into a nest of scorpions. This here feller was too free and easy, when he oughter have been kind of stand-offish, considering the gold he's supposed ter have, and that we aer four ter his one. Jest kick Tom and Abe gently."

"What'll yer do?" asked the former hoarsely, when Jack had roused him, stretching his neck so as to place his mouth close to Steve's ear. "Seems to me as we might easily walk right away now. Thar's only this man Ted to stop us, and reckon we could soon fix him."

"Ef he was alone, which he ain't," came cautiously from Steve. "Thar ain't a doubt but what we're cornered. The men who aer in with this man here are 'way up there on the hillside. Likely enough they've been thar ever since we reached the spot, and aer jest waitin' fer the time ter attack us."

"But," argued Abe, "ef that's the case, why have they waited? The risk fer them'll be the same now as earlier in the evening, or, fer the matter of that, the same as it'll be when the light comes."

"With jest this difference," urged Steve, still in the same cautious whisper, "last evenin' they might have been disturbed, for this road has a goodish number of travellers on it. In the early dawn thar ain't likely to be anyone, so they'll be able ter make their attack and get away without a soul save us seeing them. And they reckon ter wipe the hull crowd of us out, so as dead men'll tell no tales. Gee, this aer a fix!"

There was silence for some little while, as each one of the party considered the matter. As they lay there, with wide-open eyes, though they took care to make no movement, they could see the bright gleam from Ted's pipe every now and again, as that worthy leaned against the side of the cart. That he had friends near at hand was certain, since Jack had heard that whistle, and it was equally sure that while Ted remained awake any attempt on their part to steal away from the camp would immediately be detected, and the aid of those comrades called in.

"It aer clear that we're in a hole, and has ter fight it out with them critters," said Steve at last after a long silence; "and, sence that's the case, the thing aer ter fix up some way in which ter meet 'em. Thar'll be eight or nine of the varmint. These bands always run ter that number, 'cos then they aer able ter break up opposition, and, 'sides, it keeps people from following. Folks get ter know that it aer useless to go after these bands of robbers onless there's plenty of boys ter help; and sence men aer mostly busy at the diggin's, why, it follows that it aer generally hard ter get the right number. It's only when a band becomes that bad, and has murdered a hull heap of miners and carters, that the sheriff can get a strong enough force together, and by then fellers like this has managed ter divide up the plunder and ter ride ter some other part of the fields. This aer a tarnation fix."

"Supposing," suggested Jack, "we were to——"

He came to a sudden halt, for Ted had turned to look at the supposed sleepers, as if he had detected a noise.

"Yer was supposin'," whispered Abe hoarsely, some minutes later, when the stranger turned away again.

"Jest let's have it, Carrots," added Steve. "Ye've took me through a fix before now. You aer bright enough ter find a way out of this."

"Not out of it. I can suggest a way in which we can get cover and best the men when they come," answered Jack. "There's the cart."

"Ay, thar's the cart," came from Steve wonderingly, for he could see nothing useful there.

"Wall?" demanded Abe.

"Ye've forgot that it's bung full of sacks," whispered Tom, "and, besides, one wheel's broken."

"He ain't forgot nothin'," said Steve sharply. "Carrots don't make mistakes like that. Out with it, youngster."

"There is the cart," repeated Jack. "The sacks in it are likely enough filled with grass, considering how light they evidently are. As for the wheel, it is an advantage that it happens to be broken. I thought we would wait till we are about to be attacked. Or, better still, seeing that the attack is bound to come, I propose that we wait only till the light gets stronger. Then we'll make for the cart, while the man there will take to his heels. His shouts will bring the others down upon us at a run, but that will be better than having them ride up openly, as if returning from the settlements with a new wheel. That, of course, is their game. They think we shall have swallowed their story, and that all they have to do now is to ride into the camp and shoot us down easily."

"Put in a nutshell. That 'ere Carrots has his haar on right enough," growled Steve.

"Wall, thar's the cart," reminded Tom.

"We make use of it much as we did of the other when the Indians attacked us. The bags will form good protection, while the cart is within nice range of our gold. If we four can't manage then to——"

A low chuckle burst from Steve, while Jack felt Abe's strong fingers close firmly round his wrist.

"H-h-h-hush! That critter's lookin'. Ef he so much as moves a toe I'll put lead into him."

It was Tom's excited whisper, while that individual went rigid to his finger tips, as the man who watched by the cart turned and stared at the sleepers. Jack felt the scout's arm steal stealthily over him, and heard the gentle click of his firelock, as his strong thumb drew it back into cocking position. And there the arm rested, while all four lay as if dead, as if turned to stone, motionless, almost without breathing.

But whatever suspicions Ted may have had, he quickly became reassured; for, to speak the truth, Steve and his friends had played their parts admirably. Though warned from the first of Steve's suspicions, they had treated the stranger with frankness equal to his own, and had entirely disarmed his suspicions. He imagined that the party of four for whom the trap had been set so craftily had been entirely taken in, and that they would fall an easy prey. He turned away from the sleepers, and, no doubt in accordance with a prearranged plan, once more strolled to the embers, dropped some powder into them, and sent his signal flashing into the sky. Then, for the second time, from a closer point it seemed on this occasion, a distant whistle echoed along the road.

"The critters!" Jack heard the little scout exclaim. "Wall, mates, it'll be light in two hours or less, so we shan't have long to wait; and sence that skunk thar ain't axed ter be relieved yet, why, we'll let him stay on watch. Time enough to clear him out when the mornin' light comes."

To the little scout those two hours may have passed easily enough, for his sangfroid was wonderful, and his accustomed coolness not easily to be disturbed. Abe seemed to find comfort in a cube of strong and particularly evil-smelling tobacco, which he thrust between his strong brown teeth and chewed

192

slowly, and with evident relish. As for Tom, he was one of that large band of Anglo-Saxons to whom fighting comes naturally, to whom the crack of weapons and the hiss of bullets is better music than even the latest instrument can supply. He lay awake longing for the hour for movement, his lynx-like eyes fixed on the watcher by the wagon. But Jack, despite the excitement of the moment, was neither elated nor expectant. He was just an ordinary young fellow, subject to the common weaknesses of mankind. And like them, too, he was possessed of the same needs. He had been keeping watch for long now, and, finding others to help him, soon began to drowse. His eyes closed, his head dropped back on his hand, and in a little while he was fast asleep. Thus he remained for more than two hours, till the light in the eastern sky was already sweeping the gloom and darkness from the land, and until the road in front and behind the little camp was commencing to become visible. It was a sharp kick from Steve and an exclamation from Tom which aroused him. He sprang to his feet a few seconds after the others, and at once became conscious of the fact that horses were approaching at a gallop.

"To the cart, boys!" shouted Steve, leading the way. "That ere skunk slipped away so sudden that I didn't notice, and ef it hadn't been fer Abe hearin' the hosses, we might be lying thar still. In we go."

There was little time for preparation, for Ted, the rascal who had told his crafty story, had stolen a march on the watchers. They had seen him leaning against the cart as if half-asleep. Then he had sauntered to and fro, as if becoming weary of his vigil. At last the cunning rascal had stepped behind the cart, and, once out of sight, had stolen off along the grass track at the side of the road. Within five minutes, before Steve or Abe had guessed that the man was gone, the rat-a-tat-tat of galloping hoofs had come to their ears.

"Pile the bags up on all sides. Don't pitch them out," commanded Steve quickly, his voice hardly raised above a whisper. "Quick, boys, fer we ain't got too much time. Now, git down and stay thar till they're right in the camp. Then, I guess, we'll be doin' some talkin'. Jack, that ere red nob of yours'll be spotted precious quick. Jest keep down below the bags."

Quick as a flash the four leaped into the stranded cart, to find that it was by no means filled full with bags as it appeared to be. They were piled at the back and round the two sides, and, as Jack had guessed, were stuffed with grass. It wanted, therefore, very little work on the part of the little band of four to erect their defences. Indeed, the task was already done for them. Promptly they dropped to the floor of the wagon, while within a few seconds ten mounted men burst from the misty cloud which still clung to the earth and enveloped the surroundings of the wagon, and galloped down upon it like a whirlwind. A minute later they drew rein where Steve and his friends had been sleeping, while exclamations of amazement, of dismay, and of anger burst from them. Jack, squeezing into a corner of the cart, obtained a view of the robbers through a crevice between the boards, and noticed that all were well mounted, that their leader and two others wore black masks across their faces, and that Ted, the rascal who had asked for aid on the previous evening, rode beside the leader.

"Not here! Why, what's happened?" he heard the latter exclaim in angry tones. "There were four, and now——"

"A minute ago they lay there, dead asleep, I could ha' sworn. Now ef that don't beat everything!" cried Ted. "Blessed ef I can understand it. Unless. Hi, boys!" he shouted at the top of his voice, "They've took ter the wagon."

At once the horses were swung round, while the leader of the band swung his arm up, as if about to protect his face. But there was a weapon in the hand, and an instant later a sharp report awakened the echoes of the valley, while the missile struck the tailboard of the wagon, perforated it as if it were made of paper, and encountering the bags of grass, passed right through the nearest, and was only arrested when it had penetrated the second as far as the far layer of canvas. Jack felt the blow, for his hand rested against the bag, and a second later his finger tips came in contact with the rounded form arrested by the obstacle.

"Three of you load up the gold bags," shouted the leader, in a voice which seemed to come familiarly to Jack's ear. "The rest surround the wagon. Thar ain't no need ter parley. We know our business. Shoot every one of them down."

He swung the arm up again, as if about to send a second bullet crashing into the cart. But the action was arrested by the sudden interposition of Steve. A low growl had come from the little scout as he heard the commands of the brigand outside, and, to the astonishment of his friends, he was seen to stand to his full height, in view of the enemy. Then his weapon cracked, and within the same instant the man wearing the mask, who was evidently the leader, toppled from his saddle and fell to the ground.

"Joe Templeton, as I live. Joe Templeton at last!" shouted Steve, as if he had suddenly lost his senses. "I warned yer last time we met, and yer knew well what ter expect. Scum like you has ter come ter the mark sooner or later, and come yer have. Joe Templeton, you aer up agin Steve this time, Steve the hunter and scout, Steve the miner, whom you robbed."

There was a pause in the affray, while attackers and attacked stared at Steve as if they could not believe their senses, and then at the leader of the band, who lay grovelling upon the road. Then, with a sharp cry Ted, the stranger who had watched in the camp all night, swung himself from his horse and rushed towards the wagon.

"Down!" cried Jack, seizing Steve, who seemed to be filled with some unusual excitement. "Down! They are coming."

But the little miner hardly seemed to hear him. Gripping one of the bags with his left hand, he leaned against the pile, his eye fixed upon the enemy. And then such a stream of bullets shot from his weapon that the rascals recoiled.

"See here!" shouted Steve, as if careless of the bullets. "Now that that man Joe aer down, and Ted with him, there ain't no call fer others to be hurt. Quit touchin' those bags and git. I'll give yer one chance. Ef yer don't take it, I swear we'll hunt every mother's son of yer down."

Crack! From a point just behind where the enemy had gathered there came the snap of a revolver, and Steve's left arm dropped helpless to his side. But he never winced or showed that he was hurt. Instead his fingers wrapped themselves round the butt of his second revolver, and the man who had just fired measured his length on the road before Jack could follow what was happening. Then began a fusillade which rivalled an Indian attack for fierceness. Maddened by the sudden and unlooked-for change in their fortunes the brigands poured their shots into the wagon, and would undoubtedly have slain Steve, had Abe not dragged him down behind the shelter of the bags.

"Aer yer crazy, Steve?" he growled. "Aer yer gone suddenly stark starin' mad. Git down, and stay thar. Boys, jest lift a bag above yer heads, and fire from under it."

But for that precaution there is no doubt that Jack and his friends would have suffered heavily. But the bags protected them wonderfully, and so sharp was their own shooting that presently the six men who now remained alive retired from the wagon.

"But they ain't gone," said Steve, cool and calm again after his unusual excitement. "Ef they had rifles with 'em they'd make it that hot this cart wouldn't hold us. Lucky they ain't spotted the guns we left amongst the blankets. Gee! ef we had 'em here we'd make 'em hop."

"Then we'll have 'em."

Jack was no laggard when brave acts were required, as he had proved to the satisfaction of his comrades. At Steve's words, he once more showed the stuff of which he was made. The brigands had retired some hundred yards, but still remained within long pistol-shot. Careless of that, our hero leaped from the cart, walked across to the blankets that marked the spot where he and his comrades had slept, and sauntered back with their rifles, a storm of bullets whistling about his ears as he did so.

JACK FETCHES THE RIFLES

"Now, ef that ain't madness!" cried Steve angrily. "Ef that ain't askin' fer a bullet!"

"And copyin' bad examples set by them as is old enough and ugly enough ter know better," growled Abe. "It's jest the answer ter yer own doin's, Steve, and Jack aer earned the thanks of all. Gee! As ef yer didn't ought ter know better."

He turned scornfully upon the little scout. Then a smile stole across his features, and stretching out a hand he gripped Steve's.

"Reckon ye'd some special call," he said simply.

There was a grim look on the little man's face as he took Abe's hand, a look which seemed to betoken that the cause for his sudden excitement and for his rashness was something beyond him, something he could hardly dare to think about.

"'Cause!" he said, in hollow tones, moistening his lips with his tongue, as if the words dried them. "'Cause——But this ain't the time to tell of Joe and his doin's. Reckon Jack aer done a fine thing ter help us. Jest get to with them rifles. Ah, them critters is tryin' another rush!"

The news was true. From the place to which they had retired the band of brigands suddenly broke into single elements, and came galloping towards the cart. As they came they sent a storm of bullets seething about it, chipping and perforating the woodwork, thudding into the bags, and hissing harmlessly overhead. Two minutes later they were within easy shot, when Jack and his comrades returned their fire, protecting their heads in the same manner; and so careful was their aim that two more of the enemy measured their full length on the ground. There were shouts of anger from those who remained. One galloped his horse recklessly right up to the cart, and was there shot dead by Jack's pistol, then the remainder turned tail and galloped away for their lives. And as they went another accompanied them. Unnoticed in the turmoil, the leader, who had fallen to Steve's shot, and who was undoubtedly sorely wounded, scrambled painfully to his feet and caught a horse belonging to a fallen comrade. He clambered unsteadily into the saddle, his mask falling from his face as he did so; and then, mustering all his failing strength, he stood up in his stirrups and shook his fist at the cart just as his comrades turned to fly.

"Steve," he shouted, "this is to warn you! I will kill you when the time comes."

Turning his horse, he clapped spurs to the flanks and galloped away. As he went a cry came from one of the inmates of the wagon. Jack rose to his feet shaking with excitement. He seemed to have caught it from Steve, so closely did it follow upon the attack which the little scout had displayed. Bending over the bags, shaking his fist furiously, he followed the movements of the escaping leader with staring eyes.

"The robber!" he shouted, tears almost in his voice. "The man for whom I have suffered. The robber! Stop him! I must take him back to Hopeville to tell his tale! It is he who should have been tried for that burglary!"

CHAPTER XXII

A Double Recognition

Utterly oblivious of his surroundings, of the friends who crowded in the cart at his side, Jack stood pressing forward against the bulwark of grass-stuffed sacks, his fingers clutching at the canvas, his attitude and expression betokening the greatest excitement. He was pale to the lips, save that a bright, hectic spot burned in each cheek, while, strangest thing of all, tears coursed from his eyes and dribbled down on his chin.

"Come back!" he shouted. "Come back! We will not fire! Come back and act like a man, if it be for the very last time."

But he might have shouted his words to the winds, for all the effect they may have had. Joe, the rascally leader of the brigands—for that seemed to be his name, since Steve had so called him—paid no attention to the calls. Crouched low in the saddle, wobbling dangerously from side to side on account of his weakness, he struck his mount savagely with the spur, and went tearing away after his comrades.

"And nothin'll stop the varmint till we put hand on him, and then he'll be up to tricks till the sheriff and his men has placed a rope about his neck and has swung him," growled Steve. "Come, lad," he went on in soothing tones, laying a restraining hand on Jack's shoulder. "Seems to me that you, too, ha' had cause ter hate that thar varmint. Wall, I thought as how I'd finished with him, same as he thought ter have done fer me, this many a year gone by. But I ain't sorry that the bullet didn't kill him, for by what you've said ye're in want of Joe's evidence. But don't count too much on it, Carrots. That 'ere man aer the cussedest, the wickedest, that ever lived in these parts, and that's the true thought of every man as has come ter really know him. Sit down. Let's have a smoke. Time enough ter git followin'. Tusker Joe aer hard hit, and reckon we'll take him."

"Tusker Joe! Tusker Joe!" Jack searched his memory. At the back of a mind, fully engaged with his own particular troubles, there loomed a certain recollection of that name. "Tusker Joe!"

"Ah!" In a flash it all came back to him. "You called him that?" he asked, turning on Steve and facing him eagerly. "Tell me, was he ever a miner? Did he work in these parts some few years ago, and was he notorious for anything in particular?"

"Jest get a grip of that 'ere pipe and pull at it," said Steve soothingly, coolly filling Jack's pipe and placing it between his lips. "Thar's the coal ter light it," he went on, stooping over the fire, and snatching a glowing ember with his fingers. "Now, boys, thar's hosses round about, and bags of gold. Let's get things tidied up, then we'll talk. Meanwhile me and Jack'll sit down. Me, because I'm wantin' a little bandagin', and Tom here'll do it fer me; and Carrots, 'cos he's shook up badly about some matter, and a man don't get the better of such troubles when he's all of a shake. We're jest agoin' ter have a dram apiece from the keg, and reckon, when you're finished clearin' things up, him and me'll be ready to talk, and fix what's to happen in the future."

As cool as any icicle, the little scout calmly filled and lit his own pipe, and then went for the small keg in which the party kept their supply of spirit. For, though abstemious himself, and conscious of the fact that Jack touched nothing of an alcoholic nature, Steve saw that something was necessary at the moment to help to pull his young comrade together. Jack, indeed, was far more agitated than he had ever been in his whole life. Not even when first accused of that burglary, and weighed down with the desperate feeling of his own innocence and helplessness, had he shown so much emotion. But it is often a fact that while a man can face danger and difficulty, can endure hardship, wrongful accusation, and even unmerited imprisonment and punishment, with a certain amount of stoicism, yet, when relief suddenly comes in sight, when there suddenly and unexpectedly appears upon the scene that something for which he has longed—oh, so much and so continuously!—his stoicism and fortitude evaporate, the revulsion of feeling overwhelms him, and in a moment he is changed from a strong man, nobly supporting his burdens, to a child, helplessly weak.

So it was with our hero. A cloud seemed to have risen suddenly in front of his eyes, a cloud which upset his vision, which turned him giddy, and mastered every fibre in his active body. He sat down trembling, obediently drank the contents of the pannikin which Steve offered him, and then mechanically sucked at his pipe. As for Steve, he doled out a dram for himself, and, having drained the tin, lay down to rest and watch his young friend. Meanwhile Tom and Abe collected five horses left by the brigands, laid the bodies of those killed side by side, and inspected their own belongings.

"It tots up handsome," exclaimed Abe at length, rejoining Steve and Jack. "We started in with our own hosses and the animals. Now we've got five fresh mounts that'll fetch a nice sum; six revolvers that belonged ter them varmint;

and, as if that warn't enough, thar's two bags of real gold dust in thar amongst them bags stuffed with grass. Reckon they was laid thar to open and show, in case you was too suspicious."

Steve went off into a roar of laughter at the news, for he was wonderfully light-hearted now that his excitement had died down.

"I never knew a band of rascals so taken in and knocked about," he cried. "And ter think as they've left us gold dust ter add to our own, instead of takin' ours! Wall, I did think ter ax that 'ere Ted ef it was real gold as he had in them bags, and ef he'd mind my squinting at it. But then, when I come to think it out, I seed that ter do that would be ter raise suspicions. He'd get thinking that I wasn't satisfied with his yarn. That would ha' made him more wideawake, instead of so cocksure that all was panning out as he wished. Then, guess we shouldn't have managed ter get ter that cart, and——"

"We should ha' been thar," said Tom grimly, pointing to the bodies laid reverently side by side.

"And now we've got ter fix what ter do," cried Steve, becoming matter of fact. "Thar's the gold to be thought of, thar's the chaps as has gone down, and in course there's bound ter be an enquiry. And, last of all, thar's them as got away. Wall?"

He turned to Abe, as if seeking an inspiration from him. The big, bony scout, reddened with exposure to the sun, and looking the strong, courageous man he was, spoke out without hesitation. His life, like that of his comrades, allowed of no hesitation. Decisions had to be come to on the spot, without delay; for often enough a life was concerned.

"Huh! There ain't two ways about it," he exclaimed gruffly. "The nearest settlement is jest three hours' ride from here, and sense ye're wounded ye'll be the one ter sit right here and keep guard. Me and Tom and Carrots'll push on quick, and place the gold in the bank. We'll warn the sheriff, too, and by evenin' we'll be back along with yer, bringing a tidy few of the boys that we'll pick up. It stands to reason that others has suffered from these varmint wuss than we have, and when they hear that the band has had a knock, they'll be out ter make an end of 'em. Wall, then, we'll get on their tracks by evenin', and ter-morrow night those of 'em as is wounded, and I've a notion that aer the case with all that's left, will ha' been surrounded and took. That's whar you and Jack comes in."

There was common sense in the arrangement, and at once preparations for departure were made. Tom set to work to prepare breakfast, for none had touched food so far, and as soon as that was finished the three friends would leave Steve behind and make for the settlements.

"And afore yer go we've got ter discuss this other matter," said Steve, nursing his wounded arm, which Jack had bandaged for him. "Thar aer this feller Tusker Joe. Now, I don't want ter ax fer any confidences, but Carrots here ha' said enough ter let us know somethin' of what's been on his mind. I've said afore now that thar was a man somewhars in America as would shoot me on sight, and fer whom I'd do the same ef I catched him. Wall, seems that that same man aer the one fer whom Jack ha' been searching. That so?"

He turned bluntly to our hero with his question.

"You have hit the right nail on the head," he answered simply. "That man, Tusker Joe, has indeed had a great deal to do with my life. I will tell you all about it. But first let us have Steve's tale."

It was an eager trio which bent towards the little scout to listen, and sorely was their patience tried as Steve filled his pipe nonchalantly, and, staring at the ground, took ample time to refresh his memory.

"Wall, you shall have it," he said, "and short and to the point. It's a dozen years ago, maybe a little more, when I came over the mountains ter try my luck in the diggin's. And luck came my way right from the beginnin'. I struck it rich, and seemed ter have a fortune in my hand, when a fever took me, and what with nussing, and sichlike, what I'd earned precious near went altogether. But thar was enough ter make a second start, and soon I was peggin' a claim down in another gully that had got a reputation fer richness. Thar was five hundred miners thar, and one of 'em was Tusker Joe. He'd come fresh that way, so he said, was lookin' fer a partner, and, havin' a bit of gold with him, was ready and willin' ter pay fer a share."

"The same tale!" cried Jack, interrupting the little scout. "But go along, Steve, I have heard the tale before. Tusker Joe practised the very same method in another part. I can almost tell you what happened."

"Then you can tell of the most ruffianly thing as ever a man did. Mates, if a man pals up with another, and they become partners, it don't say as thar won't be quarrels. Rows do occur. I've seen 'em, and seen shootin' follow. But partners don't murder one another. They don't go behind the back of a man whose hand they've shook friendly an hour before, and let off a gun right at 'em. That are the work of an utter scoundrel."

There was indignation in Steve's voice, and the words he uttered brought sympathetic grunts of agreement from Tom and Abe.

"Reckon a chap like that aer one of the worst men that's ter be found," cried Abe. "This Tusker Joe, he war the man? Eh? He did the shootin'?"

Steve nodded curtly.

"We'd struck it rich. Leastwise, I had, fer he pretended ter be ill, and didn't work. Thar was a store of gold dust that was worth the havin'. Wall, this here critter, all friendly as one would think, stepped down to our claim one evenin' when it war almost dark, and when all the other miners had gone back to their shanties.

"How's luck?" he asks, setting down.

"Same as afore," I answered. "This here claim's rich. It'll pan out handsome fer us, and then it'll sell when we're tired of it."

"'Good,'" he says, "and then, all of a sudden, I knew nothing more."

"Shot?" demanded Tom in a whisper.

"From behind," answered Steve, flicking the ash from the bowl of his pipe. "See thar. That's where the bullet caught me."

He turned his head and pointed to a long, white streak behind the right ear.

"Enough ter kill a man," he proceeded, "but Steve aer a hard nut."

The very thought made the little scout chuckle. "A hard nut," he repeated. "Tusker reckoned he'd wiped me out, but he hadn't, and, what's more, he didn't have another chance, fer some miners happened ter be passing. But he cleared from that 'ere camp with every ounce of dust we'd gained, and with my bag of dollars into the bargain. Gentlemen, when a man gets treated like that he takes an oath, and when the time comes round, as come it must, he 'lows as he has a sorter right ter shoot on sight the ruffian what's left him fer dead. Ter kinder execute him. That aer the long and the short of the story."

The pipe went to the mouth, the cheeks caved in a little as he sucked, and then a cloud of smoke emerged from the hunter's lips.

"I aer acted up ter that oath," he said quietly. "Reckon no one can blame me."

"Not the sheriff hisself," growled Abe. "Even ef this Tusker chap hadn't been one of the band as attacked us, and ye'd hit up face ter face with him in the settlements, yer had a right, accordin' ter minin' law, ter shoot him down without warnin'. Steve, it aer clear that it war meant fer you ter get the best of this here Tusker. Reckon his chances of gettin' off ain't worth a how of chips."

"I will follow him till my horse drops, or until he shoots me."

It was Jack who had spoken, and as his three comrades turned to look at him, they saw on the face of the young fellow who had worked so well and so cheerily with them such decision and determination that all but Steve were astonished.

"You ain't seen Carrots like that afore," explained Steve, "but I have. I mind the time when he treated me as ef I war a kid, and started in with his orders. Jack aer got some better reason than I have fer following Tusker. Out with it, lad."

"Then listen." Briefly, bluntly, Jack told the tale of his own father's death, how a man named Tusker Joe had entered into partnership with him at the mines, had picked a quarrel with him when gold dust in considerable quantity had been obtained, and, having shot him down in a saloon after the pretence of a quarrel, had decamped with all the gold.

"Then you ha' got good reason fer following this here scoundrel of a Tusker," cried Abe. "Reckon when a man's father aer shot down like that, the son has got ter have a say with his murderer. I ain't one as believes in revenge. Thar's One above"—the sunburned scout swept his hat from his head for a moment and paused—"thar's One above as sees ter sech matters as that as a general rule. But ef a father's killed in cold blood, it aer plainly the duty of his son ter find the murderer and hand him over to justice. Jack, give us yer fist. I'm proud ter know as ye've been a good son."

Each in turn gripped his hand, for rough scouts such as these were could and did appreciate fine qualities in other people. Already Jack's willingness to work, his unfailing good temper and his common sense, had won their esteem, while the tale of his behaviour when Steve was incapacitated had not failed to leave its impression on them. Believing that he had come to California with one object in view, and that to discover his father's murderer, they felt he was a man they could honour, though in years he had not reached man's estate. But Jack quickly undeceived them.

"Stop!" he cried peremptorily. "You are mistaken. I did not come to California to discover my father's murderer. It was another man I was thinking of. I came this way to escape the law; for, my friends, I am a runaway prisoner."

In a few words he told them of the misfortune which had befallen him, how he had been put on his trial, and how, despairing of obtaining evidence which would acquit him, he had bolted from the prison, with the object first of making himself secure from the officers of the law, and, when that was securely accomplished, with the firm determination of hunting for that man who had come to the smithy in Hopeville, and for whom he had forged that fatal key.

"Gentlemen," he cried, "that is the man I have been searching for, with the feeling all this while that some day or other I should drop across him. It was to clear myself from the accusation wrongly put upon me that I came to California, and at last I have seen the man. Strange though it may seem to you—almost unbelievable—yet it is the truth indeed. That ruffian who murdered my father is the identical man who, a few years later, induced me to forge a key, and for whose crime I was placed in the dock. I have double reason to follow and take him."

"Thunder!" shouted Steve.

"Ef that don't walk right away with the prize!" growled Abe, his teeth closing with a sharp click on the stem of his pipe.

"And ye've got as good cause, better still, ter shoot the ruffian when next yer set eyes on him," exclaimed Tom. "Jack, it aer clear as it aer fer you ter deal with this here Tusker Joe. Steve has a call, and he's already had an innings. Reckon it aer fer him ter stand back a while and let yer have a turn."

"No. I would not harm a hair of his head," responded Jack solemnly. "Listen here, mates. If I got to shooting this man, where, then, should I be able to obtain evidence of my own innocence? I should destroy it myself, and with that evidence goes all hope of my ever clearing myself, or of my being able at any time to return to Hopeville and the State of New York."

"Right! Right to a 'T'," cried Steve. "The lad aer dead on it when he says that, and I'll tell yer. Ef we meets that man, or any of the others yer hope ter bring back with yer from the settlements, then thar ain't ter be any shootin'. He's got ter be taken alive. And afore any sheriff kin hang him he aer got ter come out with a confession. Mates, in these parts it's lynch law. Ef a man robs another way back in settled parts he gets imprisonment. Ef he does the same in Californy, amongst the diggin's, or away on the plains, he gets short shrift—trial out in the open, jedgment by the sheriff, ef there happens ter be one, and ef thar don't, then by his mates; and in the last case, ef he's declared guilty, he's shot out of hand or strung up ter a tree. That's what'll happen ter Tusker. But, first of all, he's got ter make that confession."

"And the sooner we follow him and his mates the better," cried Abe. "Let's git. So long, Steve! we'll be back aginst evenin'."

They strapped their bags of gold on the horses, and, leading the captured animals, set off at a brisk trot, leaving Steve comfortably seated before the fire. Some three hours later they reached the township for which they had been aiming, and promptly proceeded to the bank, where the gold was carefully weighed out before their eyes, its value appraised, and a receipt given for it. Then Abe led the way to the sheriff's residence.

"We've come on business," he said in his blunt, direct fashion. "We come up agin Tusker Joe and his band last night, and nigh dropped into a muss. They'd set a trap for us, and thought ter take us nicely. But they hadn't ter do with miners only on this occasion. We're all hunters and scouts, leastwise with the exception of Jack here. We seed thar was something queer, and when they opened with their game we was ready, so it's Tusker and his men as fell inter the muss. Thar's five killed, and t'others is hurt I should say. Tusker's nigh killed."

"Then you have broken up the band. Gee! That aer good," said the sheriff, who had been a miner before he attained to his present position. "That Tusker's been the terror of the camps fer the last three months. They'd heard of him before out in these parts, and, ef tales aer true, he ought to ha' been had up fer murder. But once he reached the diggin's, whether he was wanted fer murder or not, he soon got wanted fer other crimes. He and his gang has held up a sight of gold convoys, and they have killed a goodish few men. Whar have they gone?"

"That's a question thar ain't no answering, boss," said Abe promptly; "but we're game ter follow, and I'll tell yer why."

Promptly he proceeded to tell the sheriff of Steve's acquaintance with Tusker Joe, of the murder of Jack's father, and, finally, of the burglary which the rascal had committed, and for which our hero had very nearly suffered condemnation to a long term of imprisonment.

"It aer clear that the man has ter be caught," added Abe, "and that fer the sake of Jack here he has got ter be taken alive."

"Jest hop in and take a cup of coffee, gentlemen," said the sheriff. "The news you bring is the best I have had for many a long day, for this Tusker has been the terror of the roads. I'll go and see a few of my friends, and I think I shall be able to persuade some of them to ride with us."

An hour later no fewer than fifteen men set off from the township with Jack and his friends, the sheriff and Abe riding at their head. The delay in the departure had enabled Tom to find a buyer for the horses, so that, beyond Steve's injury, the little party was substantially better off after their affray with the brigands than they were before. That evening, as the shades were lengthening, they rode up to the stranded cart, to discover Steve smoking his pipe placidly and warming himself in front of the fire.

"Not a soul has passed the camp all day," he reported, "so I set to ter get on the tracks of them 'ere fellers. Ef it's the same to you all, gentlemen, we'll have a feed and then push on. The moon'll be up by nine, and thar ain't any reason why we shouldn't make the most of the light. Tusker won't be expecting such haste, most like, and so thar'll be a better chance of taking him."

Accordingly the party slipped from their saddles, slackened their girths, and, having watered the horses, sat down to a substantial meal. Two hours later they mounted again, and, led by Steve, who carried his injured arm in a sling, they trotted beneath the rays of the moon down the straggling road, and, some three miles along it, turned on to the grass border, and struck across towards the mountains which cut across the skyline.

"Somewhars up thar you'll find Tusker Joe, the murderer, and his mates," said Steve solemnly, pointing to the mountains.

CHAPTER XXIII

Steve Leads the Way

Weirdly strange were the shadows cast by the moonlight upon the earth as the party of miners and hunters turned from the road towards the mountains. The huge gleaming and silvery orb hung in a cloudless sky, typical of gorgeous California, and cast her beams from a point behind the party, so that the shadows of the horses danced in front of the men, thin, and angular, and misshapen, and stretching so far in advance that the lines of the horses they rode, actually so pleasant to look upon, were transfigured and made hideous and absurd. Above these same shadows were those of the men, jogging this way and that, topped by a sombrero, and often enough by a sharp-cut shadow, denoting the rifle the man carried.

"The gun that's got ter do with Tusker," said Steve as Jack trotted along beside him. "I believe ef it warn't fer men of his breed, and fer the saloons and the bad spirit that's sold in 'em, thar wouldn't be no need fer weapons out here, save, in course, fer use agin them Injun varmints. Fer California ain't free of them altogether, and ef it war, and we was unarmed, the critters would be pourin' over the ranges in their thousands, huntin' fer scalps. Boys, jest take a word o' warnin' from one as has been on games same as this afore. Don't ride in a bunch. Scatter, and spread yerselves out. Then, ef there's a man 'way up thar with his gun ter his shoulder, the chances aer he'll miss. Savvy?"

The men did savvy. The band who were riding out to capture the last of the gang of ruffians who had terrorized that part of the goldfields, and between them had committed many murders, was composed of individuals with an abundance of experience. For, as Steve had said earlier on, California was infested by brigands and ruffians of the worst description, who preyed upon the miners, and against whom the strictest measures were necessary. There were constant alarms, gold convoys were often held up, and not infrequently the sheriff was compelled to call upon the citizens of some little place to ride with him with the object of exterminating some of the ruffians. So it happened that there were always men to be found who had accompanied such expeditions, and who, therefore, knew what precautions to take, and how necessary it was to use cunning and care when approaching the enemy.

"Jest wait a bit," cried Steve after a while, when the party had traversed some three miles of the grass-grown plain and were already on the foothills. "It ain't so easy ter slide from yer saddle when ye've an arm in a sling. But I kin do it if the hoss aer still. Now then, mates, ef one of yer'll lead that hoss I'll shift along on foot and follow the trail. Thar ain't no difficulty hereabouts, fer a child could see their marks. But we're comin' ter rocky parts, and then it'll be a conundrum."

Half an hour later the climb had become steeper, though not too much so for the horses. But what Steve had mentioned had already occurred. They were on rocky ground, though some herbage appeared amidst the boulders. But as yet the little scout, his eye fixed upon the trail, went steadily upward and onward, never hesitating for the particle of a second.

"They know as well as I do thet any chap could follow so far," he said after a while. "Thar ain't no finding a road free of grass and soft places hereabouts. But up thar it'll be different. Then we shall have ter nose round a bit, and even then we're pretty safe ter be bothered."

It was not until they had traversed another mile, and were approaching very steep ground, that Steve raised his hand, and brought the whole party to a halt.

"Jest as I expected," he cried, dropping on hands and knees, and managing to scramble along in spite of his damaged arm. "Them artful critters rode this far, and then halted ter look around and choose a safe line. There ain't a blade of grass above us, and, in course, they've gone right on. But they may ha' turned ter the right or ter the left, and this here mountain aer long enough ter give 'em shelter and a hidin' place whichever way they go. Mates, jest stand fer a bit. Thar may be a trace, and it'd be best not ter override it. Abe, slip outer yer saddle and take a look round."

It was ten minutes before either of the scouts ventured to speak, meanwhile the remainder of the party dismounted, and, hitching their reins over their shoulders, filled their pipes and lit them. Steve and Abe, often on hands and knees, covered the ground in circles, and seemed as if they would continue in the same occupation, till of a sudden a cry came from Abe.

"Helloo!" he shouted. "Jest hop along up here. Here's somethin'."

It proved to be a dark stain on a patch of whitish pebbles, and both he and Steve pronounced it without a moment's hesitation to be a blood stain.

"That 'ere Tusker," declared Steve with a grunt. "He was feelin' queerish, most like, and called a halt. He rolled out of his saddle and lay jest here till one of his mates come and picked him up. Yer can see thar was more than one. Them stones is kicked about. This aer a find! I 'low as I war bothered back thar. Them critters seemed ter have clean slipped off into air."

"Reckon they took this line ter the right," answered Abe, "and I've a sorter notion that we'll be able ter follow, fer seems ter me as there's more of them stains. Maybe one of the hosses is hurt, and aer leavin' a trail as he goes."

In a little while Jack and his friends did indeed have displayed before them an example which many might take to heart. He and the little band of pursuers had arrived at a part where, if the enemy were cunning, as they undoubtedly were, they ought to be able to disappear without leaving so much as a track, a broken blade of grass, or a hoof-print to guide those who followed. Yet, with all their caution, a clear trail was left, though they knew nothing of it. For one of the horses, shot in the leg perhaps, imprinted a blood-stained hoof every yard of the way they had followed, making pursuit to men like Steve and Abe a simple matter. It was an indication of the fact that, while circumstances may for a while be favourable to evil-doers, sooner or later there comes some unforeseen event which trips them up.

"I've know'd a thing same as this afore," said Steve. "It war after one of them Injun raids 'way over them mountains, when the critters had come out on the warpath without so much as a warnin'. Wall, they killed and scalped every man, woman, and child as they could drop on, and fired the settlers' farms over fifty miles. George Trueman, he war a settler, and it seems he'd been 'way over the border ter see a man as was lookin' ter buy cattle. He comed back ter find the farm a mass of blackened cinders, his cattle gone, and the box as he kept his dollars in taken clear away. Trueman war wild. He war fixed up ter get married, and though he could put up with the burnin' of the farm, the loss of the money would pretty nigh ruin him. Yer kin guess what happened."

"Followed the critters, I suppose," suggested Abe.

"Sure. Got a band o' men together, same as we aer, and sets off. Wall, I war one of the band, and pretty soon I gets on ter a trail like this, made by a hoss that war wounded, but not so bad as he couldn't go. That trail ran on fer thirty mile, till you'd have thought the hoss would ha' fallen dead, and in the end we dropped into them critters, and George recovered the money."

"While this time we recover the man," laughed Abe. "Jest you hop into yer saddle agin, Steve. Ye'll ride easy thar, and it don't do that arm no good walkin' in these rough places. Reckon I kin follow the trail."

Thanks to the spots of blood, sometimes scattered sparsely on the stones, and at others imprinted in the form of a hoof Abe was able to stride along without a halt. For an hour he led the party without turning aside. Then suddenly he faced up the mountain, and began to clamber.

"Them critters brought their hosses up," he cried over his shoulder, "so guess yer kin do the same. But the goin' aer bad, and ye'd best be skeary, and look out fer holes."

The place was, in fact, difficult for horses, and it needed much care on the part of the riders to take them up such a steep and rough place. However, it was not long before the ground sloped a little less steeply, and then became almost flat. Abe led the way across this without a falter, and very soon Jack became aware of the fact that he and his friends were actually descending.

"A kinder hollow," explained Steve. "Precious soon things'll be happenin'."

Scarcely five minutes had elapsed, in fact, before the nerves of these hardy miners and hunters were somewhat startled by a loud report. A single shot rang out from some point in advance, and high up above them, while one of the horses squealed, plunged heavily, and then stood shivering and shaking.

"Wall, of all the critters!" cried one of the miners, slipping from the injured animal's back. "I didn't think as a man could see us down here in the hollow, let alone train a gun on us. Reckon it war lucky we war all spread out. Gently, lass. Yer ain't badly hurt. This here aer no wuss than a pinprick. The ball catched her two inches from her withers, on the very edge of the neck. It ain't worth mentionin', old gal."

He patted his mount soothingly, and soon had her in a happier frame of mind. Then, dropping the reins on her neck, he left her to herself, and within less than half a minute she was seeking for grass tufts amongst the boulders. Meanwhile the other men had dismounted, while Steve and Abe discussed matters with the sheriff.

Bang! From a point some seventy yards above the heads of the party, and a considerable distance away, there rang out another report, while a splotch of flame leaped from the mountain side. But it was gone in a moment; and when Jack fixed his eyes in that direction it was to see merely brown rocks and boulders tumbled haphazard on the mountain side, and all bathed in the rays of the moon, rays which gave a ghostly, eerie appearance to the surroundings. As for the bullet which had been discharged, it hummed through the air, striking a rock at our hero's feet with a resounding clang, and afterwards glissading off into space, where the ricochetting object set up a piercing scream that added to the uncanny effect produced by the moonbeams.

"And no one hurt. That's luck!" sang out the sheriff. "Now, gentlemen, it aer clear that them fellers way up thar ha' got the drop on us. Down here the moon throws our shadows, and, even ef they can't see us, a shadow is close enough ter aim at, and is bound to bring a bullet precious near before long. Leave the hosses and make fer the hill. Thar ain't no use waitin'."

"None," agreed Steve promptly. "Ef we stay down here, sooner or later, as Mr. Sheriff says, some of us'll be gettin' in the way of a bullet, and that ain't sense. But, seems to me, we might spare three or four who aer good shots ter lie down amongst these boulders and give them critters a shot whenever they show whar they aer located. Thet'll keep 'em from payin' us too much attention."

The trusty little scout was not the one to neglect or to forget a precaution at such a moment, and his advice was hailed with eagerness. It was dangerous work this pursuit of criminals, and more often than not men were killed; for the rascals who infested the goldfields knew what capture meant. It ended, in nearly every instance, in a hasty trial and summary execution. Consequently there was no thought of giving in. The contest was always one almost to the death.

"Supposin' Steve stays right here," sang out Abe. "He ain't no good fer climbing with that arm of his, and, sence it's his left, he'll be able ter hold a gun with his right and rest it on a boulder. Lively does it, mates. Ef we stay jawin', them critters'll soon be gettin' the range of some of us."

As he finished speaking, as if to impress his words upon the band of pursuers, four shots rang out from the mountain side above them, and again was heard the thud of bullets, while splinters of stone were scattered broadcast.

"Wall, get to it, Steve," called out the sheriff, "and you too, Bill Hendy and Frank Gorman. Let 'em see as you know how ter pepper 'em with lead, and keep at it with your guns till we're pretty close and handy. Thar ain't any fear of your shootin' into us, 'cos the moon's that bright yer can see easy. So long! Make it hot for them scoundrels."

Promptly Steve and the two men detailed for the work dropped on their faces amidst the boulders, and, each selecting a large rock which was high enough to give him shelter from bullets fired from above, proceeded to unsling his rifle. Nor was it long before the opportunity came to them to fire. Once more the same red splotch of flame spurted from the mountain side. It was answered almost instantly by three shots from below, and within the space of half a minute by an echoing scream from above. Then a dark, ill-defined figure started up from the mountain side, and for a moment a man stood erect, his shadow cast on the brown earth and rocks behind him. One arm was raised above his head, and the rays of the moon showed that the hand gripped a rifle. Thus he stood for a few seconds, as if staring down into the hollow where Steve and his mates lay. Then, pitching forward suddenly, he fell headlong, bringing an avalanche of smaller stones and boulders chasing after him.

"Fetched him," said Steve coolly. "Thar ain't no sayin' whose shot it war. Reckon me and these two mates of mine ha' had occasion to fire in similar sarcumstances afore. I give him a range jest a foot below the flame of his rifle, and I guess it fetched him. Ah! There's another of them."

One after another the shots rang out from the mountain side, while Steve and his friends replied as rapidly as they could. While they did so, Jack and the others raced from the hollow and, using hands and feet, clambered up the steep slope. Not a sound came from their ranks, for all their breath was required for the task before them. They never paused to look above them, nor noticed when the defenders of the position stood out from their lair and discharged their rifles at them. They clambered steadily and quickly upward, leaving the three friends below to look to their defence, and to pour in such a fire that the rascals would not dare to expose themselves.

"There they are! Close in on them!"

In his eagerness to come upon the ruffianly Tusker Joe, and capture him, Jack forged ahead of the others. He was younger than they and more agile, and, without being aware of the fact, had rapidly outstripped them. And now he suddenly came upon the lurking place of the enemy. Clambering round a boulder of unusual proportions, he came to a level spot, a narrow pathway which ran on either hand till it was lost on the face of the steep slope. Here, some six yards to his left, four men were crouching, one of them being in the act of firing down at the hollow as he looked.

"Rush them! Down with them!" Jack shouted. "But don't shoot Tusker."

Careless of the consequences, blinded to his own danger by the excitement of the moment, and urged to strenuous exertion by the ever-present thought that here, almost in his own hands, was the evidence for which he sought, Jack raced along the ledge, dashed into the centre of the group of men, and became engaged at once in a desperate struggle. A man seemed to rise up before him, and in a moment they were locked together in an embrace which nothing but the death or disablement of one or other would terminate. They stood on the very edge of the ledge, the steep slope running away precipitously below them, and swayed to and fro, swayed so far over the edge that it looked as if they must lose their footing and fall.

As they staggered this way and that, others of the gang of desperadoes clubbed their rifles and made every effort to bring the butts crashing on to Jack's head. But always some frantic twist or turn of the combatants, some violent change of position on his part, upset their aim and caused them to fail in their object.

Meanwhile Steve and his two friends below had ceased firing, and stood watching the contest with staring eyes. For the little scout the moments dragged heavily. The struggle he witnessed up there on the mountain side was more than momentous. It stirred him to the deepest depths, for he had more than a friendly feeling for our hero.

"Back him up!" he bellowed, placing his hands to his mouth. "Can't yer see we can't help him. Git to and rush them, or they'll kill him. Gosh! Ef only I war there. I'd——"

He came to a sudden stop and stood rooted to the spot, his heart in his mouth, a sudden and unusual feeling of depression about him. For help had not yet reached our hero. The brilliant rays of the moon showed the other members of the band of pursuers almost within reach of the ledge, but not quite there. It showed also the figures of five men struggling furiously on the mountain side, and one of those from his height and build was undoubtedly our hero. The mob of men seemed to be thrusting him from the ledge, and as Steve stared he saw Jack striking out valiantly with his fists, for the man who had gripped him had suddenly let go his hold. Then there was a shout, and one of the rascals attacking him leaped forward and wound his arms round Jack's body. Steve shut his eyes and shuddered.

"Gone," he thought. "They'll throw him down."

But no. When he looked again the position of affairs had not altered. Jack was there, on the very edge of the ledge, staggering to and fro in the arms of the ruffian who had gripped him. While the others had of a sudden turned their attention to the pursuers who were now within striking distance. There came on a sudden the sharp, distinctive snap of a pistol, and then a shout from Steve which awoke the echoes. For Jack had disappeared. A second before he and his antagonist had been poised on the edge of the ledge. Now they were gone, there came only the clatter and rattle of boulders and stones which came rolling and leaping down the mountain side.

"Killed!" groaned Steve. "Thar ain't a doubt but that they've done for him."

"Not they. Jest let's go and look for him," sang out Bill Hendy. "I've knowed a man fall heavier and farther by far than that, and have nary a scratch ter show fer it. 'Sides, he's young, and young bones take a deal of breakin'. He warn't shot, that I'll swear. It war the sheriff's shot as ended the struggle."

His mind full of doubt and misgiving, and yet, with his accustomed courage, still hopeful that Jack would prove to have escaped, Steve led the way up the mountain side till he reached a spot some forty feet below the ledge on which the brigands had taken refuge. And there they found our hero, wedged in between two boulders, breathing very shallowly, and quite unconscious. Beneath him lay the body of the man who had held him so firmly in his embrace.

"Dead?" asked Steve, hardly daring to ask or to touch our hero.

"No more nor you nor me," came the hearty answer. "Jest knocked silly, which ain't ter be wondered at, seein' as he's fell nigh fifty feet. Reckon this here fellow saved the fall for him. He's dead. Dead as mutton."

"Not a bone broken, or I am much mistaken," exclaimed Steve, running his hands over Jack's limbs, for in his eagerness and anxiety the little scout had slipped his wounded arm from the sling. "Stunned. Then he'll take no harm. He'll sleep well to-night, and to-morrow he'll eat as good a breakfast as ever he did. Wall, mates, what's the tale?"

The contest was entirely over by now, and, within five feet of the spot where Jack lay, one of the miners was seated on a rock stolidly smoking, while a companion bandaged up an ugly wound in his thigh.

"Jest a snap shot, like," he explained pleasantly to Steve as he sucked at his pipe. "Thought he was downed and done fer. But he warn't, the critter! He sits up sudden and let's fly, then dropped back as dead as t'others."

"Then you finished 'em?" asked Steve.

"There was five beside Tusker Joe," explained the sheriff, coming up at the moment. "I got in a shot at the man who had collared young Jack, and I dessay you saw 'em both come tumbling. Then two more was shot and wounded afore yer could count the seconds. But they got clear away in the scuffle. A fourth fell to a ball fired from one of you three as we was mounting the hill, while the fifth got hit by a ricochet. Anyway, when we arrived, there he war lyin' insensible beside Tusker."

"And him? He's dead too?" asked Steve, anxiety in his voice.

"Jest livin'. Played out after ridin' so far after sich a wound. He'll go ef we ain't careful."

"And with his life all chance of Jack gettin' his evidence," cried Steve. "See here, Sheriff, it means a hull lot fer this young friend of mine, and seein' what's happened I feel I kin count on you and the other mates ter help. We'll send along fer a surgeon, and meanwhile rig up a cover fer Tusker and the other man. Ef tryin'll do it, we'll save the man who killed Jack's father and then led the young chap hisself into sech a scrape. I can kinder count on you?"

"Yer kin," was the emphatic answer. "You and your special mates have saved us a hull heap. Tusker and his gang were a real terror, and we and other folks are grateful. In course we'll stay. As soon as the mornin' comes we'll fix up a shanty, and meanwhile I'll send one of the men back to the settlement."

They were a practical lot, those miners and scouts, and in a little while one of them was speeding from the spot mounted on the best horse and leading another. Meanwhile Jack was laid on some piled-up blankets, where he quickly recovered consciousness, for he was merely stunned by the fall.

"You aer jest ter lie thar as ef you was properly dead," smiled Steve. "That'll bring yer round sooner than anything. Thar's some coffee in my haversack, and in a while, when thar's been time to get a fire goin', we'll brew some of it extry strong. It'll clear yer head. A good sound sleep after that aer all that's wanted."

The little scout had picked up a fund of information in a practical school. His was the class of knowledge which, combined with a vast amount of experience and with common sense beyond the ordinary, is of real service in such cases as Jack's. It was not with him a little dangerous knowledge, as is sometimes the case.

"We aer got ter be particular careful with this here Tusker," he said, when Jack was securely tucked in his blanket. "His life are more valuable I guess than even Jack's, and thet's sayin' something, fer the lad thar aer a bright one. Let's jest have a look at the man."

They carried the wounded and unconscious robber into the shadow cast by a rock, and there Steve carefully inspected his wound.

"Plumb in the chest," he said, as he opened the shirt, and rolled Tusker over. "It aer clear that the bullet has broke through into the lung, and as fer as I can see it don't make much odds whether it's gone right through or remained inside. But we'll make sure."

By dint of the greatest care he and the man who was helping him rolled Tusker over still farther, only to discover that the ball which had struck him in the chest had wounded the lung, but had failed to emerge. It seemed, indeed, at first sight, as if there was little left for such inexperienced surgeons to do save to place the man in a comfortable position, shield him from the sun, and await his return to consciousness. But Steve was a knowing little fellow.

"I tell yer his life's extry valuable," he said, standing up beside his patient, "and we are got to move ef we want to save it. Not that he aer likely ter pull through. Reckon this aer Tusker's last call. Now, mate, lend a hand. We'll put some sort of a dressing on the wound, and then, seeing as he's still losing blood, we'll have ter make shift ter stop it. Yer see, it ain't the bleeding from the outside wound that matters. It's what's coming from the lung."

This important fact had not escaped Steve and his comrade. There was a deathly pallor about the robber chief which showed that he was desperately hurt, and that the hæmorrhage had already been severe. Then, too, the corners of his mouth were discoloured, while a few red drops hung on his chin.

"It stands ter reason," said Steve, speaking as if he were arguing the matter out with himself, "that nature aer doing her best ter help Tusker. He aer scarcely breathing, fer the simple reason thet ef he was moving his chest same as you and me, and with it his lung, why the movement of the one that's wounded

214

would make the loss of blood even wuss. Thet bein' so, we'll take a lesson from nature. Lend a hand. Reckon we'll roll him on ter the side that's damaged. The weight of his body will hold the ribs still, and so rest the wounded lung."

Very carefully and tenderly did they set to work. An old but clean piece of linen was folded to form a dressing, and was saturated with clean, cold water. This was firmly secured to the wound in the chest by another strip of linen. Then a long pad was made with the help of a handkerchief, and some soft grass, and, having laid their pad over the dressing and its bandage, and round the chest, Steve cleverly passed a saddle girth under his patient, brought it round over the pad, and pulled it taut, till it seemed that he would arrest all movement of the ribs. Then the patient was gently rolled on to his wounded side again.

"Thet aer takin' a lesson from Mother Nature," said Steve, surveying Tusker with some satisfaction. "He is still losing blood from the lung, as you kin see from what's coming from his lips. But that 'ere girth, and layin' him on his side, will quieten the movements of his chest, and jest give him a chance. Gee! I never worked harder to save a man. I feel as anxious about him as ef he war my father, and, I kin tell yer, it means a hull heap ter young Jack thar ef Tusker pulls round."

No two nurses could have tended a patient with greater care and devotion than Steve and his fellow worker showed. They sat down in turn beside Tusker Joe, moistening his lips with water every now and again, whisking the flies away when they would have settled on his face, and holding themselves always in readiness to turn him if the position in which he was placed should appear to be harmful. But it quickly became apparent that Steve's common sense and his most valuable habit of close observation were to be rewarded. Nature, indeed, responded to the treatment, and before long it was clear that Tusker's condition, though still desperate, was slightly improved. The pallor of his face was not now so marked, while there was little if any bleeding from the lung.

"He ain't likely ter die of loss of blood now, I reckon," said Steve, surveying him critically. "It aer the shock of the wound that's going ter kill Tusker. Jest set down beside him, mate, while I have a look at Jack."

Late that evening the man who had ridden off to the settlement with a note from the sheriff returned, and with him a young surgeon. By then Jack had awakened, and, but for a slight headache and a good deal of stiffness, was himself again. Therefore there was no need for him to have attention. The surgeon at once went to Tusker's side, and for half an hour devoted all his skill to him.

"If he lives I shall be surprised," he said at last, when he had done all that was possible. "I calculate that the ball was travelling in such a direction that it must have perforated the upper part of the lung—a part, in fact, of vital importance, seeing the size of the vessels there. In any case, the man who looked to him at first and bandaged him deserves a medal. It was the only treatment to adopt. I couldn't have done more myself. You can see for yourselves that, beyond replacing the dressing with one of suitable material, I have made no alteration."

Steve went red at such commendation. "Yer don't live out on the plains fer nothing, mister," he growled. "Still, I'm glad we did the right thing."

"You can take my word for it that you did," was the hearty answer. "All that I can suggest now refers to nourishment and covering."

The night which followed was an anxious one in the camp. Jack could scarcely sleep for worrying, while Steve was on his feet continually, hovering about the wounded man; for it was by no means certain that Tusker would live even long enough to regain consciousness, and, if he were to regain his senses, who could say whether he could or would provide that evidence which was of such vital importance to Jack, and alone could clear him of the accusation for which he had been tried, and so nearly imprisoned. It was yet to be seen if our hero would ever clear his name, or be able to return to Hopeville in safety, and there prove, beyond a question of doubt, that he was entirely guiltless.

CHAPTER XXIV

A Great Acquittal

Let the reader imagine with what anxiety Jack and his friends watched the struggle between life and death taking place in the case of Tusker Joe. There were days and days when the man lay an inert mass, unconscious, and too weak to move. Days when it appeared as if each minute would prove his last. Then, when all seemed lost, the brigand's extraordinary vitality gave him strength to rally. He turned the corner, mended slowly, and was at length strong enough to speak.

"And now we kin move him ter the settlement," said the sheriff, who had been in almost daily attendance. He had, in fact, been a stanch friend to Jack and his mates, and had sent tents and provisions to them. "Once we have him and his comrade in the settlement, we'll get a couple of lawyers to come along with us, and we'll hold a sorter court, with witnesses ter take note of everything. In course he may refuse to speak. But Tusker aer on the long road. He's mended so far, but that hurt aer goin' ter prove fatal."

That, indeed, had been the opinion of the surgeon, who also had made more than one trip out to the temporary camp beside the mountain, where the last of the brigands had been run to earth.

"Shot through the chest," he declared grimly, "and may or may not make a recovery; but in any case it will be but temporary. My experience teaches me that the man's days are numbered."

However, Tusker improved to such an extent that it became possible to move him. He was taken in a cart to the settlement, his wounded mate riding with him. As for the latter, he was even more grievously hurt, and his life still hung in the balance.

"We might wait here a month and he be still the same," said the surgeon. "We will risk moving him. There is no other alternative."

All this while Jack had been careful to keep away from the injured men. He had ridden back to the mine to report to Tom and the others what had happened, and had found them industriously delving and washing dirt in the cradles. They declared to him that the yield was, if anything, improving, and that there seemed to be a wealth of the shining metal still to be regained.

"There ain't a doubt but what we've hit it rich," declared Tom the evening Jack arrived, "and ef we get the stuff ter the bank without meeting with any of the gentry as tried ter waylay you, we'll all have fortunes to our name. So you've got that man at last, Carrots? Don't you be downhearted. That Tusker will out with his evidence, and ye'll be cleared. They'll shout themselves hoarse when yer get back to Hopeville. Meanwhile me and the mates go on, and shares are divided same as before, so you, and Steve, and Tom, and Abe'll lose nothing. That's doin' things fair and square, same as we've always done."

When Jack got back to the settlement, where Tusker was being cared for, Steve greeted him eagerly.

"He'll talk, he will!" he cried. "I've been in ter see the man, and, I tell yer, he's changed. He reckons he's got the last call, and ain't much longer fer this world. He jest begged me ter overlook old days, and forgive him for what he's done. That bein' his mood, seems ter me as you'd best see him."

That very evening, in fact, the surgeon having been consulted, Jack was ushered into the little wooden shanty where the wounded brigand lay. He was propped up in bed, and our hero was shocked at his appearance. The man was desperately thin and cadaverous, while there were heavy lines under his eyes.

"Tusker," said Steve solemnly, "I've brought a young friend of mine ter see you, and afore yer take a look at him, or git talkin', I'd like to give you his history. Aer you game ter listen?"

The wounded man motioned Steve to a chair, and scarcely looked at our hero.

"Speak!" he said in a voice little above a whisper. "I will listen."

"Then, here's the yarn. Jack Kingsley aer the son of a man called Tom—Tom Kingsley, from New York State—known in the minin' camps a dozen years ago as 'Lord Tom'. He war shot in a saloon by one called——"

"Stop!" Tusker Joe's voice rose almost to a scream. "I know—I know the tale only too well. Believe me, mates, I would give the whole of my past life if I could undo what I have done. The memory of those crimes haunts me. And this is the son? I beg of him, I—I——"

"That's done with, mate," said Steve kindly. "Thar comes a day when every man, as he looks back, sees things as he might ha' done better, things that shame him and make him wince. Ef ye've turned, as I believe yer have, why, then, I reckon your sorrow aer downright genuine. Yer can't give Lord Tom's life back to his son, so we'll let the matter be a bygone. But thar's more to tell, Tusker; more as has ter do with your actions. Listen for a spell."

The little scout moistened his lips, and looked from Jack to the sick man. At any other time he would have despised himself for tormenting a poor wretch with such a tale, for torment the words he had uttered had been to Tusker. The man's drawn face showed it. It was cruel to persevere with the story, yet here, on this man's slender life, lay the success or failure of Jack's existence.

"Wall, you've got ter hear it," said the little hunter, as gently as he could, "fer Jack here ain't never done nothin' ter harm you. He's as clean and straight and plucky a young fellow as ever I met, and ef ye're true to yerself, Tusker, he'll be able ter go back home ter his friends, and hold his head up before the world. Tusker, thar was a man same as you came to a town called Hopeville, this many months back, and got a young smith ter forge a key, stuffin' him with some simple yarn. That young chap war Jack here. He got suspicious, and happened by chance ter discover that the man fer whom he'd made the key were about ter attempt a burglary with a mate. He followed them, got right inter the house, and then war set upon by a caretaker who took him fer one of the burglars. Jack here war floored, and then the caretaker war shot by the burglars, who got clear away. Wall, when the officer came, the man as war hurt declared that Jack war one of the gang, and then died right off. Thar warn't no one to clear Jack, no one ter prove as he wasn't one of the gang, and he war put up fer trial. He'd have had ten years' imprisonment ef he hadn't bolted, and ef he ever goes back east he's sure to be taken. Tusker, the man who come fer that key war you. You're the only one as kin clear Jack and set him on his legs agin."

It was a long speech. Steve had probably never before made such a lengthy one, and at the end he drew his hand across his forehead to wipe the perspiration away. Jack stepped into the centre of the room, where the light fell full upon him, while the sick man sat upright and stared eagerly into his face. Then he fell back wearily.

"Everywhar the tale is the same," he groaned. "I have indeed done miserably with my life. I acknowledge that I was that man. Show me how I kin help ter right the wrong I have done."

Waiting outside were the surgeon, the sheriff and two lawyers, besides a couple of independent witnesses, and Steve promptly ushered them in.

"He'll speak," he said. "He acknowledges all."

"Then we will get to business. See here, Tusker," said the sheriff kindly, taking the sick man's hand, "ye've got a real good chance ter do a good turn ter one ye've harmed. We've witnesses here. Tell us the tale of this burglary. Describe the place, the house, the rooms you entered, everything, in fact, that happened. Then, when the evidence is sent to Hopeville, thar won't be a shadow of doubt but that you war the man."

It took more than an hour to take down the evidence, and true to his word Tusker gave every detail. Sketches were drawn of the house from his directions, the name and address of the owner of the cart he had hired were

219

forthcoming, while he was even able to give the name of the man who had received the goods he had stolen.

"And now," he said, more cheerfully, as if his action had taken some of the load from his mind, "I've heard that James Benson war the only other man of the gang caught alive, and that, like me, he ain't much longer fer this world. Wall, I said I'd do all I can. James war in that burglary too. Ef you want corroboration of the evidence, see him. Tell him I've spoken. Take his evidence separately. Thar won't, then, be a shadow of doubt."

The other man, who alone with Tusker had lived to be captured, promptly agreed to tell his story when he heard what his chief had done. And, as may be imagined, the sheriff and his witnesses very carefully entered every particular, getting the man to sign his confession just as Tusker had done.

"That's enough to clear a judge," said the sheriff, delight in his voice, when they had retired from the house. "Now, there's jest one more thing as the lawyers advise, and I agree with them that it would be well ef it war done. We'll call in two more sheriffs from the nearest townships, read this evidence over before them, and before Tusker and the man James, and then get them to attach their signatures and official seals. The expense will be trifling, and I'm sure havin' everythin' so up to date and orderly will prevent any little hitch arising. In course, ef it war possible, I'd say: Take Tusker and the other man right east with you to Hopeville. But that ain't ter be thought of. The journey would kill them."

A week later our hero set out for San Francisco, Steve and one of the lawyers accompanying him.

"It aer worth the expense," said Steve, when it was first suggested that a lawyer should be taken. "He'll be able ter prove the papers and the seals, and kin act as defence for yer. In course ye'll have ter surrender ter justice, and then apply fer bail. We'll draw some of our gains before movin'."

Two months later they arrived in Hopeville, and Jack nearly startled the kindly James Orring out of his senses when he suddenly appeared at the forge. James stared at him as if he were a ghost, gripped his hand, and then, sinking his voice, and looking hastily over his shoulder, drew his late apprentice into the back of the smithy.

"Glad, right glad to see yer, Jack," he said heartily; "but this aer rank foolishness. Thar's never a day passes but what Simpkins the constable gits nosing round here, as ef he expected ter suddenly find yer. He ain't been to-day. Guess he'll be about afore very long. Wall, what aer it? Short of money, lad?"

Jack laughed, and, dipping his hand into his pocket, pulled out a roll of dollar bills. "Thanks, no," he said, still smiling. "I've come to hand myself over to the constable, please. Will you send for him?"

It was a day of excitement for Hopeville, and for James and his wife in particular. Quick as a flash the news spread that the young smith who had made such a sensational escape from prison, and was being tried for burglary, had suddenly returned to face the justices. The rumour brought the pompous Simpkins bouncing along, and in a trice he had apprehended Jack.

"At last!" he cried in triumph. "Back you come to the jail."

"Stop, constable, I am a lawyer. I hold in this bag certain evidence of Mr. Jack Kingsley's innocence," exclaimed the lawyer, stepping forward. "My client hands himself over to the authorities of his own free will. We will walk to the office quietly, if you please."

The lawyer's air of authority, and Jack's obvious elation, cooled the ardour of the constable, and, seeing that recourse to harsh measures might lead him into trouble, he surlily agreed to accompany them to the station. Once there, Jack was placed in the dock, for the justices happened to be sitting; and within an hour he was set at liberty, on bail. There is no need to describe how he was again put on his trial, and how, within two days of its commencement, he was acquitted, and discharged, amid the cheers of the populace. Indeed, he was become a hero, for Steve's tongue had been wagging more than it had ever done before. The people of Hopeville knew now that the young smith was not only entirely innocent, but that he was a lad after the real heart of an American, and one of whom they ought to be proud. Moreover, he was rich. Yes, Jack was rich, and proved it; for when he set his face again for California he left James Orring and his wife comfortably housed in a place of their own, with a goodly sum to keep them, and a man installed in the smithy to help with the work. His mother and other friends had also tasted of his generosity, while the constable and he had buried the hatchet, and were become fast friends.

Jack returned with Steve to the mine in California, and, when it was sold, went back to New York State. But he did not idle his time away. He set up a number of smithies throughout the country, and managed them ably. When he was not travelling between one and another, he devoted all his time and energies to a special hobby. Recollecting his own strange and anxious experience, Jack studied the records of all criminal cases where the evidence had been contradictory and there seemed a possibility that an innocent man had been convicted. Expert lawyers and detectives advised him, and though he was not often successful, yet it is pleasant to have to relate that, now and again, in the course of years, he was able to bring relief to some poor fellow. Thus did he make good use of the gold he and Tom and the others had obtained in California. He married in due course, and lived to a fine old age. To-day there is no name held in higher esteem or remembered more kindly than that of Jack Kingsley.

The End